The politics of Latin American development

Second edition

Gary W. Wynia
Professor of Political Science
University of Minnesota

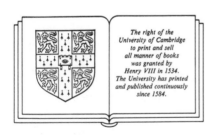

The right of the
University of Cambridge
to print and sell
all manner of books
was granted by
Henry VIII in 1534.
The University has printed
and published continuously
since 1584.

Cambridge University Press

Cambridge
London   New York   New Rochelle
Melbourne   Sydney

Published by the Press Syndicate of the University of Cambridge
The Pitt Building, Trumpington Street, Cambridge CB2 1RP
32 East 57th Street, New York, NY 10022, USA
296 Beaconsfield Parade, Middle Park, Melbourne 3206, Australia

First published 1978
Second edition 1984
Reprinted 1984

Printed in the United States of America

Library of Congress Cataloging in Publication Data
Wynia, Gary W., 1942–
The politics of Latin American development.
Includes bibliographies and index.
1. Latin America – Politics and government –
1948–   .   2. Latin America – Economic policy.
I. Title.
JL960.W9   1984   980'.03   83-15156
ISBN 0 521 26120 1 hard covers
ISBN 0 521 27842 2 paperback

The politics of Latin American
development

Contents

Maps and tables

Maps

Tables

Preface to the second edition

Three things distinguish this edition from the first one. First, each chapter was rewritten and, to varying degrees, reorganized in order to improve the exposition and, in Part II, to make the treatment of each type of politics more complete and the comparisons of countries more meaningful. An entire chapter has been devoted to Mexico, for example, and the discussion of the Allende regime has been moved from the chapter on revolution to the one that deals with democratic reform politics in order to stimulate a discussion of the limits of constitutional government. Second, insights gleaned from recent scholarship are added in several places, including the sections on the church, the military, authoritarian government, and economic dependency. And third, the analysis has been updated with the addition of new material on the 1982 Brazilian elections, the Argentine military's rise and fall between 1976 and 1983, the Nicaraguan revolution and its aftermath, and the world financial crisis and its impact on the region in the early 1980s.

The book was never intended to serve primarily as a summary of current events, but rather as an introduction to some of the fundamentals of Latin American politics and public policy. That remains its purpose. Nothing has happened to alter these fundamentals. Legitimate governments remain scarce, Latin America is as vulnerable to external forces as ever, the region's militaries, though ruling in fewer countries now than a decade ago, still believe that it is their right and duty to govern whenever they see fit, few of the benefits of economic development have trickled down to those most in need, revolutionaries continue to struggle against heavy odds, and American presidents still believe that they are obligated to block radical change within the hemisphere.

As in the first edition, no effort has been made to present every theory or interpretation of Latin American politics offered by students of the region. No work could do so without sacrificing much of its coherence. The approach taken here is intended to provoke meaningful discussion, which I hope will cause those who disagree with it to undertake the kind of study needed to generate conclusions of their own.

Nothing is more pleasing to a teacher than to learn, as I have during the past six years, that many people have gained from one's work. I can only hope that the readers of this edition will discover even more than their predecessors did in the first one.

G.W.W.

Preface to the first edition

Latin America is an enduring source of fascination to the student of politics. Within the territory that lies between the Rio Grande and Tierra del Fuego there exist exceptionally diverse forms of political life ranging from the very traditional to the revolutionary. Fundamental issues of politics, economic development, and social justice are still intensely debated throughout the region, and governments continue to experiment with competing forms of political rule and public policy. But Latin America is also a source of frustration to those who try to comprehend its public affairs. Its immense variety and diversity defy simple description, and the behavior of its leaders repeatedly confounds observers. It is no wonder many students of the region prematurely abandon their quest soon after they have begun, convinced that the analysis of Latin America's intrigues should be left to the expert or those involved in its daily affairs.

Some of this frustration is justified, of course. Latin America is a vast region where 316 million people of European, Indo-American, African, and Asian heritage occupy an area larger than the United States. Its politics is complex, the motives of its leaders often obscure, and its range of experience great. Yet, it is the thesis of this book that Latin American politics, though complex, is comprehensible and that a few basic tools of analysis, consistently applied, can take us a long way toward the development of understanding. To begin with, despite their diversity, the Latin American nations do have many things in common that facilitate systematic analysis. They have, for example, shared a long colonial experience that has had a lasting impact on their social values, economic structures, and political institutions. Most also gained their independence at the same time and spent their formative years struggling with similar nation-building problems. And most important to the student of the contemporary scene, they now share several conditions, including widespread poverty, uneven and irregular economic growth, and heavy dependence on the more affluent industrialized nations, which provide markets for their exports and financial capital and technology for their development.

There is no better place to begin to develop an understanding of Latin American politics and public policy than with these last three conditions and the ways governments have dealt with them. A rich and diverse array of measures has been tried in recent times. You can still find a few traditional autocrats who endeavor to hold back the forces of change even though self-imposed isolation is no longer possible. There are others who have placed their faith in democratic politics, hoping change will come peacefully through citizen participation in the resolution of development problems. Still others have rejected democracy, claiming that their citizens cannot accept responsibility for self-governance or that a firm authoritarian hand is needed to impose the kinds of growth-stimulating policies that can overcome the region's underdevelopment. And some have decided that only through a revolutionary transformation of their societies under the direction of a mass-based political party can development and social justice be achieved.

The purpose of this book is to introduce you to these governments and to give you some of the intellectual tools needed to analyze their conduct and assess the effects of their decisions on the welfare of Latin Americans. When you complete it, you will not only have become familiar with the different ways governments have dealt with poverty, inadequate economic growth, and dependency, but you will also have acquired some of the skills needed to explore the world of Latin American politics on your own.

A book of this kind cannot be written without drawing on the research of others who have studied Latin American politics and economic life. I am especially indebted to the path-finding work of Charles W. Anderson, William Glade, Celso Furtado, Albert Hirschman, Helio Jaguaribe, Guillermo O'Donnell, and Kalman Silvert. Of course, I alone am responsible for the way their ideas have been interpreted and joined in this book. I have spared the reader footnotes and instead have listed at the end of each chapter the principal English language monographs that were consulted. It is my hope that these brief bibliographies will also serve as points of departure for readers interested in pursuing each topic further. Most of the works cited contain excellent bibliographies of relevant material available in Spanish, Portuguese, and English. In addition, maps of Latin America are provided at the end of this Preface, and data describing each nation's economic and social conditions are included in the Appendix.

This undertaking is the product of several years of teaching Latin American politics to university undergraduates. It represents the culmination of successive attempts to meet the challenge laid down each year by students who insist that they be taught how to understand the political behavior of the Latin Americans who share the hemisphere with them. Had they been less demanding, this project never would have been begun. I have also gained immensely during the past fifteen years from the wisdom of the Latin American public officials and private citizens with whom I have discussed the region's affairs during my visits to their countries. I can only hope that this book faithfully communicates their insights.

Several colleagues have read the manuscript and contributed to its improvement. In particular I thank Roger Benjamin, Peter Johnson, and Sue Matarese of the University of Minnesota, along with Sue Brown, who typed the many drafts. I am also grateful to Professors Lawrence Graham of the University of Texas, Richard Clinton of Oregon State University, and William Garner of Southern Illinois University, who gave much needed criticism and advice at each stage of the project's development. Finally, I owe my greatest debt to my teacher, colleague, and friend, Charles W. Anderson, whose intellectual influence on this project is greater than either of us cares to admit.

G.W.W.

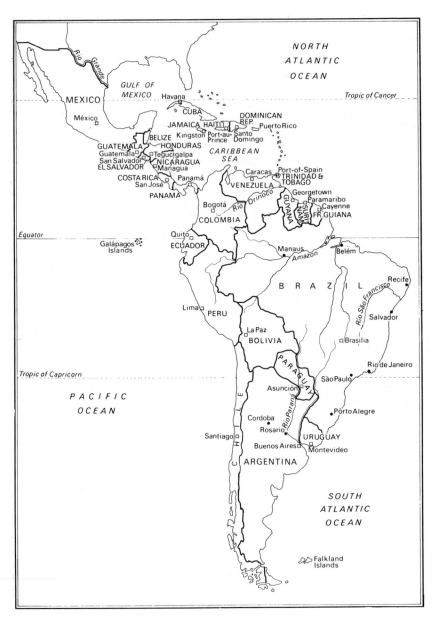

Map 1. Latin America

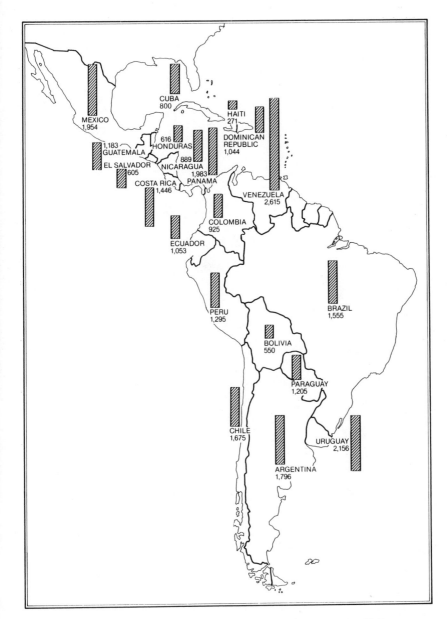

Map 2. Per capita gross domestic products 1981, measured in 1980 U.S. dollars. (*Source:* Inter-American Development Bank, *Economic and Social Progress in Latin America*, 1982, p. 351.)

Part I

Understanding Latin American politics

1. Latin American conditions

Dissatisfaction with the way things are runs deep in Latin America. But that is hardly surprising since much of what Latin Americans covet, be it wealth, security, liberty, community, or legitimate government, seems to be in short supply.

North Americans have shared few of Latin Americans' worries and frustrations. Not until OPEC raised petroleum prices in the early 1970s did an affluent postwar generation discover the meaning of economic dependence on other nations. And only after experiencing double-digit inflation a few years later did we learn about victimization by forces that seemed beyond anyone's control. A generation raised on the notion that society's problems could be solved in reasonable and relatively painless ways learned that there were few easy answers after all.

No doubt Latin Americans were surprised by none of this, for they had been short of easy answers for some time. But their problems are quite different from those of their prosperous northern neighbors. Not only are their economies more dependent on foreign markets, their poverty much greater, and their political inconstancy more persistent, but their adversities are more intransigent. And whereas North Americans confine most of their public disputes to the selection of officials and the choice of public policies, Latin Americans still clash over the nature and purpose of government. Unlike their neighbors to the north who study Plato, Aristotle, Machiavelli, Marx, and Mill primarily to understand their political heritage, Latin Americans study them in search of help with problems yet unsolved.

To appreciate the Latin American condition we must examine more closely the region's history and its legacies. We will start with a tale told by a make-believe president just elected on a platform of economic and social reform. Our fictional leader does not represent all Latin American presidents; no single example could. Latin American nations share many things, but they also differ in important ways, and a single narrative cannot capture their diversity. What follows

3

then is one leader's understanding of the Latin American condition. Its author, unlike some of his contemporaries, still retains a belief in democratic politics and the possibility of reforming economic and social structures without bloodshed. His solutions are products of these beliefs. As you read them, judge for yourself whether they have anything to offer the people he intends to govern and whether there is any hope of achieving his objectives in the world he describes.

Development problems and prospects: a presidential proposal

A brief description of our country is presented in Table 1.1. We have approximately 15 million inhabitants, most of whom are *mestizos* or mixed-bloods (Hispanic and Indian), though 5 percent are Negro or mulatto, 10 percent are still classified as Indians, and approximately 5 percent are descendants of European and Asian immigrants. If you divide our gross national product by the number of inhabitants, we have a per capita product of $1,000, which is below the Latin American average of $1,300.

As you can see from Table 1.1, we are primarily an agrarian nation, though mining and industry contribute much to our economy. We depend very heavily on the export of a few products – primarily coffee, sugar, cotton, and iron ore – to the industrialized nations, especially the United States. Our principal domestic industries are food processing, textiles, and clothing, although in recent years we have added chemical and pharmaceutical industries. Most of our public utilities are owned by the state, having been nationalized by the government during the past thirty years. But we have also welcomed foreign investors in areas where we lack technology and capital. Today, foreign companies are majority shareholders in two of our banks, our iron mines, retail fuel companies, and chemical and pharmaceutical firms.

Since the early 1950s we have received loans and grants from international agencies and the United States government to finance our development programs. At the end of last year they totaled $1.5 billion in loans, which we are now repaying with some difficulty, and $600 million in grants. We have also borrowed heavily from foreign private banks, especially since the price of imported petroleum rose in the early 1970s. Using loans and grants, we have also tripled the length of our paved roads, modernized our ports, built a hydroelectric

Table 1.1. *Country profile*

Population: 15 million

Size: 500,000 square miles

Literacy: 50%

Gross domestic product per capital: 1,000 U.S. dollars

Ethnic composition
Mestizo:　80%
Negro:　5%
Indian:　10%
European:　5%

Class structure		*Land tenure*
Upper stratum:	5%	Richest 5% owns 60% of land
Upper middle stratum:	15%	Middle 20% owns 30% of land
Lower middle stratum:	30%	Poorest 75% owns 10% of land
Lower stratum:	50%	

Distribution of gross national product
Agriculture:　35%
Industry:　25%
Mining:　10%
Services:　30%

Trade patterns

Exports to		*Imports from*	
United States:	40%	United States:	50%
West Germany:	20%	Japan:	20%
Japan:	10%	West Germany:	10%
Great Britain:	10%	Great Britain:	10%
Latin America:	8%	Latin America:	5%
Others:	12%	Others:	5%

facility, improved our telecommunications, built new schools, constructed hospitals, and financed several domestic industries. Yet there is still much to be done if we are to provide our citizens with a decent life, as the following review of our social and economic conditions makes clear.

Social conditions

Undeniably the structure of our society has changed a great deal since the beginning of this century, especially under the impact of postwar industrialization and urbanization. Nevertheless, one thing has been constant throughout our modern history: the continued concentration of wealth and power. In contrast to the more industrialized Western European societies, where the wealthiest 20 percent of the population receives approximately 40 percent of the national income, our wealthiest 20 percent receives 70 percent of our national income. Rural poverty persists, and the number of urban poor increases rapidly due to population growth and migration from the countryside.

Because census information is incomplete, our social structure cannot be described in detail. Nevertheless, we know enough to make some estimations. At the top there is an "upper stratum" of approximately 5 percent of the population; this includes what is left of the landed elite as well as the owners of the country's largest commerical and industrial firms, banks, and import–export businesses. The next 15 percent, or "upper middle stratum," includes managers in industry and commerce, professionals (e.g., doctors, lawyers, and engineers), the larger commerical farmers, top government bureaucrats and technicians, and high-ranking military officers. Below them comes the 30 percent that makes up the "lower middle stratum" of unionized laborers, along with schoolteachers, merchants, lower bureaucrats, non-commissioned military officers, and small farmers. Finally, there is the remaining 50 percent of our population, composed of urban and rural poor. Although this group is quite diverse in its composition, its members share the condition of poverty. It includes seasonal rural workers, subsistence farmers, peasants who work on landed estates as sharecroppers, part-time menial laborers and vendors, and domestic servants.

Clearly this last group has benefited the least from our economic development and now requires the greatest attention if we are to increase economic production and improve social welfare. At present these persons neither take much from nor contribute much to our national economic and political life. Their concerns are local and are dominated by a preoccupation with survival in a hostile world. Although most of the urban and rural poor tend to be passive politically, accepting the status quo as something that is beyond their power to change, we know from the experiences of our neighbors as well as our own past that their frustrations sometimes lead to their support of revolutionary causes. If we are to promote sustained economic growth and create a durable democratic order, we cannot afford to ignore this marginal population, for if it is left in poverty it will have little choice but to join those who advocate violent revolution.

Before we can discuss the development problems raised by our present social structure and suggest ways to deal with them, an understanding of that structure's origins and persistence throughout our history is required. There are, of course, hazards in looking to our past to explain our present condition. One is always tempted to blame our Iberian and Indian heritages for our plight today. But self-pity serves no useful purpose. We are products of our past, to be sure, and remnants of colonial and nineteenth-century institutions and values remain with us. But we are much more. Imported ideas and technologies, along with the ingenuity and industry of our people, have changed many of the ways we do things. To assume that we are nothing more than our past is to ignore nearly 200 years of struggle.

Until early in twentieth century our society was characterized by the domination of the masses by a small rural elite. The origins of this condition can be traced back to the conquest of the New World. The first *conquistadores* brought with them social values that had been formed during the last stages of the reconquest of the Iberian peninsula from the Moors during the fourteenth and fifteenth centuries. The reconquest was a long and bitter struggle that had a lasting impact on Iberian society and heavily influenced Iberian rule in the New World.

The reconquest required daring and determination. A premium was placed on military skills, and the heroic military leader became the model against which all leadership was judged. For their efforts, the valiant warriors of the reconquest were rewarded not only with the glory of military victory, but also with power and wealth, usually in the form of property, which the Crown disbursed in large quantities to those who had expanded its domain. For future generations the lesson of the reconquest was clear: The quickest route to fame and fortune was through heroic deeds on behalf of the king and queen.

Opportunities for such deeds were opened anew by the conquest of the New World at the beginning of the sixteenth century. Hernan Cortes, Francisco Pizarro, and the other ambitious adventurers who explored the New World were determined to serve God and the king and to get rich. Most were of modest origins in a society where rank and social distinction were derived from the ownership of land and the command of peasant laborers. Monarchs sent them to secure gold for the royal treasury, promising that if they succeeded their descendants would be given a place in the nobility. The *conquistadores* were many things – valiant, cruel, sentimental, aggressive, selfish, and occasionally altruistic – and were sustained by the belief that they would secure fame and fortune if they triumphed and Christian salvation if they did not.

The *conquistadores* also brought with them the patrimonial political values that had taken root in the Iberian peninsula during the reconquest. Their approach to politics was uncompromisingly authoritarian, stressing hierarchy and ordered relationships between governors and the governed. Authority moved in only one direction, from the monarch downward to his or her subjects. Individual citizens were not free agents who could seek out any place they chose in the political order; with few exceptions, they had to accept the station into which they were born. According to the Iberian view, authority was not delegated by the people to public officials; rather the people relinquished their autonomy to those who by heritage or conquest had come to prevail in society. This approach to politics differs sharply from the eighteenth-century liberal notion of political authority, which called for the selection of leaders by the citizens they govern. To the sixteenth-century Iberian elite such a practice was incomprehensible. Citizens were subjects who had no right to withdraw their consent whenever they wished, for by living under the monarch they had accepted the monarch as their sovereign. Only the administration of the laws was subject to appeal, but even that had to be done through courts controlled by the Crown.

The New World proved fertile ground for the transplanted reconquest values and institutions. Military victories over the Aztecs, Incas, and other indigenous peoples came with relative ease; precious metals were found and shared with the Crown; and thousands were converted to Catholicism. Through the institution of the *encomienda*, a right granted by the Crown to landowners and mineowners that allowed them to extract labor or tribute from Indians within their domain, the new nobility created a system of mines and large landed estates that gave them wealth, social prestige, and political power.

The landed estates, termed *latifundios*, were very different from the mode of land tenure developed in North America outside the Deep South. In Latin America land was distributed by the Crown immediately after the conquest. Even though many areas remained unoccu-

pied until the late nineteenth century, most of the best land had been
allocated through royal grants by 1600. What made the *latifundio* possible was the availability of conquered laborers. In North America, in
contrast, much of the farmland was secured after Independence and
distributed gradually in relatively small parcels by the government to
immigrant farmers after indigenous populations had been liquidated
or moved. As a result, except for slavery in the plantation agriculture
of the South, labor was scarce, forcing farmers to limit their holdings
to what they could work by themselves. For them, land was primarily
a means to a modest livelihood; for Latin Americans it became not
only a source of production for domestic and foreign markets, but also
the basis of social control. It made possible the creation of a privileged
class who believed it deserved its disproportionate share of economic
and political power. From it we inherited a rural society composed of
landed aristocrats and peasants, whereas North America escaped the
legacy of both.

The institutions, values, and social structures created during the
colonial era have not survived unchanged. With the expansion of commerce and trade in the late nineteenth century came substantial adjustments, most evident socially in the emergence of citizens who
were neither members of the elite nor part of the rural masses. It was
they who eventually formed our upper and lower middle class, composed of professionals, merchants, bureaucrats, and organized laborers, whose number increased rapidly after 1930. What we now find is
neither the simple two-class society we inherited from the colonial era
nor a completely transformed one evidencing the values of a modern
middle class. Today, remnants of the traditional society coexist with
the institutions of a more modern one. In the countryside one still
finds some traditional *latifundios* and plantations as well as very productive modest-size coffee farms. But alongside them are thousands of
landless peasants and tenant farmers who subsist on relatively few
acres. In the cities, on the other hand, are descendants of our traditional elite alongside foreign-trained technicians and aggressive merchants and industrialists. Thousands of poor live there in slums, surviving precariously through their unskilled labor and petty commerce
and services. Ours is a society in which the old tolerates the new and
the modern coexists with the traditional. It would be satisfying to
conclude that we are swiftly moving from one stage of development to
another and that the vestiges of traditional society are giving way to

the modern, but we cannot be so sure. Instead, we seem to have become stuck somewhere in midstream, unable to generate and distribute enough wealth to meet the needs of most of our people.

This brings us back to the problems I mentioned at the outset of this survey of our social conditions. Our contemporary problem is not the lack of economic growth and modernization per se, for we can proudly point to the transformation of our capital into a modern metropolis, the growth of manufacturing, and the rise of something resembling a middle class as evidence that we are indeed making progress. Our problem is the failure to extend the benefits of economic growth to a majority of our citizens. For those with easy access to the culture and skills of modernity, life is changing rapidly, and new opportunities are continually arising. But others, who begin without such advantages, have little hope of sharing in these opportunities. Instead they are trapped within a vicious circle of poverty that has not been broken by the kind of economic development we have achieved to date. Nearly 50 percent of our citizens lack the skills and capital needed to escape their very low level of productivity; their low output, in turn, brings them little income with which to purchase goods and services in our economy. Thus they neither contribute much to our economic growth nor gain much from it. But our economic task will not be completed until we transform them into productive members of our society.

Economic underdevelopment and its causes

Since colonial times we have been primarily an agrarian nation devoted to the production of commodities for export and domestic consumption. As we have seen, landed estates were granted to the *conquistadores*, who used them to build local empires, which they governed paternalistically but harshly. Our economy began as an extension of an Iberian imperial system that ruled us through its stifling bureaucracy. During the colonial era we were confined to the cultivation of indigo, sugar, and cacao, the extraction of silver and gold, and the raising of cattle on unpopulated plains. With Independence at the beginning of the nineteenth century, we finally escaped the grasp of the Spanish Crown. Yet, instead of pursuing new lines of production, we stayed with what we knew best – the export of agricultural goods. We were, like our neighbors, a primary product export economy organized to feed the industrializing nations of Europe. The only real change was that England and France replaced Spain and Portugal as our primary trading partners.

The principal impetus to economic growth in the years before 1900 came from the increased commercialization of cash crops such as coffee and cotton under the leadership of ambitious rural entrepreneurs and traders. As our exports increased we enlarged our ports, modernized our capital city, and built railways using foreign investment and expertise. Our leaders were proud of their achievements, convinced that we had found our place in the modern world. What they ignored, of course, was the continued poverty of the majority of our people, many of whom had lost what little land they owned to the coffee and cotton producers who, with the government's help, confiscated peasant lands and transformed their former occupants into seasonal laborers.

Our economy changed slowly during the early twentieth century. First came the discovery of iron ore in 1915. Mining had been important during colonial times, but this was the first major discovery since then. With the mines came foreign investors, who exploited our minerals after making sizable capital investments. They shared a small portion of their profits with the government and gave employment to several thousand former peasants. Like coffee had mining also increased commerce and banking. Though in comparison with the industrial nations of Europe and North America we were still a poor country, especially if one looked at our per capita income of only $200, we had changed since colonial days, and our business, farm, and political leaders could take credit for these achievements.

Unfortunately, our self-satisfied leaders never recognized the precariousness of the economic edifice they had constructed. There had been occasional economic crises in the past, such as the one brought on by the interruption of trade during World War I, but they were tolerated as temporary setbacks that could be absorbed by a system that had otherwise performed well. But in 1929 our leaders were shocked from their complacency by a worldwide depression that undermined our faith in the primary product export economy. There we were, suddenly without markets for our agricultural products and cut off from the suppliers of manufactured goods.

At first we did little but adapt ourselves to hard times, as there seemed no feasible alternative but to continue a way of life that had served our affluent elite so well for so long. Gradually, however, we came to recognize that the time had come to revise our economic strategy. Like many other nations, we turned to industrialization for help. It was a difficult and controversial choice. Industrialization's proponents were opposed by the producers of export commodities, who feared that the growth of domestic manufacturers would upset our traditional trading partners and prevent the renewal of bilateral trade once the depression-induced economic crisis had subsided. Nevertheless, other leaders, convinced of the need for change, struggled on, using government policy to stimulate industrial growth during the 1940s and 1950s.

Where have these changes left us today? I would like to conclude that our economic transformation has been completed, that we no longer depend on the export of agricultural commodities and minerals for our economic survival, and that we now produce all the manufactured goods we need. Unfortunately, I cannot make that claim. The past three decades have, in fact, been frustrating ones. Although our economy has changed a great deal and our industries now generate as much of our national product as does agriculture, we have not escaped irregular growth, widespread poverty, and foreign trade crises. Many of the development policy issues that divided us in the past continue to divide our political leaders today.

Finally, there is the matter of population growth. The number of people we must employ increases every year. Between 1900 and 1950 our population doubled; it took only twenty-five years for it to double again. Our capital city holds 4 million people today; it will be the home of 9 million in twenty years. Since the growth rate is highest among the poor, it makes the reduction of poverty even harder. Over the objections of the Catholic hierarchy and some of our more nationalist parties, our government has begun family planning programs, but even if we achieve our objectives, our population will double again before the end of the century.

Political life: past, present, and future

We have already noted the influence of the Iberian conquest on our political heritage. Until Independence we were governed by a distant monarchy and its colonial bureaucracy in an authoritarian manner. Though we were obligated to obey colonial authorities, we developed the habit of avoiding its most onerous laws whenever we could get away with it. Our disobedience reached the point of political rebellion in the early nineteenth century. Those who led our revolt were motivated by many things, the most important being their longing for liberation for the colonial trading system, the termination of arbitrary and harsh rule by the Crown's administrators, and a desire for some form of constitutional government similar to that created by the American Revolution. But however one interprets the achievements of Independence, one fact is inescapable: The Independence struggle may have freed us from the Crown, but it did not liberate us entirely from Iberian political values and social institutions. What Independence did was impose the idea of the "social contract" onto our tradition of hierarchical political authority. By severing our ties to the Crown we had hoped to open the door to the creation of government based on popular consent. Yet, what we achieved was not the construction of democratic government, but only the superimposition of a democratic veneer over a traditional, autocratic political system in which our leaders gained their authority more from their social-economic status and military might than from the popular will.

Despite some valiant efforts to make democracy work, post-Independence governments were overthrown with regularity by local leaders and their private armies. Such leaders, called *caciques*, or *caudillos* when they controlled large regions, dominated politics for fifty years after Independence. Their objective was the preservation of local autonomy in the face of central government efforts to create a unified nation-state. Some wore military uniforms, called themselves generals, and fought continuously with the government and other *caudillos*. The ambitious and astute defeated their rivals and seized the government for themselves, often relying on brutality and intimidation to govern until they were deposed violently. Little acutally changed during the rule of the *caudillos*, for despite frequent upheavals, our landed elites retained their wealth and privileges.

By the 1860s political parties began to appear. Initially, we had only two parties, one calling itself the Conservative party and the other the Liberal party. These were not parties in the modern sense; rather, they were elite cliques lacking constituency organizations or mass appeal. More characteristic was their use of patron–client relationships in which individuals of lower status were made to depend on those of higher status to gain access to resources under the latter's control. Peasants, for example, relied on landowners; the landowners depended on local *caudillos;* and they, in turn, depended on national political leaders. From the landowner the peasant received access to land and protection against natural and human enemies in exchange for deference, cheap labor, and support for the landowner's political causes; similarly, landowners were given physical protection by *caudillos* in return for financial tribute and political support. Patron–client politics remains part of our political life. Upward mobility within the political process depends heavily on patronage, and survival in office requires that one serve as a broker between clients and the government agencies that provide the services needed by industrialists, farmers, union leaders, peasants, and the like.

Given the elitist nature of nineteenth-century politics, it is not surprising that there were few differences between the Conservative and Liberal parties. The Conservatives, as their name implies, favored the traditional social order, the economic status quo, and the dominance of the Roman Catholic church in society. The Liberals, though also elitist, were anticlerical and promoted the opening of economic opportunities by encouraging the seizure of church and Indian lands by ambitious producers of coffee and cotton. It was under the rule of the Liberals during the late nineteenth and early twentieth centuries that our economy began to grow at a faster pace, aided by the foreign-financed construction of the railways and ports needed to transport our coffee, cotton, and iron ore to foreign markets. The Liberals gave us unprecedented political stability, holding five consecutive elections without violent interruptions. Of course, only 10 percent of our adult population participated in those elections, as the franchise was limited to literate male property owners; moreover, those who did vote were often the victims of threats and other forms of intimidation. What the Liberals failed to do was create any sense of nationhood among our people. We were taught that it was our function to supply the rest of the world with food and minerals and leave public affairs to a small elite and their foreign allies. For most of our people, there was no distinct nation to identify with, but only a village or region that from time to time was harassed by a distant central government.

We have already discussed how the 1929 world depression undermined our export economy and prompted efforts to industrialize. The drive for industrialization was accompanied by the growth of nationalism and the emergence of new political forces that challenged the traditional elite and its monopoly over economic and political power. In less than two decades our political process was transformed from one in which a few political leaders settled all policy questions among themselves to one in which the representatives of industrial, professional, and labor groups became actively involved in the policy-making process.

The transition had actually begun around 1900. With the growth of our foreign trade and domestic commerce had come a rapid increase in the number of merchants, lawyers, and white-collar employees. Simultaneously, there arrived on our shores several hundred thousand immigrants from Europe. Many started new lives as tenant farmers, merchants, and laborers, and some, inspired by European socialism and anarchism, organized our first labor unions. It was not long before these new groups demanded admittance to our political process. Some were incorporated into an expanded Liberal party, but many others formed their own political parties and campaigned for electoral reforms that would give them competitive advantages. However, it was the military, not the new political parties, that finally ended the elite monopoly over public office. Frustrated by the Liberal party's inability to deal with the economic collapse and social protests that followed in the wake of the 1929 depression, the military reluctantly seized the government, ending five decades of civilian rule by the agro-exporter elite. Although it tried to remain neutral, the military did much to promote the growth of our industries by nationalizing railroads and several public utilities, creating an industrial development bank, and raising tariffs on imported goods that were produced domestically. At the same time, however, it ignored the rural economy, leaving its management to the *latifundistas* and commercial farmers who had dominated it for the past fifty years.

After World War II our political life became quite complicated. The military was now in politics to stay. Even though it has returned the government to civilians after its interventions, it continues to influence the way the country is governed. Our political party system has grown. In addition to the Liberal and Conservative parties, there are small Socialist and Communist parties and my own Popular Democratic party, which we created in the late 1930s. In 1936 the military held an election that was won by the Liberals; however, amid charges of corruption and incompetence it removed them again in 1944. When elections were held again in 1960, my party won for the first time. But when we hastily enacted an agrarian reform program and adopted a progressive income tax, we alienated many in the upper class and they persuaded the military to depose us in 1963. Now after several years of military rule, we have won another election and will try once again to implement our reform program. This time we will have to be more cautious, as we received only 45 percent of the popular vote compared with the Liberals' 25 percent, the Conservatives' 15 percent, and the Socialists' 10 percent, and we are just short of a majority in both houses of Congress.

New interest groups have been added to our political process as a result of the economic and social changes of the past forty years. The Roman Catholic church (now divided between progressive and conservative factions), *latifundistas*, commerical farmers, exporters, bankers, and foreign investors have been joined by large and small industrialists, labor unions, and peasant leagues. Some of these groups, such as bankers and foreign investors, are well organized and financed and enjoy great influence, whereas others, like the peasant leagues, are grossly underrepresented in the policy-making process. Respect for democratic institutions varies considerably, depending on how well such institutions serve particular interests. It is not uncommon for some, especially the more conservative ones, to urge military intervention whenever their interests are seriously threatened by the government. My party has tried hard to secure the support of several groups, especially the new peasant associations and the labor unions, but our campaigns have been only partially successful because many peasants still submit to landlord pressure to vote for the Liberals or Conservatives, or do not vote at all, and some of the laborers prefer the Socialist party to ours.

An even tougher problem is the hostility of many powerful interests to our reform program. Foreign investors are very concerned about our nationalization proposals, landowners are fearful of our plans to expropriate inefficient estates, bankers oppose our desire for government control over the allocation of credit, and industrialists do not agree with our plans to create more state industries. If we are to succeed, we must somehow overcome the threats posed by such formidable opponents, who will undoubtedly try to block passage of our program and obstruct its implementation through the use of the many resources at their disposal.

Finally, there is the question of our ability to sustain the democratic process in a country that has frequently rejected constitutional government. The democratic rules of the game have served my party well because our ability to organize large numbers of voters has earned us the opportunity to rule. But others have not gained from democratic politics. For conservative political and economic groups representative democracy has always posed a threat because it offers an avenue through which representatives of the masses can deprive them of their wealth and power. At the other extreme, many peasant and labor groups who were denied their rights under the old elite-run system worry that democracy is little more than window dressing for the continued domination of the poor and powerless by the wealthy. We are, it seems, caught in the middle between those who fear that we might do them harm and others who are convinced we will do nothing at all for them. The more we threaten the former and disappoint the latter, the harder it will be to sustain any kind of democratic process.

What can we do?

The task that lies ahead is not an easy one. We must alleviate poverty as much as possible, increase our national economic independence, and build a solid foundation for our political democracy. In order to prepare for the task of governing this country, I have, with the assistance of my economic advisers, prepared the following report on the economic reforms we plan to implement, as well as an assessment of the obstacles we will face once we have begun.

We must begin by recognizing that we are still a long way from completing the industrialization of our economy. We continue to import some consumer goods and nearly all our iron, steel, machinery, and electrical goods. We also suffer from what Dr. Raul Prebisch of the United Nations Economic Commission for Latin America (ECLA) has called adverse terms of trade with industrial nations, which have forced us to expand increasing amounts of our commodities to pay for the same quantity of imported industrial goods simply because the prices of manufactured goods have risen faster than those of sugar, coffee, cotton, and other primary commodities. This is precisely why we must continue to push hard for as much industrialization as we can afford.

But industrialization will not come easily because we are still plagued by a shortage of financial capital. There are several reasons for this. First, we lack domestic savings. Savings derive primarily from individual savings accounts in financial institutions and from government taxation. Private savings are relatively scarce because nearly half our population is too poor to save. Those who can – property owners, merchants, professionals, and skilled laborers – do so at a lower rate than their counterparts in industrial nations because of well-founded fears that our persistent inflation will reduce the value of their savings. Under such precarious conditions they prefer to consume goods today rather than save now and then purchase the same goods at higher prices later. And when they do save, they usually place their money in foreign banks or use it to buy more secure foreign stocks and bonds. Despite repeated government efforts to prevent capital flight, it persists.

The shortage of private capital makes the government the financier of last resort. Through its taxes, it can force private entrepreneurs and wage earners to contribute to national savings by taking income from them and transferring it through government banks and investments to industrial activities. Unfortunately, this works better in theory than in practice. Traditionally, our government has relied primarily on import and export taxes for public revenues because of the ease of their collection. Only after 1945 did we initiate income and capital gains taxes. Both are still resisted even though their rates are less than half what they are in Western Europe and the United States. In fact, tax evasion permeates our society. We estimate that only about 30 percent of taxable income is declared annually; unfortunately, we can do little to prevent tax evasion because our bureaucrats lack the skill and technology needed to tighten tax collections. Consequently, the forced savings that might be captured by the public sector continue to escape our grasp.

Another obstacle to industrialization is the small size of our national market. We cannot achieve economies of scale in our manufacturing as long as half our population is outside the market economy. In a sense we are a victim of our own underdevelopment and widespread poverty. Gradually our agrarian reforms and rising urban employment will expand our domestic markets, but until they do our industrial growth will be constrained. Meanwhile, we should work for regional economic integration within Latin America to increase our markets. Separately each country lacks sufficient consumer demand to generate efficient production, but collectively we can grow by allowing one another free access to our domestic markets. To succeed, we must first agree to a division of labor and specialization in our industrial output in order to avoid duplication of effort and then integrate our markets through regional agreements that abolish tariffs on goods traded within our region and increase the free movement of labor and capital among member nations. We are cautiously optimistic that we can still build a common market among the Latin American countries that will help alleviate the problem of insufficient demand. Of course, we recognize that in order to succeed we must overcome many obstacles, not the least of which are traditional rivalries and distrust among our neighbors as well as the costs of industrial specialization, which will necessitate our closing some industries.

Regional economic integration may help with our market problems, but we still face the problem of capital shortage. If domestic private investors and the state cannot supply what is needed, we must borrow abroad or encourage foreign investors, often in the form of multinational corporations, to finance our industrialization. That, of course, raises an issue that greatly concerns my administration: the risk of excessive reliance on foreign suppliers of capital and technology. There is nothing unique about our turning to foreigners for assistance with our development; other nations have done it with much success, as have we in the past. Foreigners built our railways, constructed our ports, financed some of our industries, and made it possible to import advanced technology. What concerns us now are the political and economic effects of increasing our dependence on foreigners in the decades ahead.

We know from past experience that with foreign capital comes foreign intervention into our domestic affairs, if only to protect investments. Moreover, as our debts to outsiders increase, so do the outsiders' demands that we adopt only those policies that favor the swift repayment of our debts. We must guard against a process of "denationalization" that transfers control over important domestic economic decisions from individuals and organizations loyal to our nation to those who are loyal to other nations or to multinational corporations. If we do not, we will find that in exchange for the benefits of foreign captial and technology, we have relinquished control over the course of our development. In particular we must guard against foreign control over industries, like mining, whose exports are critical to our national development. The arrangement we choose should leave our citizens in the dominant position, to assure that foreigners do not use their economic power against us. We must also develop regulations that curb the export of profits from foreign investments. Although the stockholders of such corporations merit a return on their investments, we must encourage the reinvestment of profits within our economy, channeling them into areas where they are more productive. There are no simple solutions to the problem of denationalization. Common sense tells us that we require some foreign investment and technology in order to continue our program of industrialization; yet a desire to control our own destiny dictates that we regulate foreign capital closely, assuring that it serves our ends as well as those of its suppliers.

Finally, we know that industrialization alone will not solve our development problems. Equally important is the modernization of agriculture. We are plagued by inefficient farms, including the remnants of the *latifundios* that have survived since colonial times; moreover, two-thirds of our rural population works at or just above the subsistence level. New taxes that penalize farmers who leave their land idle or exploit it inefficiently are essential to encourage higher productivity. But if we are going to improve the condition of the rural poor, something more than tax reform is needed. We must also implement an agrarian reform program that expropriates land from the larger, less efficient producers and transfers it to landless peasants. With adequate technical assistance the latter should increase their productivity, improve our food supply, and raise their personal incomes. And higher income will make them consumers of the goods produced elsewhere in our economy, thus contributing to economic development generally.

We face a challenging task. Our economic growth is not sufficient to meet the needs of our expanding population as well as the aspirations of most of our citizens for an improved standard of living. We have tried to free ourselves from our dependence on an agricultural economy and its raw-product exports through a gradual and costly process of industrialization. We are now less dependent on the importation of consumer goods than ever before; yet we must still import fuels and other raw products to operate our industries. We are also becoming increasingly dependent on foreign investors to complete our industrialization. Our economic performance continues to rise and fall with the market value of our exports. Moreover, we have on occasion been plagued by inflation rates as high as 60 percent owing to a variety of causes, including unproductive government spending, the failure of our industries to meet the demands of urban consumers for particular goods, our farmers' inability to supply enough food to local markets, and occasional wage–price spirals touched off by unions trying to get ahead of prices and management trying to cover its costs.

We can begin by reforming our economic institutions and stimulating the growth of our rural and industrial economies. Our goal is not only rapid economic expansion, but also the inclusion of greater numbers of citizens in the modern economic sector where they can share the benefits of our growth. Should we fail to elevate them, we will be faced with an ever-increasing number of marginal poor, rising social tensions, and the growth of political movements advocating solutions that are more radical than ours.

The obstacles we face

We are not so naive as to believe we can achieve our objectives without confronting intense opposition. Our agrarian reform program, for example, will be opposed by the landowners whose property we propose to expropriate, the Liberal party, which is hostile to rural reform generally, and even the Communists and Socialists, who view our solutions as threats to their campaigns for peasant support. There are many technical problems associated with agrarian reform as well. First, much of the peasantry, imprisoned by tradition and fear, may not respond to our initiatives. Second, we face the question of which lands to include within our reforms. Should we, for example, encourage colonization of public lands or depend entirely on the expropriation of private ones? If the latter, should we expropriate land currently in production or only that not in use? And once it has been expropriated, how should it be reallocated: into individual family farms, cooperatives, or state farms? We know that in trying to improve the welfare of the rural poor we may actually reduce production, at least temporarily, because it may take some time for peasant farmers, who lack technology and know-how, to raise their productivity.

Our tax reform program which is aimed at ending tax avoidance and increasing the tax burden borne by the richest 20 percent of our population and the foreigners who invest and work in our country, can expect opposition from industrialists, professionals, landowners, and foreign investors. These groups will be helped by the fact that it will not be easy to administer our new tax laws. To succeed we will have to end the practice of bribing public officials. Many of our low-paid bureaucrats have succumbed to the temptation to accept bribes and other favors in exchange for ignoring those who evade the law. Unless we can reduce this practice, we will never end the cynical abuse of our tax laws.

Nor will it be easy to operate the foreign-owned mines we plan to nationalize. Of course, we are not without precedents in this area, as our military governments nationalized foreign-owned railways and telephone companies in the 1940s. But in extending state ownership from utilities to extractive enterprises we are embarking on a new and risky course, one that may frighten foreign investors in other sectors. As they have done elsewhere, the mining companies will exert pressures on foreign banks who have lent us money and on foreign governments who supply us with development assistance in an effort to persuade them to punish us if we go ahead with our plans. Our vulnerability to such pressures is well-known. Our dependence on foreign loans and technology is what makes it so hard for us to chart our own economic course. Here again we seem to be caught in a vicious circle, for the more we try to develop our economy, the more we must depend on foreign help; but the more we accept the latter, the harder it is to develop on our own terms.

Finally, we face the more general problem of how to hold on to public office in the face of likely attempts to bring our government down. Our party's first try at public office ended, it will be recalled, with our overthrow by the military at the urging of the other political parties. Conservatives and Liberals feared that our reforms would undermine their economic power; Socialists worried that our success might undercut their campaigns for popular support. What we have learned from that experience is that we cannot merely announce our programs in the expectation that everyone will step aside and let them take hold. Nor can we assume that our election under the democratic rules of the game will in itself prevent a military coup. Like most reformers we must find a way out of our central dilemma: If we move too swiftly we will encourage our opponents to block us in the legislature, obstruct the execution of our program, or encourage the military to overthrow our government. Yet, if we move too slowly, our supporters will become disillusioned and our reforms will not develop the momentum needed to carry us through. What we now need more than anything else is a plan of political action that will guide us through the many obstacles that lie ahead.

A challenge and a promise

You have just read the story of a fictitious Latin American president-elect who is searching for ways to implement a program of reform and development in his country. The example we used happened to be that of a democratically elected, reform-oriented president, but we could just as easily have used a conservative, military, or revolutionary one. Whatever government officials' motives and objectives may be, they will confront political and economic legacies similar to those just described. There are no certain solutions to the problems they face or easy ways to overcome their opponents. In each case hard decisions have to be made and high political risks taken.

Now the time has come to turn the tables and consider what you would do if you were in the position of our fictitious president. How would you search the recent past for lessons that might help you implement a development program? Which political forces would be most critical to your success or failure? What would be your chances of serving out your term without a military coup? How would you deal with your opponents: by compromising with them, by ignoring them, or by repressing them? What would be the costs of compromise or repression to you and your program? Are the development problems you face solvable in the long term or is the country doomed to poverty and continued dependence on foreigners? And what about the chances for reform in general? Can you explain why so many reform governments in Latin America in recent years have ended in military dictatorships? And finally, can reform work at all under such conditions? If it cannot, is revolution the only real alternative left?

But wait a minute, you say; you are not prepared to deal with these questions after reading only one brief summary of the problems faced by the leader of a make-believe country. Do not be discouraged; if you could answer them satisfactorily, you would have no need for this book. Our purpose in the chapters that follow is to discuss some ideas that will help you analyze Latin American political life and to suggest how to go about finding answers on your own. The remainder of this book is divided into two parts. In the first we will examine the rules of the Latin American political game, the players who participate in it, and the economic strategies they use to achieve their ends. In the second part you will learn how to apply these tools to the analysis of Latin American political systems. Examples of four different types of

24   Understanding Latin American politics

governments will be described in some detail. Our objective is to develop analytical skills while learning about the contemporary politics of several Latin American countries.

Further reading

Arciniegas, German. *Latin America: A Cultural History.* New York: Knopf, 1967.

Cardoso, Fernando Henrique, and Enzo Faletto. *Dependency and Development in Latin America.* Berkeley: University of California Press, 1979.

Furtado, Celso. *Economic Development of Latin America.* Cambridge: Cambridge University Press, 1977.

Gibson, Charles. *Spain in America.* New York: Harper & Row, 1966.

Glade, William P. *The Latin American Economies.* New York: Van Nostrand Reinhold, 1969.

Glassman, Ronald M. *Political History of Latin America.* New York: Funk & Wagnalls, 1969.

Griffin, Keith. *Underdevelopment in Spanish America.* London: Allen & Unwin, 1969.

Herring, Hubert. *A History of Latin America: From the Beginnings to the Present.* New York: Knopf, 1962.

James, Preston. *Latin America.* New York: Odyssey Press, 1969.

Keen, Benjamin, and Mark Wasserman. *A Short History of Latin America.* Boston: Houghton Mifflin, 1980.

Lambert, Jacques. *Latin America: Social Structure and Political Institutions.* Berkeley: University of California Press, 1967.

Morse, Richard M. "The Heritage of Latin America," in Louis Hartz, ed., *The Founding of New Societies.* New York: Harcourt Brace & World, 1964, pp. 123–77.

Odell, Peter R. *Economies and Societies in Latin America: A Geographical Interpretation.* New York: Wiley, 1973.

Olien, Michael D. *Latin Americans: Contemporary Peoples and Their Cultural Traditions.* New York: Holt, Rinehart and Winston, 1973.

Pike, Frederick B. *Spanish America 1900–1970: Tradition and Social Innovation.* London: Thames and Hudson, 1973.

Prebisch, Raul. *Change and Development: Latin America's Great Task.* Washington, D.C.: Inter-American Development Bank, 1970.

Roxborough, Ian. *Theories of Underdevelopment.* Atlantic Highlands, N.J.: Humanities Press, 1979.

Stein, Stanley J., and Barbara Stein. *The Colonial Heritage of Latin America: Essays on Economic Dependence in Perspective.* New York: Oxford University Press, 1970.

Tannenbaum, Frank. *Ten Keys to Latin America.* New York: Knopf, 1962.

Veliz, Claudio. *The Centralist Tradition in America.* Princeton, N.J.: Princeton University Press, 1980.

Wagley, Charles. *The Latin American Tradition: Essays on the Unity and Diversity of Latin American Culture.* New York: Columbia University Press, 1968.

2. The rules of the Latin American game

A civil war raged in El Salvador. Across the Caribbean Venezuelans held their sixth consecutive presidential election between candidates from two evenly matched parties. In neighboring Cuba a communist regime directed by Fidel Castro celebrated its twenty-fifth anniversary while far to the south the military officers who deposed elected Socialist Salvador Allende a decade before still ruled Chile with a heavy hand. One could not find a more diverse array of political regimes anywhere in the world, nor a region more inviting and challenging to the student of politics.

Latin American politics can be studied in several ways. We can, for example, scrutinize governments, focusing on presidencies, legislatures where they exist, and judiciaries. Despite the fact that they are often abused or ignored in practice, formal government organizations do influence political conduct. We might also look at less formal institutions such as political parties and interest groups. Political parties may have unusual functions to perform, but they are sometimes critical to a government's survival. And interest groups may not be as well organized in Latin America as elsewhere, but distinct political and economic interests do exist and are represented in politics by designated individuals and organizations. A nation's political heritage and culture also merit attention, for even though current beliefs and habits are not exact replicas of those of days past, they cannot help being influenced by them. And finally, we must examine the economic and social structures that distribute political power within and among nations, for seldom will politics change without their changing too. In short, we cannot afford to bypass any of these things as we try to increase our understanding of Latin American politics.

What we are faced with then is not a need to decide what to study but a need to determine how we can incorporate so many different things into an analysis that generates coherent and defensible explanations of Latin American political conduct. What we want is something that will make our task manageable by helping us sort out the things that are relevant from those that are not.

The political game

One way to do this is to study politics as if it were a game. The game concept is helpful not because politics is primarily a form of recreation; as we know, it is deadly serious. Rather, the game idea is helpful because it forces us to structure our inquiry with an understanding of politics as a dynamic process involving human decisions, public conflicts, and self-interested participants.

The genesis of politics lies in human beings who act, affecting others as they do. In studying their behavior it does little good to assume that they are like physical particles whose actions are entirely predetermined and, therefore, always predictable. Many things influence human decisions, but it is up to us to determine what they are and how they affect individual and group behaviors. The game approach does not offer explanations per se, but it does force us to make sure that we regard the people we study as social beings who, though prone to like behaviors under similar conditions, do change their conduct in ways that iron filings do not. In other words, the game approach forces us to search for the variables as well as the constants in human affairs.

We can begin our quest by recalling that when trying to satisfy their needs people may work with or against each other. If relations among us were always harmonious, then the game idea, with its emphasis on conflict and its resolution, would be of little use. But disputes are common since most of what people want is either in short supply or is monopolized by a few people, making it impossible for everyone to secure what he or she wants most of the time. Many disputes are settled privately, but some require resolution by public means, and it is the latter that interest us. In particular, we want to know why public conflicts arise, how societies deal with them, and who gains and who loses when they are resolved.

Games come in many different forms. One of the most familiar is the kind in which contestants are closely matched and each has some chance of winning. Most parlor games are like that. But few political contests are so competitive. More common is a type of competition in which the chances of winning are very unevenly distributed, in some cases because the rules discriminate against some players and in others because the resources needed to win are distributed unequally. The rules that govern in a monarchy, for example, favor the monarch, whereas communist rules give advantages to party members and liberal democratic ones favor vote getters and interest groups. To think of politics as a kind of game, then, does not mean that we assume that it is always highly competitive or democratic. On the contrary, games can be easily rigged by anyone who has the power to write the rules, and rules can be ignored by those who can get away with it.

Equally important, games are not played in a vacuum. To begin with, each nation has a culture that we must take into account when we try to comprehend its politics. As we learned in Chapter 1, Latin American politics began as an extension of Spanish and Portuguese cultures through the physical domination of indigenous peoples. Contemporary life is not a carbon copy of this heritage, but neither is it free of its influence. Cultures change slowly and with them political attitudes and personal values. But cultures are also constantly on the move, borrowing things from one another. Some cultural elements are highly contagious, like modern science and technology are currently, and compel their assimilation even when they are not congenial. Others are deliberately sought and adapted for local use, such as political ideologies and economic strategies. Latin Americans have been energetic borrowers, constantly looking for innovative ways to deal with their problems. The result is a rich and varied mix of beliefs and technologies ranging from the indigenous to the most modern and sophisticated. If we omit tradition and culture from our inquiry we not only ignore a primary source of a nation's political rules, but we also risk losing sight of the meaning of politics to the players themselves.

Equally important is the material world in which the game is played. Man may not live by bread alone, but he cannot live without bread. You do not have to believe that politics is merely an expression of economic forces to acknowledge that it is influenced in many ways by the forces of production. Economic factors set limits on the range of options available to politicians and citizens alike. Consequently, the distribution of wealth, property, and technology in a society has important consequences for the way the game is played. This is so in a nation's relations abroad as well as internally. Few conditions limit the options available to Latin American governments as much as those created by economic decisions made in other nations and in world markets regarding the prices of their goods, the cost of desperately needed imports, and the availability of capital for investment. Rather than taking it for granted that Latin Americans can solve their economic development problems in any way they choose, we must try to see the world as they do, keeping in mind the forces that limit their choices.

A closer look at the games played in Latin America is necessary before we go any further. We will begin by inquiring into the status and content of political rules in the remainder of this chapter. Then in Chapters 3 and 4 we will acquaint ourselves with the principal players, followed by a review in Chapter 5 of what is at stake.

Identifying the political rules in Latin America

When someone speaks of political rules, we think first of a constitution or legal codes that specify how the government is organized, how public officials are selected, and how citizens are to be treated. We consider agreement on such rules to be essential to the creation and maintenance of a political society. But where do such rules come from? Their origins are as varied as their content. They may evolve slowly over time, commencing as local customs and later becoming formal laws. The ruling monarch of Saudi Arabia, for example, governs under rules that have changed little over the centuries. Rules may also arise from agreements on fundamental principles ratified by a nation's citizens or their representatives as in the case of the United States Constitution. They may also be imposed by force; the majority may disagree with the prevailing rules but, nevertheless, obey them for fear of punishment for disobedience. In Poland, Russian-backed Polish troops intervened in 1981 to restore a system of rules many Poles had discarded; the military prevailed for the moment, not because of its popularity but through the use of physical force. Similarly, throughout Latin America the military has frequently overthrown a popularly elected government and imposed a new order despite the opposition of a majority of citizens.

But are the rules contained in constitutions or other documents the only ones that guide political conduct in Latin America and, therefore, the only ones that should concern us? Obviously not. Our interest in formal rules should not be allowed to blind us to the many unwritten, informal ones that influence much of the behavior of political activists. In some cases, informal rules develop simply because constitutions ignore important practices; most of the constitutions written in the eighteenth and nineteenth centuries, for example, did not address themselves to the regulation of either political parties or influential private interest groups. Informal rules also arise when formal ones are ignored or temporarily suspended, such as occurred frequently in colonial Latin America when local elites refused to obey Spanish and Portuguese laws that they regarded as unjust or inconvenient. Informal rules are enforced by common practice in accord with the self-interest of players rather than by legal authorities. For example, in no Latin American country is it written that the military coup is the legal method for removing presidents. But most players at one time or another have accepted the coup as an appropriate way for dealing with their enemies. Nor is it written that landowners have the right to harm peasants when they fail to vote for their landlord's candidate; yet many have done so knowing that they would not be charged with a crime even though assault is prohibited by law.

In order to grasp the essential character of the Latin American game, an understanding of the ways players use political rules is essential. To begin with, we should remember that the acceptance of rules by individual players is as important as what rules say. In other words, we cannot assume that official rules enjoy the same status in Latin America as they do in the United States or Great Britain. It is also possible that rules supported by one player may be ignored by another. Some players may, for example, compete under one set of rules only to abandon them in moments of intense conflict and then return to them later. Or the majority may live by one rule while the minority subscribes to another. What this means in practice can be more readily comprehended if we look at the effects of the status of rules on three aspects of Latin American political life: the winning of public office, presidential conduct, and the treatment of political opposition.

How public office is won and lost

Few matters concern political scientists more than the selection of political authorities. Diversity rather than uniformity characterizes the way people select their leaders. Citizens in liberal democracies are guided by the principle of popular sovereignty, which holds that political authority is derived from the consent of the governed as expressed through some form of election. But liberal democracies are the exception rather than the rule, a minority among the world's nations. In communist regimes, in contrast, popular consent comes not through elections, but via the creation of a collective consciousness, which has its origins in fundamental ideological principles. Another point of view, quite common among Third World military regimes, justifies authority in terms of necessity rather than consent, arguing that strong authoritarian government is required to overcome internal racial, linguistic, ethnic, or economic conflicts. Still others stress the importance of tradition, claiming that public office should be passed from one member of a royal family to his descendents. Finally, public office can be won and held through the use of charismatic or personal appeals, where citizens obey leaders because of emotional attraction to them.

Latin Americans have known all of these methods. If you had observed Latin American countries at any time during the 1970s, you would have found liberal democracies governed by political parties, traditional autocracies ruled by a small elite, military regimes that expressed little concern for popular consent, and revolutionary regimes that sought to establish new ideological foundations for legitimate government. But it is not just the diversity among Latin American nations that is intriguing. Even more striking is the discovery that if we examine Latin American countries over time, we find diversity not only among nations but within them as well. A nation that organized its politics along liberal democratic lines one year would be under military rule the next. A country ruled by a conservative elite at one point a few years later would be a military dictatorship and then a decade later governed constitutionally. Of course, not all Latin American governments have undergone such frequent changes, but the fact that many have and continue to do so raises some challenging questions about the rules of the political game in these nations.

The diversity of political rules within many Latin American countries is primarily the product of a failure to solve the fundamental problem of political legitimacy that arises in all political systems. Political order and the governing of a nation are usually more easily achieved and maintained when political authority is made acceptable to a nation's citizens. If citizens agree on the principles under which the government is organized and its occupants selected, most citizens will play by the formal rules they have agreed to. And when they do, authorities do not have to expend a great deal of time coping with rule violators. But where agreement does not prevail, authorities will contend with such problems continually.

Disagreement over formal political rules was the norm rather than the exception throughout Latin America during the nineteenth century. When most of the region's nations achieved their independence around 1820, they adopted a set of constitutional rules modeled on those written in the newly independent United States of America, which called for the regular election of public officials who governed according to principles established in law. But the new post-Independence rules were not universally accepted. In fact, they were followed by only a small minority. Most citizens were either unaware of the new rules or ignored them because they threatened their status and power. What resulted were not stable democracies but political systems in which traditional forms of localized power and authority contended with the newly imposed liberal democratic rules, usually to the disadvantage of the latter. Neither the old Iberian values of hierarchy and centralized authority nor the new democratic ones gained enough legitimacy among active players to prevail. Instead, there developed a strong and lasting habit throughout the region of using whichever set of rules gave greatest advantage to one's cause. Consequently, Latin America has been plagued during much of its modern history by the kind of fundamental disputes over questions of political legitimacy and authority that many other nations resolved long ago.

The failure of constitutional democracy in Latin America after Independence should not be surprising. Democratic rules are vulnerable to attack, especially from belligerent oligarchs. Democratic government will not work simply because some citizens desire it, for though popular support is necessary, it is hardly sufficient. What the many want the few often subvert in order to defend their narrow interests. North Americans should recall that the success of their constitutional democracy was due not so much to the popularity of constitutional rules as to the fact that, unlike European liberal democrats, the founding fathers were not opposed by a landed aristocracy determined to retain privileges it had enjoyed for centuries. Imagine what the United States would have been like had the English colonists been mere instruments of a monarch who rewarded their conquests with huge tracts of land on which indigenous peoples supplied free labor.

The landed aristocracy would have used its power to subvert and destroy constitutional rule after Independence, just like it did in Latin America.

If Latin Americans do not always agree on a single set of political rules, what determines the way the game is played? To answer this question we must look not to general principles but to a closer examination of the players and their resources.

A player is any person or group that wants to occupy public office or influence the decisions of those who do. Political resources are those things that players use to compel or induce others to help them attain their political ends. The most common resource is physical force. When we cannot persuade others to comply with our wishes, we sometimes force them to do so. Physical intimidation and government repression remain the ultimate resource in Latin America, as they do elsewhere. Usually identified with military rule, physical force is used by other players as well. Right-wing death squads, leftist guerrillas, and terrorists also prefer the gun to the bargaining table.

Wealth is another resource. Although it seldom guarantees political influence, it can secure it. The rich can purchase official favors that the poor cannot afford, for example, and they can influence upwardly mobile politicians by admitting them to their social circles. Economic power is not exercised only in exchanges between individuals, however. Political influence accompanies the ownership of industries, financial institutions, or rural properties. Officials who prefer capitalist economics rely on private entrepreneurs for their country's economic development. Their dependence on private business, in turn, strengthens businessmen who use their influence to secure high tariffs to protect them from less expensive imports, prevent tax increases, and restrict the activities of organized labor. Were wealth the only resource allowed, the rich would easily dominate. But even though it is not, the wealthy still enjoy enormous advantages in capitalist societies where their contributions to economic development are heavily relied on.

Expertise is a third resource. As governments increase their responsibilities, they must rely more and more on professional advisers and bureaucrats trained in economics, development planning, engineering, and other sciences. And with expert knowledge comes influence for those who possess it. Latin American governments are staffed at the highest levels with corps of technocrats charged with responsibility for solving many of their nations' problems. They are joined in policy-making circles by advisers from international agencies and foreign governments as well as those representing domestic and foreign firms. Their politics is that of the technical report and the closed meeting, but that does not make it any less influential than that of groups who rely on the ballot box or the street demonstration.

Players also appeal to principles to secure their ends. These we label normative resources, for instead of force or money, the players try to convince others that a particular principle justifies their claims over those made by their competitors. Religion is the most common source of normative principles. The Ayatollah Khomeini and his followers adroitly exploit the Islamic faith to maintain their leadership in Iran, and in Latin America today many clergy are trying to lead the masses into social action using reformist church doctrines. Secular ideologies compete with religious ones for influence in politics. Nationalism is a powerful force employed by political movements, some of which, like the ruling party of Mexico, have held office for decades by cloaking themselves with it. Liberalism, socialism, and fascism also compete for influence, and the region's history is littered with governments who claimed to have lived by the principles of one or the other. Knowing how much normative principles actually influence conduct is never easy since it is always possible to prohibit people from acting according to their beliefs, but we cannot overlook something with so great a claim over human minds.

Finally, there is the resource of mass action. As with each of the other resources, mass support alone does not guarantee that one will prevail. If elections are held, the rules of secret ballot make the size of one's following the determinant of one's success. But if electoral rules are prohibited or their effects ignored, mass support matters little, unless the masses can disrupt the status quo in other ways, like demonstrations, which may provoke political change. Few things are harder to measure than the influence of the masses and their movements in games where elections are prohibited. Of course, the problem is not ours alone, for neither the leaders of such movements nor the governments and players they oppose know for sure how much clout they have.

What one can achieve in politics depends primarily on how one's resources are regarded by those against whom they are used. We can seldom predict the outcome of an encounter knowing who holds how much of what. Players do not behave that mechanically. Instead, they constantly estimate what others will do along with the probable effects of their own actions. They calculate, bluff, take chances, act, and suffer the consequences. Patterns of behavior emerge because people tend to act in similar ways under like conditions, and we discover their routines not by measuring resources but by examining how people fare when they put their resources to work.

What distinguishes Latin America is not the variety of resources used by its citizens to capture or influence government. Force, wealth, expertise, normative principles, and mass following are not peculiar to Latin America, but are present to some degree in political systems throughout the world. What makes Latin America different is that resources are used not only to capture public office or influence policy, but also to undermine the formal rules of the political game. In the liberal democracies of Anglo-America and Western Europe the ability to win elections determines who governs because rules place a premium on the electoral decision. To be sure, economic power and expertise also influence policy, but it is the election, with all its imperfections, that regulates the choice of political leaders. But in much of Latin America no single resource or set of resources consistently determines the selection of public officials or the making of public policy. From time to time one may appear to gain a foothold, but more often than not it will be replaced by another before it becomes secure. Thus, if asked how public office is gained and held in Latin America, we have to answer that there is no single rule that has become definitive in most instances. Instead, there are several.

First, there are elections. The fact that modern Latin American history is littered with presidential elections might lead us to conclude that voting is the dominant mode of selecting public officials. Each year elections are held somewhere in Latin America; in 1982, for example, they occurred in Mexico, Colombia, the Dominican Republic, Costa Rica, Brazil, and El Salvador. However, on closer examination we discover that the preferences of the voters are not always respected. Elections have been rigged, annulled, and ignored by incumbents. Moreover, the inauguration of an elected president does not guarantee that he will complete his term of office. Military intervention, assassination, and rebellion have been used to depose presidents. What matters is not the election itself but who accepts its results.

The military coup is a second way of taking office. For those who have lost an election or intensely oppose a president and his policies the coup is a convenient instrument of last resort. It is not only the military's desire to govern that makes the coup so common throughout the region, but also the fact that few players have resisted the temptation at one time or another to urge its use against a government they could not dislodge through any other means.

Elections and coups are the primary ways of ending the life of a government in Latin America, but not the only ones. Public protests aimed at undermining presidential authority are another. Tactics vary, but the most common is the mass demonstration or general strike intended to cut off basic services and undermine public morale. It is most effective at securing a change in government policy, but the mass demonstration can also create enough disorder to force military intervention.

Insurrections and guerrilla warfare are also used to depose governments. Peasant uprisings aimed at evicting local ruling elites from their property and national political leaders from their offices have occurred several times in the region since Independence. More recently, opponents of incumbent governments inspired by the success of national liberation movements elsewhere have organized small armed units and employed guerrilla tactics to undermine authorities by frustrating and humiliating the armies that try to protect them. Some operate in the countryside, where they seek to develop peasant support for their struggle; others go to the cities and use kidnapping, assassination, bank robberies, and the destruction of public facilities to promote a collapse of public authority.

Governments can also be changed through the efforts of powerful elites who use their resources to apply economic pressure on public officials. Farmers, bankers, and industrialists may slow production in order to damage the economy and thereby reduce public confidence in the government. Domestic groups are not, however, alone in such efforts. Foreign governments, international agencies, and multinational corporations, separately and together, may from time to time try to end the life of governments they oppose. By cutting off desperately needed loans, boycotting a country's exports in foreign markets, withdrawing investments, or supporting opposition groups, they endeavor to weaken a nation's economy and force the replacement of its government.

By now it should be apparent why most Latin American countries find it so hard to live by a single set of rules. Groups and individuals who discover that the prevailing rules favor others more than themselves may prefer to undermine the rules rather than obey them. The leaders of large political parties may prefer elections because their strength rests in their mobilization of large numbers of voters. But groups who do not have large followings may oppose elections, especially if the elections result in victories for parties that threaten their interests. For example, conservative economic elites may try to block elected governments using their economic clout and influence within the military to depose the incumbents. Similarly, labor unions persecuted by a conservative government may shut down critical industries or take to the streets to force a change in policy or bring down the government.

The number of players in the game has grown gradually during the past century. Admission to the ruling circles was seldom easy and never went unchallenged. Some still are on the outside looking in. No doubt the stubborn resistance of the oligarchy to the admission of the middle classes and organized labor contributed to the suspicion, hostility, and distrust still present today. The repression of rivals who threaten an elitist way of life does not contribute to the growth of an ethic of compromise and reform. Instead, those on the outside cannot help convincing themselves that the defeat and removal of their opponents, and perhaps even their exclusion from the game, are the only ways to play.

It is not just the oligarchs who have tried to exclude their rivals from the government. Revolutionaries have done much the same thing. The leaders of the Mexican revolution were determined in 1917 to break the power of the church, landed elites, the military, and foreign investors. They did not succeed completely, as we shall see later, but for a time they did reduce the influence of each significantly. To consolidate their domination they erected a new power structure in which they ruled organized labor, peasants, and the emerging middle class using a national party organization. The regime has survived for over sixty years, making Mexico the deviant case among Latin Americans. The Cuban revolutionaries went even further after they took over in 1959. They seized 70 percent of the nation's farmland, nationalized nearly all private businesses, and enforced a set of rules drawn from Marxist-Leninist thought and Soviet practice, leading eventually to governance by the Cuban Communist

party. And in Nicaragua the Sandinista movement, which defeated
the National Guard of dictator Anastasio Somoza Debayle in 1979,
created its own military and placed all of the Somoza properties, over
one-third of the economy, in government hands. In each of these cases
one set of players prevailed by eliminating some of their rivals.

How rules affect presidential conduct

We turn now to the matter of presidential behavior. What is intriguing about Latin American presidents is not the amount of power
they appear to wield, but how they use their power to cope with the
uncertainty that arises when a consensus on political rules is lacking.
Traditionally, Latin American presidents have been freer of legislative
and judicial constraints than their North American or European counterparts. Not only do their constitutions assign them more authority
over legislation, law enforcement, and foreign affairs than do most
liberal democratic constitutions, but in actual practice Latin American
presidents have managed to dominate their nations' political life to a
greater degree than have their counterparts in constitutional regimes.
Throughout the nineteenth century, when the central political issues
were national unification and the expansion of the authority of the
state at the expense of the church, it was the president who organized
the armies and maintained the peace. The legislature has always been
the weaker partner in this relationship, making checks and balances
among the different branches of government more myth than reality.
Countries where legislatures achieved significant strength, such as
Uruguay and Chile before 1973 and Costa Rica since 1948, are the
exception rather than the rule in Latin America.

What limits the exercise of presidential power is the ability of other
players to constrain the president by using their political resources
against him. During the late nineteenth and early twentieth centuries,
especially in the less developed Latin American countries, the president assumed the role of the "man on horseback," or strong-armed
ruler, and employed physical force to create and maintain political
order. Since then, many other types of presidents have come and
gone, ranging from the very cruel and autocratic to weak leaders,
easily manipulated by other players.

Presidential conduct is influenced by the status as well as the content of political rules. Where a single set of rules prevails, the presi-

dent tends to be more confident and can exercise his power with a steady hand. But in countries where the rules are contested or ignored, the president is insecure and to survive is forced either to balance interests and manipulate rules or to use autocratic methods to fortify himself against potential opponents. When everyone plays by the rules, he knows more or less how they will behave and how to respond, but when they do not, he must always guess what they will do, never certain what steps to take to protect himself against them.

Examples of well-institutionalized presidencies are few, but their strengths are readily apparent. Take Mexico, for example. The Mexican president is elected every six years to a single term. Since the late 1920s, Mexican elections have been held on schedule and without interruption. During those years the Mexican presidency has become the dominant institution in the country's political life, with its occupant functioning as both the leader of the ruling party and the head of government. The revolutionary tradition requires that the president appear to be responsive to the interests of the party's constituent organizations and devoted to the goals of the revolution; to achieve these ends, it gives him control over a huge state bureaucracy and a national party organization. Whether he is an autocrat or a democrat in practice is intensely disputed in Mexico, but regardless, it is apparent that the public acceptance of the Mexican rules of the game has made him a very powerful political leader.

The same is true, for somewhat different reasons, in contemporary Cuba. Undoubtedly Prime Minister Fidel Castro derives much of his power from the strength of his character and his leadership of the insurrection that ended the tyranny of Fulgencio Batista. But his authority is maintained not through personality alone but also through the organization of a new revolutionary power structure under the leadership of the Cuban Communist party. Castro and his associates are able to prevail because they have created a consensus of sorts on the way the country should be governed. Cubans have come to know what to expect from Castro and his party and bureaucracy, and the latter in turn know what the citizens they govern expect from them. The point is not that Cuban citizens control every action of their leaders, but that both know where they fit into the existing political order. Regardless of the means used to achieve the consensus, one cannot deny its effect in strengthening Cuban leadership.

There are nonrevolutionary examples of the strong presidency as well. Interestingly, they are found primarily in the more traditional countries that are the least politically complex and sophisticated. This should not surprise us for it is in the very traditional society that a single set of rules most easily dominates. In Paraguay, which has been governed by General Alfredo Stroessner for over three decades, or Nicaragua, where the Somoza family presided for nearly half a century, one found strong presidents who faced few political constraints and little uncertainty over the rules that governed political life in their countries. In the latter case, of course, change did come, but only after a bloody revolution that overthrew the Somoza dynasty in 1979 and replaced it with a drastically different political order.

But what about the powers of the president in those countries that are plagued by lack of agreement on the rules of the game? The president may claim as much legal authority as do his more secure neighbors, but in practice he often finds himself constrained by the uncertainties created by the lack of political consensus and his vulnerability to the use of political resources by his opponents. In contrast to a president in a consensual system, who knows how and in what form his critics will assault him, the less secure president does not know for certain how far his opponents will go or which resources they will bring to bear against him. He is beset by uncertainty, never knowing when laborers may riot to block his policies or when the military may launch a coup to depose him. Haunted by a politics of rumor and conspiracy, he will spend most of his time consorting with his allies to disarm and isolate his critics.

An outstanding example of this can be found in postwar Argentina. Even though it is one of the most affluent nations in Latin America, Argentina has been plagued by political instability, especially since 1955 when President Juan Perón was overthrown by the military. Between 1955 and 1982 three presidents were elected, but none completed his term. Twelve military presidents came and went during that time, some yielding to elected governments and others being deposed by fellow officers. Argentina's elected presidents, despite substantial constitutional authority, have faced repeated attacks on their leadership by civilian and military opponents. Among the civilian players are a militant and well-organized labor movement that demands that its Peronist party be allowed to rule and opposition parties and an upper class that often ask the military to intervene on their behalf. There is no easy escape from the dilemmas faced by

Argentine presidents. For example, when they resort to force to deter militant workers, they provoke more illegal protests that threaten political order; yet when they yield to labor's demands, they often cause the intervention of antilabor military officers. In the face of such competing pressures, the president can either try to bargain with each side in the hope of securing temporary compromises, or he can retreat from the battle, conceding that he lacks the support required to lead the nation. The contrast between the vulnerable Argentine president and the very strong Mexican one is striking. The formal constitutional authority of the two is quite similar, but the civilian Argentine president has been forced by the lack of consensus on political rules to struggle, unsuccessfully, to survive, whereas the Mexican president has enjoyed the security of his well-organized political organization and broad political consensus.

We have seen that presidential power is a variable rather than a constant in the Latin American political game. Both the amount of presidential power and the manner of its use are heavily influenced by the content and status of the rules operative in each nation. Rules may give the president much latitude for governing the nation, or they may restrict his authority, forcing him to share it with others in the government. And where there is widespread agreement on the rules, the president is spared the insecurity that comes from the unregulated give and take of political warfare. In contrast, where there is no agreement on fundamental rules, uncertainty prevails, often forcing the president to behave as a ruler under siege rather than as the leader of a well-organized governmental process. One of our objectives in Part II will be to examine the behaviors of presidents who operate under each of these sets of conditions.

How rules affect political opposition

One of the most critical relationships in politics is the one that exists between a government and its opponents. The rules that guide this relationship are a principal defining characteristic of a political system. Liberal democracy, for example, is defined in part by its toleration of political opposition; authoritarianism, in contrast, is distinguished by its intolerance. Most Latin American systems conform to neither of these idealized models. Instead, we usually find players who lend their support to public officials when it serves their needs and oppose the government when their vital interests are threatened, and governments that tolerate some opponents while repressing others. Policy making under these conditions is a dynamic process involving actions by authorities and critical reactions by other players. It also frequently involves intense conflicts between political ins and outs, especially when governments try to promote development by redistributing resources from one player to another. Those who find themselves threatened may not only try to block the execution of adverse policies, but may also seek to bring down the government and end the threat it poses. At the same time, it is not unusual for authorities to anticipate such reactions and repress potential opponents before they can mobilize an attack.

The treatment and behavior of political opponents also affect the creation of a political consensus in a society. The more the rules give all players a sense that they are being treated fairly in the competition for public influence, the more likely the players are to accept them. On the other hand, the more the rules threaten their interests and deny them an opportunity to capture public office or influence public policy, the more they are forced to break the rules to protect themselves from those in power. It is the latter circumstance that contributes to much of the extralegal protest behavior found in Latin America.

One cannot place all the responsibility for coups, riots, and demonstrations on governmental abuse of opponents, but it is not hard to understand why opposition players express themselves through such means when they feel ignored or abused. We have already seen how different players prefer to follow the rules most favorable to them rather than those selected by opponents who seek to rig the game against them. It is also apparent that when they are threatened by the existing rules, many opponents of the government prefer confusion to the rule of law, convinced that they will have more freedom to pursue their interests when disorder reigns than when strict enforcement of a single set of rules prevails. Their choice is never an easy one, since political confusion may do everyone harm eventually, but in the short run it may give them the freedom they need to counterattack against authorities.

Latin American governments have developed an arsenal of methods for dealing with political opponents, each of which reflects an application of particular rules and strategies. The most familiar is the conventional competitive process, modeled on the practices of Western de-

mocracy, in which groups strive openly to influence government policy and political parties compete for public office in elections. Very
few Latin American countries have fulfilled the requirements of this
purest form of the competitive model for extended periods of time,
though Uruguay from 1903 until 1973, Chile between 1932 and 1973,
Venezuela since 1958, and Costa Rica since 1948 have come close.
More common is a less conventional competitive system in which
some players are restricted while others participate in elections, lobbying, and protesting. It is not unusual to find public authorities in
such systems using all legal means and some illegal ones to weaken
certain opponents in the hope of defeating them more easily in subsequent elections.

Another departure from the pure competitive system is the one in
which the government co-opts or attracts its potential opponents to
its regime, securing their temporary cooperation by sharing public
authority with them. The most familiar mode of co-optation is
through a coalition government in which the leaders of the ruling
party invite other political parties to share cabinet posts and legislative leadership. Chilean governments during the 1940s and Venezuelan ones in the 1960s used the coalition technique with some success.
Its more impressive application, however, occurred in Colombia after
1958, when the country's two largest political parties ended a decade
of bitter civil strife by agreeing to form a national front government
in which for sixteen years the presidency was alternated between the
two parties and all cabinet positions were divided between them. In
essence, the Colombians agreed to suspend the normal competitive
rules of the game, which had led to violent interparty conflicts during the 1950s, and substitute new ones, which froze the competition
so that each of the dominant parties was assured a place in the
government.

Co-optation and coalition building do not apply only to political
parties in Latin America, but are also a means for dealing with economic and social groups. The practice of linking private groups formally to the government has been quite common in Western societies,
ranging from the schemes of the extremist fascist regimes of the 1930s
to the contemporary industrial societies of northern Europe, where
labor unions, farmers, and business groups are used by government as
instruments of political control and economic management. The co-
optation of private groups has taken several forms in Latin America.

In some countries it involves only informal agreements between groups and public officials; in others, like contemporary Mexico, groups representing laborers and peasants are included in a corporatist-type ruling party. In each case the practice of co-optation represents an attempt by public authorities to alter the rules of the competitive game so that they can better coordinate and control its outcome. Their objective is to replace the open conflict of poorly regulated competitive processes with a system of well-defined channels of communication between authorities and private groups that officials can use to resolve conflicts to their advantage.

Two other sets of rules have been applied to political opposition throughout Latin America. Under one, the government's opponents are seen but not heard; the other seeks to eliminate them altogether. The first is found in countries where opposition parties exist, but are never allowed by the incumbent party to win public office. Mexico is again a good example of this. The Mexican government encourages the participation of opposition parties in elections and in the legislative process, while at the same time using all resources at its disposal, both legal and illegal, to limit their success. Though in many ways very different from Mexico, post-1964 Brazil is another example of circumscribed opposition. Its military regime organized two political parties, one to control the legislature and the other to act as a loyal but impotent opposition. In both Mexico and Brazil political opposition was tolerated, but only up to a point; its criticisms of the government had to be muted, its acceptance of the official rules complete, and its expectations of capturing the presidency or an electoral majority repressed.

Why is an opposition tolerated at all when a government has no intention of letting it capture important public offices? Some argue that the ritual of democracy is important to leaders even though the fact of democracy is not. First, it may help the country's image in the exterior by satisfying those nations who insist on democratic institutions as a precondition for the maintenance of relations. More plausible, however, is the fact that it offers a means, albeit a crude one, through which opposition pressures can be channeled and controlled without doing harm to the regime and its policies. It may also give officials an effective tool for mobilizing its own supporters, since an exposed opposition offers a visible threat against which to unite one's followers.

Oppositions are treated even more harshly in those systems where the government strives for political unanimity. The most notable example is Cuba, where opposition parties are considered irrelevant to the needs of the Cuban Revolution. Fidel Castro candidly admits his preference for a one-party regime. He argues that there can be only one true revolutionary ideology and, therefore, only one party to interpret and enforce that ideology. Dissent over policy, if it occurs at all, should come from within the party and other official organizations. The communist regime is not the only one, however, that has sought to eliminate opposition parties. Some contemporary military regimes, like those that governed Argentina, Uruguay, and Chile in the 1970s, abolished political parties without creating new ones in their place. They claimed that political parties were divisive forces that undermined social order and therefore served no useful purpose.

This brief review of political opposition and the rules that govern its behavior in Latin America would not be complete without mention of "antisystem" oppositions. Most of the opposition groups we have discussed thus far are ones whose principal political objective is to capture public office or to acquire political influence within the existing political game. But Latin America has a history of opposition groups whose aim is not playing the game but transforming it through revolutionary means. Both the Mexican and Cuban revolutionaries were of this type before they gained power. During the 1960s and 1970s, antisystem groups proliferated throughout the region, often taking the form of rural guerrillas or urban terrorists intent on defeating the political elite and its military defenders. They succeeded in Nicaragua in 1979, fought hard in El Salvador and Guatemala in the early 1980s, and were brutally repressed in Argentina and Uruguay in the mid-1970s.

The next step

You are now familiar with the concept of political rules and the role rules play in the game of politics. We have discovered that they come in many forms and can be found in constitutional codes and informal norms that guide political expectations and behavior. They influence how political office is won, how presidents behave, and how political opposition is treated. The concept of political rules offers a point of departure in our quest to understand Latin American politics and public policy. It is a tool you can now use to study and compare individual Latin American political systems.

The study of political rules cannot provide all the answers we seek, but it does take us a long way toward asking the right questions. For example, henceforth when you examine a Latin American political system you can begin by asking: What are the current rules of its political game and who respects them? To what extent is a single set dominant and followed in practice? Are there informal rules that shape behavior? If so, what are they and what is their effect? And what about the consequences of the rules of the game? To whose advantage do they work and how do they affect the process by which development policy is made and implemented? More specifically, who benefits most and who benefits least from the nation's politics?

Further reading

Adams, Richard Newbold. *The Second Sowing: Power and Secondary Development in Latin America.* San Francisco: Chandler, 1967.

Anderson, Charles W. *Politics and Economic Change in Latin America: The Governing of Restless Nations.* New York: Van Nostrand, 1967.

Bailey, F.G. *Stratagems and Spoils: A Social Anthropology of Politics.* New York: Schocken Books, 1969.

Chilcote, Ronald H., and Joel C. Edelstein. *Latin America: The Struggle with Dependency and Beyond.* Cambridge, Mass.: Schenkman, 1974.

Collier, David, ed. *The New Authoritarianism in Latin America.* Princeton, N.J.: Princeton University Press, 1979.

Fagen, Richard R., and Wayne A. Cornelius. *Political Power in Latin America.* Englewood Cliffs, N.J.: Prentice-Hall, 1970.

Jaguaribe, Helio. *Political Development: A General Theory and a Latin American Case Study.* New York: Harper & Row, 1973.

Lambert, Jacques. *Latin America: Social Structure and Political Institutions.* Berkeley: University of California Press, 1967.

Linz, Juan, and Alfred Stepan, eds. *The Breakdown of Democratic Regimes: Latin America.* Baltimore: Johns Hopkins University Press, 1978.

Liss, Sheldon B., and Peggy Liss, eds. *Man, State and Society in Latin American History.* New York: Praeger, 1972.

Malloy, James M., ed. *Authoritarianism and Corporatism in Latin America.* Pittsburgh: University of Pittsburgh Press, 1977.

Mercier Vega, Luis. *Roads to Power in Latin America.* London: Pall Mall Press, 1969.

Needler, Martin. *Political Development in Latin America: Instability, Violence and Evolutionary Change.* New York: Random House, 1968.

Powelson, John. *Institutions of Economic Growth: A Theory of Conflict Management in Developing Countries.* Princeton, N.J.: Princeton University Press, 1972.

Silvert, Kalman. *The Conflict Society: Reaction and Revolution in Latin America.* New York: American Universities Field Staff, 1966.

3. Players – I

Now we can take a closer look at the players in the Latin American game. In Chapter 2 we defined the player as any individual or group that tries to gain public office or influence those who do. Political parties, wealthy landowners, and businessmen come immediately to mind. But there are many others: military officers, peasant leaders, labor unions, foreign governments, multinational corporations, priests, and students, just to name a few. Unfortunately, labels and titles tell us very little about political activists who often contrive reputations to augment their power. To know who players are, what they want, and how much clout they possess we have no choice but to examine each one, observing its behavior under a variety of rules.

Before meeting them we need to recall that their political world differs in many respects from that of the liberal democracies of Western Europe and North America. First, most political organizations in Latin America are less well organized than those found in more industrialized and technologically sophisticated nations. Moreover, leaders who claim to represent large constituencies often are in contact with far fewer followers than they allege due to the difficulty of organizing them and communicating with them. Second, given persistent disputes over political rules, politics demands much more of players in Latin America than it does of those who operate in settings where a single set of rules is widely accepted. As we saw in Chapter 2, Latin Americans contend over rules as well as policy, constantly risking their exclusion from the game. Therefore, we cannot assume that their political parties and labor unions will always behave like parties and unions in Western Europe and the United States. And third, we should not forget that although players do change, forever adapting their tactics to take advantage of opportunities given them by changing rules, their reputations usually lag behind, creating an image out of step with reality. Landowners who were powerful in the past may no longer be so despite their claims to the contrary, and government technocrats who were once minor figures in an impotent bureaucracy may make decisions affecting the welfare of the entire population but go unnoticed.

To organize this introduction we will ask four questions about each player. First, who are the people involved? What do they share in common and how united are they economically, socially, and politically? Second, what do they want from politics, if anything? We should acknowledge at the outset that most people in Latin America, as elsewhere, do not devote their lives to politics. Many are uninterested; others expect their leaders to make decisions for them. Some players, in fact, want only to be left alone, free of public authorities who seek to tax, regulate, or otherwise deprive them. Others want favors or subsidies to gain advantages over their competitors. So instead of assuming that they are active merely because they share in some objective political interest, we must inquire about their subjective interests and whether these lead to any form of political participation. Third, what resources do players have at their disposal and how do they use them to influence the outcome of the game? The mere possession of resources does not assure that they will be put to effective use; they must be employed with skill and good timing to be effective. And fourth, which set of rules do players prefer and how successful have they been in determining which rules dominate the playing of the game? Because players are just as likely to do battle over the rules as over public policy, their influence over the way the game is played is even more important than their effects on its policy outcomes.

In this chapter we will focus on social classes and the people who speak for them in order to learn about the importance of social and economic position in politics. Economic elites, the middle class, and the masses will command our attention here. Then we will turn to more organized interests in Chapter 4, focusing on political parties, the military, the church, bureaucrats, and foreigners. Since players come in many forms, it is imperative that our study include both large collectivities and narrow, highly organized interests. What follows then are general, introductory observations. Deviations from the trends described will be left to the discussion of individual countries in Part II.

Rural elites

For centuries Latin Americans have complained of the *oligarquía*. It is the *oligarquía*, we are told, that has monopolized wealth, corrupted politicians, manipulated the military, conspired with foreigners, exploited the masses, and obstructed progress. But who in fact are the oligarchs? Is the *oligarquia* a small group of conspirators or a sizable social class? Do its members control most resources or just a few that they have exploited for strategic advantage? And are they the same today as they were a century ago, or has their membership changed with industrialization in recent times?

Today few observers agree on who the oligarchs are and how much power they exercise in politics. To be sure, no one denies that a minority possesses a disproportionate share of wealth and power and enjoys immense political and economic advantages. But that is true in all nations of the world. What we want to know is not whether there is an elite, but who belongs to it, how much power it has, and how it has used its resources in each Latin American country.

We can begin in the countryside, where wealth and power traditionally have been concentrated. The first thing we discover is that the rural elite is neither as small nor as cohesive as it once was. Landowners remain powerful in the less industrialized nations of Central America and the Andean region, but most compete with other players in the more industrialized ones like Brazil, Argentina, and Mexico. Though quite willing to exercise what influence they can on the national scene, landowners have always been strongest at the local level where people are most dependent on them, their wealth, and the employment they provide. In political matters landowners have relied heavily on their ability to control local judges, police, and voters when elections were held. But two things have always threatened them: the confiscation of their property through its seizure by peasants or government agrarian reform programs and their loss of control over cheap labor. When the threat of either arises they are quick to use what power they have at the national as well as the local level to protect themselves.

Landowners share many needs and concerns, yet they are not a very homogeneous group. What each wants is influenced by whether he produces primarily for domestic or foreign markets, his use of modern technology, the size of his operations, and the value of his produce. Equally important are geography, demography, and local traditions. Of the many ways of classifying rural elites one of the most helpful to the political analyst is to distinguish between *latifundistas* and modern farmers. Within the *latifundista* category are those who

are more devoted to traditional forms of life than to maximizing economic gain. Normally they own large tracts of land, but cultivate only
small sections intensively, renting the rest to sharecroppers or leaving
it as unimproved pastures. *Latifundistas* employ very little modern
technology, but rely instead on manual labor supplied by peasants.
Their goal is the preservation of the *latifundio* as a social institution
through their control over land and peasant laborers and the production of enough goods to sustain their aristocratic lifestyle.

Modern farmers, in contrast, are devoted primarily to the maximization of economic gain. Their operations tend to be more capital
intensive, as they make use of modern technologies wherever profitable. Intensive commercial farming is not new to Latin America.
Since colonial times there have been plantations and *haciendas* organized primarily for profit maximization. But not until the twentieth
century has intensive commercial farming come to dominate the rural
economies of most Latin American countries. To be sure, these two
categories are a bit imprecise. Those whom we have classified as
latifundistas occasionally adopt modern modes of production, and some
commercial farmers still rely on traditional technologies. Nevertheless, it is useful to distinguish among landowners on the basis of
differences in their social values and economic goals because it helps
explain their varied policy concerns and political activities.

The *latifundista* has been on the retreat throughout Latin America in
recent times. Some *latifundios* have been divided by inheritance; others
have been transformed into productive commercial operations by a
new generation of farmers. They have also been eradicated by land
tenure reforms aimed at promoting higher production and improving
peasant welfare. In Mexico, Nicaragua, Venezuela, Chile, Peru, and
Cuba, extensive holdings have been expropriated by the government
and redistributed to peasants or reorganized as cooperative or state
farms. Yet, as successful as these efforts have been in some parts of
the region, the *latifundista* is not yet extinct. Many tradition-bound
landowners still struggle tenaciously to withstand deliberate attacks on
their way of life. They are now on the defensive, but they can still use
their wealth, family ties, and local influence to keep government reformers from encroaching on them.

What, in addition to their self-preservation, do the *latifundistas* want
from politics? Very little, actually, for besides high prices for their
limited produce and control over cheap labor, they want primarily to

be left alone. They require few government services and have little use for most of its regulations. All they have wanted from the central government has been economic stability and occasional protection against peasant organizers and other disrupters of the status quo. Since World War II, few *latifundistas* have sought public office, led political parties, or controlled the making of national development policy. They have relinquished these tasks to the urban professionals, party politicians, and military officers. Instead, they have concentrated their efforts on the bureaucracy and the courts as they enforce the law. Through personal influence, bribes, and obstinacy, *latifundistas* have sought, often successfully, to escape laws aimed at depriving them of their wealth and power.

What about the political resources of the *latifundistas?* Obviously, they have wealth and social prestige, especially if they are descended from the post-Independence ruling class. But how can wealth and social prestige be translated into power that will deter reform governments? We have already mentioned bribery, a practice that has proved effective in deterring tax collectors, land surveyors, and judges, among others. It also secures the help of low-paid local police officers. Social status and familial ties also help gain favors from public officials, many of whom seek admittance to higher social circles. Traditionally, *latifundistas* have made excellent use of regional political bosses on whom the government sometimes depends for political control at the local level. The exchange of favors between landowners and local politicians builds mutual obligations that are used to halt the enforcement of undesirable laws. And when all else fails they have hired assassins to kill *campesinos* who defy their rules, as they have recently in Central America. At one time the landed elite also enjoyed the support of the military, but since few officers are now recruited from the upper class, the wealthy can no longer take military support for granted. In sum, the *latifundistas'* political strength is greatest at the local level. They are not without influence on the national scene, but it is their ability to hold off enemies who try to intrude on their domains that sustains their survival. It takes a strong, well-organized, and determined bureaucracy to penetrate Latin America's local political systems; insecure governments, even if popular with large numbers of people, are seldom capable of dislodging landed elites.

Finally, which rules of the game do the *latifundistas* prefer? Obviously they see little advantage in electoral democracy. Even though they can sometimes control votes within their regions, the votes are seldom enough to defeat urban political parties. They may, of course, join with commercial farmers and urban elites to organize a conservative coalition, but such coalitions receive no more than one-third of the popular vote in most countries. The *latifundistas* want a set of rules that circumscribes reform-oriented, mass-based political parties and, when the latter are elected, limits their power. They need a government that is either uninterested in penetrating and reforming local power structures or too weak to do so, in other words, an elitist constitutional government, as was common in the late nineteenth century, or, in the contemporary age of activist masses, an autocratic one devoted to the protection of the propertied classes.

If our analysis of the landed elite were confined only to *latifundistas*, we would be guilty of ignoring a majority of those who wield power in the countryside. Gradually but steadily, a more intensive type of farming has spread throughout the region. Today, plantations and large family farms outnumber traditional *latifundios* in many countries. They are important not only to the welfare of those who own and manage them, but to national economies as well. Modern, or intensive, agriculture includes units of all sizes, making it impossible to draw a line between the elite and the rest of the modern farmers. But that should not prevent us from studying the behavior of this large and very powerful community.

Some modern farmers are descendants of *latifundistas* who transformed their estates into modern commercial enterprises; others are the heirs of the commercial farmers of the late nineteenth century who produced coffee, cattle, and other commodities for export. Some come from immigrant families, primarily from Europe but also from Asia, who came to Latin America after the turn of the century, began as colonists and tenant farmers, and gradually expanded their enterprises. Modern farms come in many forms and operate with varying degrees of efficiency, ranging from well-organized plantations employing several hundred laborers to family farms engaged in mixed cropping. On the whole, their owners are less prominent socially than the traditional rural elite, though many have achieved social status from their wealth. They are, however, not as isolated from other economic sectors as the *latifundistas*; some, in fact, are also deeply involved in food processing, banking, and commerce. Many of their enterprises are modern, efficient operations comparable to those of

North America, although the majority operate at lower levels of efficiency, handicapped by the high cost of technology and their reliance on unstable international markets. In sum, Latin America's modern farmers are a diverse and sizable group that includes, among others, the grain producers of Argentina, Uruguay, and southern Brazil; the coffee producers of Colombia, Brazil, and Central America; the Mexicans who raise fruits and vegetables for export to the United States each winter; the truck gardeners near most large cities; the sugar barons of Brazil and the Caribbean; the banana producers of Ecuador and Central America; and the cotton farmers found throughout the region.

Modern farmers want more from government than do *latifundistas*. First and foremost, they want policies that promote high prices for their produce. In addition, they lobby for cheap transportation and storage facilities, and against land taxes and agrarian reform. Like farmers elsewhere they want to be protected against adversity but allowed to take advantage of opportunity. And like their counterparts in Europe and North America, they have created organizations to represent them before government officials. Some farmers' organizations unite the producers of a single commodity; others follow regional lines. Modern farmers covet membership on government boards and commissions as a means of gaining control over agricultural policy making. Though they do not ignore political parties, they prefer to deal directly with the officials who make policy, avoiding the broader political issues in favor of more narrow agrarian matters.

Success in the political arena depends not only on organization and access to public authorities, but also on the resources one can bring to bear on particular issues. The modern farmers' strength derives from the economy's dependence on their produce. Most Latin American economies rely heavily on the export of agricultural commodities for desperately needed foreign exchange. Any interruption in the flow of exports can quickly undermine the economy. Moreover, rapidly growing and increasingly urban populations must be fed by domestic production if the foreign exchange costs of imported food are to be avoided. Thus, no matter how hostile they may be to rural elites in principle, most governments are forced to rely on them. Conversely, by using the country's dependence on them to good advantage, the rural elite can often persuade officials to meet their demands.

Finally, there is the question of preferred political rules. Do farmers have a preference for one set of rules over another? Latin American farmers, like farmers elsewhere, prefer stability in all things. There is already enough uncertainty in their world caused by natural forces without the addition of political instability. They desire a political game that offers few uncertainties and a government that is sympathetic to technical economic argument over the demands of voters. It is not so much the form of the government that matters to them as its stability and its performance. Like the *latifundistas*, they tolerate democratic government as long as it is orderly and not hostile to rural interests. On the other hand, they also accept autocratic government, especially if it is well managed and able to carry out supportive economic policies. As they are for most players, for the commercial farmers the rules are a means to an end rather than ends in themselves, and whichever set of rules secures their objectives is the one they are most likely to support.

We now have some idea of what rural elites expect from politics. Nevertheless, our work is not completed. The rural elite is quite complex; moreover, its members often act covertly, seeking personal favors from public authorities. Consequently, when we study the behavior of *latifundistas* and modern farmers, we have to look at what they do in specific instances to determine how influential they are. We cannot assume that they always dominate contemporary politics because they did in the past, nor can we assume that they are powerless in nations where populations and wealth are now heavily concentrated in urban areas.

Business elites

Wealth has never been a monopoly of rural elites in Latin America. Since colonial times merchants, traders, and bankers have prospered. In the late nineteenth century native businessmen were joined by immigrants, many of whom have amassed great wealth. Today the *Who's Who* of business in Brazil, Argentina, or Venezuela, for instance, reads like a United Nations roster, listing Italian, English, German, Jewish, and Lebanese surnames as well as those of Spanish and Portuguese origin. The 1929 depression shattered many Latin American economies, but it also opened the door for enterprising investors who seized on the opportunity to manufacture goods no longer supplied by a collapsed Europe. Long held back by rural elites who feared that industrialization would offend their European trading partners, native and immigrant entrepreneurs built industries in the larger countries that soon contributed more income than did agriculture to national economies. And the more important industry became, the more governments were obligated to protect it with high tariffs, subsidized credit, and improved transportation and utilities.

The study of business elites should be sensitive to three issues. First is the familiar matter of whom to include within the elite category. Obviously the very large firms belong and the more numerous small ones do not, but that leaves many in between. To complicate matters, most of the middle-size firms belong to the same national business organizations as the larger ones and benefit from their influence over public policy. What this means is that on some issues, labor policy for example, all firms, regardless of their size, have a common interest, whereas on others, such as the subsidization of small business, the large and more secure firms may oppose the interests of the smaller ones.

Second is the issue of ownership. Many of the largest firms in Latin America are foreign-owned, and in this book we will treat foreigners separate from domestic business because of their origins and obligations to foreign shareholders. In reality they are not entirely separate in their interests and political activities, of course. Moreover, the line between foreign and national ownership of individual firms is deliberately blurred by government policies started in Mexico several years ago that require joint foreign–domestic ownership of firms in an attempt to limit external economic control.

Third, there is the matter of the relationship between rural and business elites, namely, whether or not they are the same people and, if not, how closely they work together. Again the answers vary by country, but the most general rule is that the more industrialized and larger the economy, the less likely it is that the same people will control both sectors. The holders of economic power in Brazil are many and their interests diverse, whereas in El Salvador they are fewer and more homogeneous. On specific issues farmers, industrialists, and bankers each look out for their own interests, sometimes coming to conflict with each other. At the same time, they share a determination to defend the capitalist system and to preserve their dominance within it.

What then do most businessmen want from their governments?

Their rhetoric to the contrary notwithstanding, few actually want completely free markets. Most industrialists started under the protection of high tariffs and easy credit and still rely upon such measures to protect them from competition with cheaper imported goods. Academic economists and ideologues, not native businessmen, are the real defenders of Adam Smith's version of market capitalism these days. When it comes to actual government policy most industrialists still prefer the helping hand of the state.

Equally high on their policy agenda is the subordination of organized labor. Businessmen have fought labor organizations since their inception at the turn of the century, always demanding their tight regulation by authorities whenever they could not control workers by themselves. Business has not always secured the advantage it wanted because vote-seeking politicians have from time to time cultivated working-class favor by giving them an edge over management, as did Juan Perón in Argentina. Fear of the populist politician has caused business leaders to become as concerned about who occupies the presidency as about the content of policy, leading some not to hesitate to summon the military to evict presidents who threaten their interests. Few things have affected politics more than the way its leaders handle this inevitable conflict between business and organized labor, as we shall see repeatedly in our study of individual countries in Part II.

The political activities of businessmen are like those of modern farmers. They have organizations that represent commercial, financial, and industrial interests before the government. They seldom work directly through political parties, though they do lobby before legislative bodies and participate as much as they are allowed on government boards and commissions. But more than any other players, businessmen seek out public officials on their own, trying to gain advantages for their individual firms, in many instances resorting to bribes and other favors to secure what they want. Businessmen, like farmers, also take advantage of their role in the developing economy to persuade authorities to meet their policy demands. When threatened by higher taxes or regulations that raise their costs they warn of the economic calamities such policies would cause. Because industrial and commercial growth is essential to most development programs, a nation's president is especially vulnerable to such threats. He has little choice but to favor business unless he is willing to call its bluff and risk the consequences. How influential businessmen are over policy will depend, of course, on the credibility of their threats and the government's dependence on each industry and enterprise. To be sure, the government is not helpless, but has weapons of its own. Businesses depend on it for contracts, supplies, and their legal standing and are vulnerable to competition from public enterprises.

Businessmen seldom agree on which rules of the game serve them best. Native small businessmen who are vulnerable to foreign competition welcome nationalistic political parties even if it means risking the election of officials who are more tolerant of organized labor than they would prefer. The managers of larger, more secure firms, in contrast, have little use for nationalists and electoral processes that might generate popular social reform governments. What they do agree on is the need for access to public authorities, convinced that regardless of the government's ideology, individually entrepreneurs can gain what they need if given a chance to influence officials.

Middle sectors

The wealthy have never ruled Latin America alone. Many things had to be done that oligarchs refused to do for reasons of tradition and lifestyle. Retail stores and banks had to be managed, post offices staffed, upper-class children educated, and goods transported. As economies grew in the late nineteenth century, so did the demand for literate and skilled persons able to fill such positions.

Scholars have never known what to call these people. Some, like historian John Johnson, prefer the label "middle sectors," in order to distinguish them from the middle classes in Europe and North America with whom they had little in common. Johnson argues that the middle sectors were neither as poor and uneducated as the masses nor as wealthy and powerful as the oligarchy. By the turn of the century middle-sector politicians began to speak out in Argentina, Chile, Uruguay, Brazil, and Mexico, denouncing the injustice of their subservience to conservative ruling elites. But lacking the kind of economic power gained through industrialization that had made the European middle class so strong politically, the most they could achieve was gradual and limited political reform, eventually permitting the election of some middle-sector leaders in the 1920s. Their programs were modest, confined primarily to expanding public education, subsidizing private business, and increasing public employment. In short, they succeeded in opening the political process to their followers without changing the structure of society. Under their leadership rural elites operated unmolested and most poor saw few benefits from their programs.

The middle sectors remain an elusive object for political analysis despite their well-known history and obvious importance. There are several reasons why this is so, all of them related to the group's unusual history and complex character. First, as Johnson pointed out, the middle sectors have not developed the kind of class consciousness that was found among the bourgeoisie in Europe and North America, but have remained a diverse aggregation of individuals. Second, they have not transformed their societies the way the middle class transformed Western Europe. Many retain traditional social values and seek admission to the old elite, allowing the oligarchy to survive by absorbing its middle-sector imitators. And third, the middle sectors have promoted an unconventional route to industrial development and in the process produced a political economy different from that which accompanied the European industrial revolution. In Europe the middle class gained influence over the economy and then captured political power. In Latin America, in contrast, the middle sectors, starting from a very weak economic base, first gained public office and then used the government to promote industrialization. The result has been the heavy involvement of the state in the subsidization of industrial enterprise and an entrepreneurial class that is very dependent on government support.

If we were to search today for the descendants of Johnson's middle sectors, we would find them everywhere. As society has grown more complex, the middle sectors have grown more diverse and even less united by a common cause. Most of the reform parties of the 1960s that championed agrarian reform and development planning were led by individuals who came from middle-sector families. So did most of the military officers who have governed in the 1970s and 1980s. Some have joined the economic elite as commercial farmers, industrialists, merchants, and bankers. And some are now the technocrats who supervise Latin American government agencies. We would be hard pressed to find a Latin American leader today whose parents did not come from these middle sectors.

The middle sectors are quite fickle in their politics. In some places

they championed the cause of electoral democracy and honored constitutional rules once in office. Few political parties anywhere were more
devoted to democratic practices than the middle-sector-led Radical
parties of Argentina and Chile and the Colorados in Uruguay. The
democratic preference was not true everywhere, however. In Mexico,
for example, the middle sectors enthusiastically supported one-party
government, and in Brazil they were content to work within the long-
established tradition of elite-dominated regional political machines.

Even more striking is the way middle-sector political preferences
have varied over time. The first to organize political parties that won
free elections, they have also backed military governments when it
served their interests. This can be explained in part by their heteroge-
neity. As we have learned, this is not a cohesive social class but an
aggregation of people who are distinguished primarily by how little
they have in common with the very wealthy and the poor rather than
by a culture or ideology of their own. In politics there is no single
middle-sector position. It is also due to the occasional incompatibility
of their political and economic wants. Those who do prefer democracy also want economic security; when democracy is accompanied
by intense political conflict and economic uncertainty, they are quick
to turn to the authoritarians for help. And even though they may at
times support social and economic reforms, they are seldom receptive
to reform when they and not the powerful upper class must assume
most of the burden for income redistribution to the poor, either
through higher taxes, wages, or inflation. In other words, when their
economic self-interest conflicts with their political ideals, they, like
people elsewhere, are willing to sacrifice the latter if necessary to gain
the former.

The masses

Before considering workers and peasants a word of caution is in order.
Two problems haunt the analysis of the masses as players in the Latin
American game. The first is the temptation to see them as a homogeneous community whose members share economic and political interests. The mere fact that they are laborers in economies run by owners
and managers would appear to give them a common identity, as do
their poverty, political isolation, and exploitation. But closer examination reveals differences among them that are as great as their similari-

ties, especially when viewed through the experience of the masses themselves. Race, ethnicity, regional identities, and short-term economic self-interest traditionally have separated Latin America's poor from one another. Moreover, their differences have been exploited by local elites determined to obstruct concerted resistance to their authority. Even today the masses are not united to do battle with the rest of society. Instead, if they become involved politically at all, it is usually through an organization that competes with other mass organizations for a share of the national pie.

The second problem that accompanies the study of workers and peasants is that few of them actually belong to the organizations that claim to represent them. Less than one-fourth of the region's urban work force is unionized, and very few peasants and small farmers have organizations. Therefore we must be cautious when attributing the views of union and peasant leaders to all of the people they claim to lead. They are important players in the political game, but that does not justify our assuming that all of those who speak for the masses enjoy their support.

Organized labor

What to do with organized labor preoccupied ruling elites at the turn of the century. It still does today. Working-class movements began in the 1890s, led by immigrant workers and intellectuals advocating socialist, anarchist, and syndicalist ideologies then popular in Europe. They achieved little at first, torn from within by ideological disputes and harassed and repressed from without by conservative businessmen and reactionary governments. They were also victims of the region's underdevelopment. Not until industries and the public sector began to grow in the 1930s in the larger countries did the working class achieve the size needed to seriously threaten the existing order through political action. But even then it was thwarted everywhere except in Mexico by stubborn ruling classes who refused to share their power with an unwelcome intruder who demanded admission to the game on its own terms.

Labor leaders learned many things from their political defeats, the most important being their inability to penetrate ruling circles on their own. How to put this lesson to work became the subject of intense debate within labor movements during the 1930s and 1940s. In the

end it was resolved not by labor ideologues but by a new generation
of politicians from outside the movement who, lacking a large political
base of their own, turned to the working class for support, offering
them in return protection by a paternalistic state. By exploiting rank-
and-file frustrations and a general malaise caused by the depression
and its aftermath, politicians like Getulio Vargas in Brazil, Juan Perón
in Argentina, and Lázaro Cárdenas in Mexico built populist coalitions
that made them presidents and secured labor a new place in national
politics.

A labor movement's political prominence depends in part on the
terms under which it gained admission to the national political game.
Nowhere is this more apparent than when we compare the political
fate of Latin American labor with that of labor unions of the United
States. The latter retained their institutional and legal autonomy after
becoming a player, and they still act as a relatively independent force,
negotiating contracts with employers at the industry level and influencing policy by supporting candidates and lobbying legislators on the
national scene. Latin American unions, in contrast, gave up much of
their autonomy when they accepted the paternalism of populist politicians. Populist law and political practice made organized labor the
ward of a powerful, centralized state. To exist legally, unions had to
be officially sanctioned by the government; moreover, the ministries
of labor tightly controlled collective bargaining, access to funds raised
by special taxes on workers' salaries, and labor courts. Regardless of
whether the nation's politics were democratic or authoritarian, the
state was responsible for the supervision and protection of organized
labor. In contrast to the United States where the government occasionally acts as a mediator of last resort when all private modes of
conflict resolution fail, in Latin America it supervises from the outset.

Populist paternalism was never as beneficent as it seemed. When
the interests of labor and those of populist presidents clashed the
latter usually prevailed by using the power of the state to keep
recalcitrant unions in line. The rank and file were often the losers in
the populist scheme, for though they gained official attention and
legal recognition they usually watched helplessly as their leaders
sacrificed their interests in order to retain the vestiges of power for
themselves. Eventually the populists were deposed or replaced, but
state control over organized labor survived them, remaining to this
day the way of life in most places.

We normally think of organized labor as speaking for the masses, but in fact it speaks primarily for itself. It is really an elite within the working class, representing a minority of workers who have to some extent "made it." Most laborers are not among this fortunate few, but are unorganized, protected by few laws, and without much clout when it comes to collective bargaining. Like most elites, organized labor has grown more concerned with its own conquests and their protection than with improvement of the welfare of those not within its organizations. Individual unions expend most of their energy on such bread-and-butter issues as wages, working conditions, and retirement benefits, while their national confederations concentrate on securing government policies favorable to them. Confederation leaders not only resort to strikes, demonstrations, and consultations with officials, but also try to secure the appointment of their leaders to the government ministries that make labor, economic, and social policies.

Nearly all economic policy decisions affect labor in some way. Take antiinflation policies, for example. Rising prices reduce purchasing power and force unions to demand higher wages to compensate for their losses to inflation. Wage increases, however, may only provoke higher prices, touching off a wage–price spiral. One solution is to freeze wages temporarily, thereby asking labor to bear some of the burden of stopping inflation. But labor leaders seldom stand by idly while they are singled out to pay the price of fighting inflation. Instead, they use all means at their disposal to see that the costs are shifted to others. In so doing they try to protect themselves from harm in the short run even if they cannot secure the long-term benefits they desire.

Organized labor has many resources at its disposal that it can use to influence officials. In a democratic game, for example, it can offer its votes to candidates who will advance its interests. Despite the fact that organized workers are a minority of the work force, they can deliver large blocks of voters to their chosen candidates. They can also mobilize their supporters for rallies and demonstrations on a candidate's behalf. But votes count only in elections, and since elections are the exception rather than the rule in many places, organized labor is forced to employ other resources to gain favor. One of the most important is its economic influence. More often than not unionized industries are vital economically. Workers in transportation, mining, petroleum, banking, and manufacturing have been organized for some time and know how to use society's dependence on those industries and services to good advantage. Through strikes they can not only threaten owners and managers, but also undermine government economic programs in order to force the government to settle a strike in labor's favor or to adopt a particular policy demanded by the labor leadership.

Finally, as a resource of last resort there is the general strike or violent protest aimed at securing a desirable presidential response. Such extreme tactics are employed to undermine public order and force presidential concessions. They are especially effective in countries where weak presidents fear military intervention if order cannot be maintained. In such cases the president must decide whether to meet labor's demands and risk criticism from antilabor elites or to deny labor and risk continued disorder and possible military intervention. Of course, labor too runs some risks when it chooses such drastic tactics. A strong president may retaliate with force to break union protests, and should the military intervene, it too might exact a high price from the protestors by closing unions and jailing their leaders.

No matter how rich it is in resources, the labor movement cannot succeed without effective organization. It is not enough for a few leaders to claim to represent the rank and file; they must also enjoy their followers' loyal support. Unauthorized wildcat strikes or, conversely, an unwillingness to join in strikes can undermine labor leaders by destroying the unity they need to maximize their influence. Disunity and internal squabbling, in turn, encourage the divide-and-conquer tactics employed by businessmen and antilabor governments to break strikes and hold the working class in check. On the other hand, unity creates problems of its own. For example, once the labor movement is joined into a national confederation, it runs the risk of overcentralization and the kind of bureaucratization that makes labor leaders insensitive to the needs of union members. The latter situation has led in some countries to the creation of rival union organizations that have sought, in most cases unsuccessfully, to break the monopoly of these unresponsive labor bureaucracies. One of the principal causes of the failure of such insurgents has been opposition to them by public officials, who over the years have worked out accommodations with labor leaders and are willing to defend them against their working-class rivals.

We might expect laborers to be partial to democratic rules since it gives them an obvious advantage over smaller groups. But it is not that simple. Remember that most unions secured their place under populist leaders or single-party governments who seldom lived by democratic rules. They learned early that what mattered most was not the form of government but the protection it gave to union organizations. Consequently, most labor leaders are more concerned with what a government does to fulfill its obligation to them than the methods by which its officeholders are selected. Whether it is democratic or authoritarian is not as important, it seems, as whether it will act as their ally and patron.

Latin Americans continue to dispute where organized labor belongs in the scheme of things. One's position depends on what one thinks it contributes to the process of national economic development. Some believe labor's involvement in the game is essential to the mobilization and allocation of the nation's scarce resources, as we shall see when we examine the populists and reformers in Chapters 6 and 7. Others still prefer exclusion, as we will find when we look at the military authoritarians in Chapter 8.

Campesinos

The rural poor are not taken very seriously despite claims to the contrary. They have been the neglected ones, ignored by politicians and bypassed by the forces of economic modernization. Their world is confined to the *latifundio* or commercial farm on which they work, the *minifundio* (subsistence farm) they occupy, or the village in which they reside. For them, effective political authority resides not in some distant capital but with landlords, village mayors, parish priests, and local military commandants.

Latin American peasants have not always accepted their subjugation by local elites passively. The region's history is filled with peasant revolts, and violence is still common in the countryside. In recent years dispersed protests have given way to organized campaigns to secure government intervention on the peasants' behalf. Throughout the hemisphere governments have responded with diverse reforms aimed at redressing peasant grievances. Agrarian reforms have yielded impressive results in a few countries, most notably Mexico, Cuba, Venezuela, Nicaragua, and Peru. Nevertheless, most of the rural poor survive at or just above the subsistence level, either untouched by agrarian reform or given land but no capital or technology to develop it. For many peasants agrarian reform has been a disappointment, little more than an instrument for promoting large-scale modern farming rather than improving the welfare of the rural poor.

To understand why reform has benefited so few, we must look more closely at the Latin American *campesinos*, their political goals and resources. By *campesinos* we mean the *mestizo*, Indian, and Negro subsistence farmers and laborers who populate rural Latin America. Nearly all of them earn barely enough for their physical survival and enjoy few opportunities for improving their condition. At the same time, they differ from each other in important ways. When grouped according to their means of employment, they fall into four distinct groups.

The first group is the *colonos*, who work as laborers on the *latifundios* or as sharecroppers or tenant farmers. They have probably resided in the same region for generations and are bound to their employers by debts incurred over several years. Some *latifundistas* have taken their responsibilities as *patrones* seriously, protecting the *colonos* and their families from catastrophe and providing them with a subsistence income in order to maintain the *latifundio* as an organic, self-sufficient community. Others have treated the *colonos* harshly, ignoring their basic needs and abandoning them during hard times. As one might expect, *colonos* tend to be isolated from national politics by their physical separation from national capitals. When they vote in national elections, they usually are closely supervised by the *patron*. Moreover, they are hard to organize politically because of their dispersion throughout the countryside and their subordination to the *latifundistas*. The latter can discourage *campesino* organizers by using the local police, economic control over their workers, and their influence in local courts. It is not difficult to understand why *campesino* movements have seldom survived without help from outside, for without public officials or party leaders to protect them from the reprisals of local elites, *campesino* organizers stand little chance of success.

A second type of *campesino* is the wage laborer. Many of the crops produced on Latin America's commercial farms are harvested by hand. This is especially true of cotton, coffee, sugarcane, fruits, and vegetables grown in areas with an abundance of labor. Many of those who work in the harvest are migrants who leave their villages and return at the end of the season. Some own their own land but must seek employment elsewhere because they cannot produce enough to meet the needs of their families. Others have become landless through population pressures or the loss of their land to creditors. They are the Mexican *braceros* who migrate legally and illegally to California and Texas, the coffee pickers who descend from highland villages in Guatemala and Colombia, and the cane cutters in northeast Brazil. Like migrants everywhere, they exist on the fringes of the political process and are seldom reached by government programs. They can ill afford to become involved in political protests during the harvest for fear of losing an entire year's livelihood. In the off-season they return to their villages and blend back into the local population, out of reach of labor organizers.

Plantation workers are a third type of *campesino*. Like the *colonos* they are bound to one place year round, but like the migrant they work on commercial establishments rather than traditional estates. Plantation workers have more in common with factory workers than they do with most of their fellow *campesinos*, for they work in highly organized settings in which modern technology is applied to the production of commodities for export. In some instances, their employers are foreign corporations like the banana companies of Central America and Colombia, though they are just as likely to work for domestic firms or individual families. The relative ease of organizing plantation workers explains in part why the number of plantation worker unions has increased. Unlike most other *campesinos*, plantation laborers work in close proximity, communicate regularly, and develop skills that are needed by their employers. Thus, if the leadership is available, they are organizable, much like factory workers. To succeed, however, they must overcome the resistance of plantation owners, who are often backed by sympathetic government officials.

Not all *campesinos* work on *latifundios*, plantations, or commercial farms; many own land or occupy small plots to which they have no legal claim. *Campesinos* employ only the most primitive technologies and farm primarily for their own subsistence, selling a small surplus in local markets. They take few risks with new seeds or fertilizers, most of which they cannot secure because of their poverty and lack of access to short-term credit. If they want to ship their small surplus to distant markets, they must rely on private traders, who easily take advantage of their isolation and dependent status. Subsistence farmers confront agrarian reformers with one of their toughest problems, for if they are given more land they may use it inefficiently because of their low level of technology; yet if agrarian reform is to lead to higher production, something must be done to increase the efficiency of such units. Usually the only alternatives considered are government financing of small-farm modernization, which is quite costly, or farm reorganization into more efficient cooperative, communal, or state-run units to maximize the use of modern technology, a solution often resisted by the very independent *campesinos*.

What do *campesinos* want from politics? Unfortunately, *campesinos* have seldom been asked what they want, and when the question has been raised, others, notably landed elites, reformers, and revolutionaries, have answered for them. Moreover, as we have seen, *campesinos* are a very diverse group, separated by economic interest, region, and ethnicity, and they seldom speak with a single voice. Nevertheless, even though they are not united by a single set of policy demands, time and again they have made their basic needs and wants clear to any who would listen.

Campesinos want to improve their life chances and the welfare of their families on their own terms. How that is to be done is not always clear. Some *campesinos* demand greater protection against exploitation by landlords and employers; some want land of their own; and still others ask only for easier access to credit, water, storage facilities, and markets. With only a few exceptions, their concerns are personal, local, and specific, rather than general and self-consciously ideological. *Campesinos* are not as opposed to innovation or the expansion of their production as is often assumed. If they appear to be risk averting, it is because they can ill afford to take chances when their annual crop is all that stands between their families and starvation. New technologies require expenditures they can seldom afford, especially if they lack access to credit. Only the government, through its supply of subsidized technology and redistribution of land, can break the vicious circle in which most *campesinos* find themselves. Thus, even though past experience has taught the rural poor that government is unwilling or ill equipped to meet their needs, it remains the only source of their salvation. Understandably, however, they continue to be suspicious of grand promises, skeptical about the possibility of progress, and alert to the betrayal of their cause. But their apparent passivity should not be mistaken for apathy, for, like other players in the game, *campesinos* want a larger share of the nation's wealth. If they lack anything, it is confidence in their ability to secure that share.

The political strength of *campesinos* is yet to be tested in most Latin American countries. Their principal resource is their immense size as

a social group, a resource they have seldom been permitted to use.
Because they are a majority in most countries, *campesinos* would appear
to have the most to gain from elections and democratic processes. Yet,
although many of them dutifully march to the polls, their votes are
usually the exclusive property of their employers or the local elites.
Only where modern political parties have recruited the peasantry into
constituency organizations, as in Venezuela and Mexico, has their
participation affected electoral outcomes. Where electoral influence is
denied them, *campesinos* can resort to violent attacks on their oppressors. But armed revolts are risky, especially against well-entrenched
rural elites and their allies in local law-enforcement agencies. Nevertheless, occasionally rural revolts have been successful, as they were
in Mexico in 1910 and Bolivia in 1952.

Given their limited influence in elections and the high risks of violent protests, how can *campesinos* affect national policy? To have any
impact at all, they must overcome several obstacles. One is organization. It is not especially hard to organize wealthy landowners, businessmen, or labor union members into effective political action groups.
They are usually united by physical proximity, an agreement on basic
issues, and their ability to finance a permanent staff. *Campesinos*, in
contrast, are separated physically, often do not perceive their common
interests, and cannot finance their own organizations. Another is the
communications obstacle. *Campesinos* are separated not only by physical
distance but also by ethnicity and regionalism, especially in countries
with large indigenous populations. As a result, issues and solutions that
satisfy one group of *campesinos* may be inappropriate to the needs of
others. The *campesinos'* organizational problems are aggravated by the
fact that their enemies exploit their weaknesses in order to limit their
success. It has been by taking advantage of the *campesinos'* isolation,
fear, and inability to communicate over large distances that the landowners and their allies have until recently so successfully prevented the
development of viable peasant organizations.

As fears of *campesino* independence have grown among members of
the rural elite, so has the brutality of their repression. In some places,
most notably Central America in the early 1980s, the appearance of
guerrilla movements drew the military deep into the countryside in an
attempt to head off *campesino* collaboration with urban-bred insurgents. Even when they chose to be inhospitable to the rebels, *campesinos* were attacked by authorities, the elite strategy being one of intimi-

dation intended to deprive the guerrillas of potential village sanctuaries. Too often *campesinos* had little choice but to flee their traditional homes in order to avoid becoming the victims of one side or other. It was not uncommon to find entire villages empty in the Guatemalan highlands, their former residents having been either massacred or forced to flee. Death tolls of several hundred *campesinos* per week were quite common.

Obstacles to peasant organization and vulnerability to landowners' divide-and-conquer strategies have made the *campesinos* more dependent on help from outside, especially from the state, than any of the other players in the Latin American game. Ambitious aspirants for public office began reaching out to the *campesinos* during the postwar years, offering agrarian reforms and other measures in exchange for political support. Central to their political strategy was the mobilization of *campesinos* into constituent organizations that could deliver the peasant vote. Modeling their tactics after the highly successful organization of the Mexican peasantry by President Lázaro Cárdenas in the 1930s, reform parties throughout Latin America have tried to break the monopoly of local elites over peasant voters and use the latter to defeat their opponents at the polls. Some *campesinos* have been organized locally and regionally much like urban labor unions and represented in national party councils and the legislature by leaders they have chosen at their national conventions. Their goals have been reformist rather than revolutionary, and in countries like Venezuela, Chile, and Mexico they have worked within the system rather than against it. In Venezuela, for example, thousands of peasants were organized by the Acción Democrática party in the early 1940s and were rewarded with an agrarian reform program after the party took office in 1947. When the military overthrew the Acción Democrática a year later its peasant organizations survived clandestinely to reemerge after the party was restored to power in 1959. The ability of Acción Democrática to win subsequent elections was due in large part to the peasant support it had retained.

Despite its many accomplishments, the kind of reformist agrarianism practiced in Venezuela, Chile, and Mexico is not without serious limitations. Democratic governments, which are vulnerable to countervailing pressures, have not always fulfilled their promises to their rural supporters. Government fears of retaliation by the rural elite or the military, as well as the desire to increase productivity by encouraging

modern rather than peasant farms, have seriously hampered the fulfillment of commitments to the rural poor. Another obstacle has been the
frequent co-optation of *campesino* leaders by governments that exploit
their desire for status and power. In short, even though reformist
agrarianism opens the policy-making process to *campesino* representatives and meets some of their demands for rural reform, it is vulnerable
to countervailing pressures that often leave the peasants short.

Campesinos need not follow the peaceful path of reformist agrarianism. They can choose instead the more direct route of violent revolt,
taking matters into their own hands and seizing land in order to force
public authorities to meet their demands. The campaign of Emiliano
Zapata during the Mexican Revolution is a classic example of this.
Zapata was revolutionary only in the sense that he wanted to change
the rural status quo. His was not a utopian vision of a new society,
but a simple desire to regain for his village the land that it had held in
the past and that had been taken away by local sugar barons with the
government's encouragement. It was a struggle of armed peasants
against tyrannical landlords who had destroyed their way of life. But
Zapata's is not the only example of revolutionary agrarianism. In
Cuba the rural cause was taken up by Fidel Castro's insurrectionists
and in Nicaragua by the Sandinistas. Theirs were not peasant revolts,
but the campaigns of urban-bred ideologues who acted in the name of
the peasantry as well as other members of the masses. Once their
revolts had succeeded, peasants were among the first beneficiaries of
the revolutionary program.

Despite these successes – or perhaps because of them – the cause of
rural revolution has been treated harshly by the region's governments
and their military defenders in recent years. Nevertheless, revolutionaries continue to struggle. Those who have chosen guerrilla warfare as
their mode of attack have been plagued by many problems, not the
least of which is the reluctance of suspicious *campesinos* to support their
cause, either directly by joining in the armed struggle or indirectly by
not betraying them to authorities. The challenge laid down by guerrillas confronts *campesinos* with a more difficult choice than might first
appear: If the *campesinos* do not support the revolutionaries, their condition is not likely to change, but if they do support the guerrillas,
they risk retaliation from landowners and local police and have no
assurance that the results of the revolution, should it succeed, will be
to their liking. This is why many revolutionaries have discovered to

their disappointment that the exploited and potentially explosive *campesinos* are often reluctant participants in their struggle.

Finally, what about the peasants and the rules of the political game? As the least active and least encouraged participants in the conventional game, they have seldom been given the opportunity to shape the rules by which it is played. Moreover, regardless of the type of political system in which they live, they still find themselves on the receiving end of decisions made by others. In traditional autocracies, for example, they are dominated by local landlords and law-enforcement agents; in reformist democracies, a few peasant leaders and government bureaucrats usually manipulate them. And in revolutionary societies party leaders and government agents reorganize their lives for them. Their choice, it seems, is among being ignored, represented by a few well-intentioned reformers, or transformed by an elite that claims to act in accord with their objective interests.

The *campesinos'* weaknesses confront them with a serious problem. Without strong allies among those in political authority, they have little chance of affecting the course of rural policy. Yet, if they do secure an alliance with other players, they risk being absorbed and used by their new allies. The fact that most leaders of peasant movements have been small-town professionals or urban functionaries with very weak loyalties to their rural constituents makes their co-optation even more likely. Moreover, internal conflicts are as common to peasant movements as they are to the interest groups of the rich, perhaps even more so, making them vulnerable to manipulation by competing peasant leaders and politicians. Whichever path they choose, the *campesinos* will end up with less than optimal results.

The economic development of Latin America depends on the progress made in the rural sector in the years ahead. The region's rural populations are increasing too rapidly and their migration to overcrowded cities is too great to be ignored. Although most governments in Latin America acknowledge this, few have demonstrated that they can do anything about it.

Further reading

Rural elites

Barraclough, Solon Lovett. *Agrarian Structures in Latin America: A Résumé of the CIDA Land Tenure Studies of Argentina, Brazil, Chile, Colombia, Ecuador, Guatemala, Peru.* Lexington, Mass.: Lexington Books, 1972.

de Janury, Alain. *The Agrarian Question and Reformism in Latin America*. Baltimore: Johns Hopkins University Press, 1981.

Dew, Edward. *Politics of the Altiplano: The Dynamics of Change in Rural Peru*. Austin: University of Texas Press, 1969.

Feder, Ernst. *The Rape of the Peasantry: Latin America's Landholding System*. Garden City, N.Y.: Doubleday (Anchor Books), 1971.

Hirschman, Albert O. *Journeys Toward Progress: Studies of Economic Policy-Making in Latin America*. New York: Norton, 1973.

Kaufman, Robert. *The Politics of Land Reform in Chile 1950–1970: Public Policy, Political Institutions, and Social Change*. Cambridge, Mass.: Harvard University Press, 1972.

Keith, Robert, ed. *Haciendas and Plantations in Latin American History*. New York: Holmes & Meier, 1977.

Nichols, William Hord, and Ruy Miller Paiva. *Ninety-Nine Fazendas: The Structure and Productivity of Brazilian Agriculture, 1963*. Nashville: Graduate Center for Latin American Studies, Vanderbilt University, 1966.

Payne, James. "The Oligarchy Muddle." *World Politics* 20: 439–53, 1968.

Smith, Peter. *The Politics of Beef in Argentina*. New York: Columbia University Press, 1969.

Smith, T. Lynn. *The Process of Rural Development in Latin America*. Gainesville: University of Florida Press, 1967.

Business elites

Brandenburg, Frank. *The Development of Latin American Private Enterprise*. Washington, D.C.: National Planning Association, 1964.

Cardoso, Fernando Henrique. "The Industrial Elite," in Seymour Martin Lipset and Aldo Solari, eds., *Elites in Latin America*. New York: Oxford University Press, 1968, pp. 94–114.

Davis, Stanley M., and Louis Wolf Goodman, eds. *Workers and Managers in Latin America*. Lexington, Mass.: Heath, 1972.

Evans, Peter. *Dependent Development: The Alliance of Multinational, State, and Local Capital in Brazil*. Princeton, N.J.: Princeton University Press, 1979.

Harbron, John W. "The Dilemma of an Elite Group: The Industrialist in Latin America." *Inter-American Economic Affairs* 19: 43–62, 1965.

Imaz, Jose Luis. *Los Que Mandan* (Those who rule). Albany: State University of New York Press, 1970.

Kling, Merle. *A Mexican Interest Group in Action*. Englewood Cliffs, N.J.: Prentice-Hall, 1961.

Lauterbach, Albert. *Enterprise in Latin America: Business Attitudes in a Developing Economy*. Ithaca, N.Y.: Cornell University Press, 1966.

McDonough, Peter. *Power and Ideology in Brazil*. Princeton, N.J.: Princeton University Press, 1981.

Purcell, John F. H., and Susan Kaufman Purcell. "Mexican Business and Public Policy," in James M. Malloy, ed., *Authoritarianism and Corporatism in Latin America*. Pittsburgh: University of Pittsburgh Press, 1977, pp. 191–226.

Strassman, Paul W. "The Industrialist," in John J. Johnson, ed., *Continuity and Change in Latin America*. Stanford, Calif.: Stanford University Press, 1967, pp. 161–85.

Middle sectors

Cardoso, Fernando Henrique. "The Industrial Elite," in Seymour Martin Lipset and Aldo Solari, eds., *Elites in Latin America*. New York: Oxford University Press, 1968, pp. 94–114.

Gillin, John P. "The Middle Segments and Their Values," in Lyman Bryson, ed., *Social Change in Latin America Today*. New York: Random House (Vintage Books), 1960, pp. 28–46.

Johnson, John. *Political Change in Latin America: The Emergence of the Middle Sectors*. Stanford, Calif.: Stanford University Press, 1958.

Veliz, Claudio. "Introduction," in Claudio Veliz, ed., *Obstacles to Change in Latin America*. London: Oxford University Press, 1965, pp. 1–8.

Wagley, Charles. "The Dilemma of the Latin American Middle Class," in Charles Wagley, ed., *The Latin American Tradition*. New York: Columbia University Press, 1968, pp. 194–212.

The masses: organized labor

Alba, Victor. *Politics and the Labor Movement in Latin America*. Stanford, Calif.: Stanford University Press, 1968.

Alexander, Robert. *Labor Relations in Argentina, Brazil and Chile*. New York: McGraw-Hill, 1962.

Organized Labor in Latin America. New York: Free Press, 1965.

Baily, Samuel L. *Labor, Nationalism and Politics in Argentina*. New Brunswick, N.J.: Rutgers University Press, 1967.

Davis, Stanley M., and Louis Wolf Goodman, eds. *Workers and Managers in Latin America*. Lexington, Mass.: Heath, 1972.

Landsberger, Henry A. "The Labor Elite: Is It Revolutionary?" in Seymour Martin Lipset and Aldo Solari, eds., *Elites in Latin America*. New York: Oxford University Press, 1968, pp. 256–300.

Payne, James L. *Labor and Politics in Peru: The System of Political Bargaining*. New Haven, Conn.: Yale University Press, 1965.

Urrutia Montoya, Miguel. *The Development of the Colombian Labor Movement*. New Haven, Conn.: Yale University Press, 1967.

Zeitlin, Maurice. *Revolutionary Politics and the Cuban Working Class*. Princeton, N.J.: Princeton University Press, 1967.

The masses: peasants

Fals-Borda, Orlando. *Peasant Society in the Colombian Andes*. Gainesville: University of Florida Press, 1957.

Feder, Ernst. *The Rape of the Peasantry: Latin America's Landholding System*. Garden City, N.Y.: Doubleday (Anchor Books), 1971.

Handelman, Howard. *Struggle in the Andes: Peasant Political Mobilization in Peru*. Austin: University of Texas Press, 1974.

Huizer, Gerrit. *The Revolutionary Potential of Peasants in Latin America*. Lexington, Mass.: Heath, 1972.

Landsberger, Henry A., ed. *Latin American Peasant Movements*. Ithaca, N.Y.: Cornell University Press, 1969.

Rural Protest: Peasant Movements and Social Change. New York: Macmillan, 1974.

Petras, James, and Robert LaPorte. *Cultivating Revolution: The United States and Agrarian Reform in Latin America.* New York: Random House, 1971.

Powell, John Duncan. *Political Mobilization of the Venezuelan Peasant.* Cambridge, Mass.: Harvard University Press, 1971.

Stavenhagen, Rodolfo, ed. *Agrarian Problems and Peasant Movements in Latin America.* Garden City, N.Y.: Doubleday, 1970.

Wolf, Eric R. *Sons of the Shaking Earth.* Chicago: University of Chicago Press, 1959.

Peasant Wars in the Twentieth Century. New York: Harper & Row, 1969.

Womack, John. *Zapata and the Mexican Revolution.* New York: Knopf, 1969.

4. Players – II

Political parties

At first glance a political party looks like any other player, doing what it can to influence the affairs of state. But, of course, it is not the same. To begin with, most political parties compete with each other in elections; other players do not. And parties usually represent diverse interests when in office, giving a variety of supporters access to authority in exchange for votes and financial support. In other words, when the rules permit, parties are in the center of the game, acting as brokers in the contest for influence over public policy.

In Western democracies we take political parties for granted, expecting them to offer candidates, contest elections, and direct governments. But it is not so everywhere. Much depends on the rules and what they authorize parties to do. For example, one of the first things we learned about Latin America was that elections are not the only means for creating governments, and even where they are, the victor is not guaranteed a full term in office. Therefore, we cannot expect that parties will always play the conventional role.

Parties play at least three roles in the Latin American game. First is the familiar one of electoral competitor. In some countries, like Costa Rica, their life is fairly simple, requiring little more than campaigns to win honest elections. But in others, like Argentina and Brazil, much more is required for them to succeed, for they cannot assume that everyone will play by the liberal democratic rules, accepting defeat as well as victory, nor that elites, military officers, and foreigners will respect triumphs. Just as important as their vote totals is their ability to keep their opponents playing by their rules.

Parties also play the role of conspirator. They may be forced to disregard democratic rules when others do so, or they may ignore them simply because they find it advantageous. Whatever their motives, conspirators need collaborators rather than votes, such as military officers willing to expel their opponents. Conspiracies generate

74

counterconspiracies, of course, and what one party does in desperation may only provoke others to do likewise, undermining civility
altogether.

Third is the monopolist role. Rather than live by competition or
conspiracy, a party may try to monopolize authority. The creation of
the one-party government, tempting though it is, is not easily done, as
many failed leaders and parties can testify. Critical to its achievement
is the ability of the party to secure and retain military approval and
substantial support from the middle sectors and organized labor, as
did the Mexicans and Cubans after their revolutions. The Mexican
party has won every presidential election since its creation in 1928.
Using its control over the Mexican state to distribute patronage and
wealth to its loyal supporters in all social classes, it has denied other
parties the constituencies needed to pose a threat at the ballot box.
The Cuban Communist party is even more monopolistic, not even
bothering with the facade of electoral competition. After eliminating
traditional parties, the Cubans created a single party to serve as the
vanguard of the masses.

From the roles played by parties we can turn to the structure of
party systems. The term "party system" refers to the number of
parties and the degree of competition among them. We usually speak
of one-party systems, two-party systems, and multiparty systems
composed of three or more parties. Within the last two categories
different degrees of competition are present; in some countries several
parties are close in their popular vote and exchange office frequently;
in others, one or two parties dominate. Party systems in Latin America are especially fascinating because within the region one discovers
examples of nearly every kind of party system. For instance, at various times during the postwar period, you could find two-party systems in Colombia, Uruguay, and Honduras; multiparty systems in
Argentina, Chile, Costa Rica, Venezuela, Brazil, Panama, and Ecuador; and one-party systems in Mexico, Cuba, and Nicaragua.

In many ways Latin America provides one of the largest laborator-
ies in the world for the analysis and comparison of party systems.
But, unfortunately, attempts to draw conclusions from studying them
are handicapped by the short duration or frequent interruptions of
most systems. In contrast to the Anglo-American democracies or even
the countries of Western Europe, many Latin American party systems
have not survived for more than a decade or two. The principal

exceptions are the one-party systems like Mexico's, where party competition is nonexistent, and democracies like Chile's and Uruguay's, whose impressive twentieth-century record of party government was abruptly halted by military coups in the early 1970s. Yet, despite the frequent interruptions of party government, there is still much to be learned from the Latin American experience, such as why some parties can govern without interruption under these conditions and others cannot. And Latin Americans can tell us a great deal about what it takes for a party to survive years of persecution, retaining enough support to be returned to office time after time.

Before we can answer these questions, we should become better acquainted with the kinds of political parties found in the region. There are many ways of classifying and comparing political parties. One can focus on professed ideology, organization, leadership, sources of support, or election strategy, among other things. In studying Latin American parties it is also important to examine them within their historical contexts. Different kinds of parties have arisen in response to particular circumstances. Some have come and gone; others have endured and still struggle. The story of the growth of the region's political parties tells much about its political evolution, for parties arose at critical turning points in history, reshaping politics as they did.

The first organizations to call themselves political parties were little more than cliques drawn from the oligarchy, which contested public office during the last half of the nineteenth century. They differed not so much over who should rule–they all believed in elite rule–but over what policies the government should follow. Those who called themselves Conservatives came primarily from the ranks of landowners and the clergy and wanted government to do little more than preserve the prevailing hierarchical social and economic structures. Their opponents, usually termed Liberals, were more ambitious, desiring to use government to promote commercial agriculture and commodity exports through the redistribution of church and Indian lands to ambitious rural entrepreneurs. Election contests between Conservatives and Liberals were exclusive affairs, involving less than 10 percent of the adult population and sometimes rigged by the party in power.

In a few countries, such as Colombia and Honduras, Liberal and Conservative parties forged deep and lasting loyalties that persist to-

day, but in most of the region their monopoly was gradually broken by
the rise of new parties at the turn of the century. As long as party
politics was dominated by the elite, the new generation of immigrants,
urban businessmen, professionals, and small farmers that emerged in
the larger Latin American countries between 1900 and 1920 had little
hope of gaining a voice in domestic politics. No matter how hard they
might try to affect government decisions, they were usually rebuffed
by the leaders of traditional parties, who were unsympathetic to their
pleas. Their only recourse was to create political parties of their own
and use them to agitate for electoral reforms that would give them an
opportunity to compete with the established parties. In several countries middle-sector politicians succeeded not only in securing electoral
reforms but also in gaining public office. Calling themselves Radicals in
Chile and Argentina and by other names elsewhere, they used urban
constituency organizations and the personal popularity of their leaders
to defeat traditional elite parties and fill the public payrolls with their
supporters while implementing some modest educational and urban
reforms, as we learned in Chapter 3.

The 1929 depression was a severe blow to the middle-sector parties,
for it revealed their inability to solve the problems raised by world
economic crises. They were attacked by Conservatives and, in a few
cases, evicted by the military. After World War II they were forced to
compete for popular support with new political movements that had
been unleashed by the depression and its aftermath. The most important of these were the Populists.

The Populists were ambitious and skillful political opportunists
who took advantage of the rapid industrialization of their countries
during the 1930s and 1940s and the rising aspirations of a growing
urban proletariat, as well as the latter's neglect and persecution by
Radicals, Liberals, and Conservatives, to build a working-class constituency. But they relied more on the personal magnetism of leaders
and the talent of their lieutenants than on sophisticated party organizations to keep the movement together. Once in office, the Populists
divided the spoils among their supporters and helped native entrepreneurs by promoting industrialization.

The Populists were never accepted by most intellectuals and professionals, who resented their demagoguery and strong-arm methods.
Consequently, at the same time populism was on the rise, other anti-
status quo politicians were busy creating the nucleus of mass-based

democratic reform parties. Their goal was to make democracy work by combining the democratic ideals of the Radicals with the mass appeal of the Populists and the sophisticated party organization developed by Socialists and Social Democrats in Europe. They sought to involve not just the middle sectors, as did the Radicals, but also laborers and *campesinos*. The two essential ingredients in their campaign were a sophisticated national organization that penetrated to the grass roots and the mobilization of rural voters through use of peasant organizations linked to their political party. They also offered their countrymen a commitment to the reform of traditional economic institutions and to development planning. Attempts to create democratic reform parties were made in most Latin American countries during the 1940s and 1950s, but they were successful in only a few – those like Chile, Venezuela, and Costa Rica, where populism had never gained a foothold and where peasants were physically accessible to party organizers.

There are essentially two types of reform parties, one secular and the other religious in origin. The first began with the APRISTA party led by Peruvian Raúl Haya de la Torre and dissident students in the 1920s who were inspired by reformist Peruvian philosophers and modern socialism. The APRISTAs have been persecuted throughout most of their history and never allowed to rule Peru except in coalition with more conservative parties. The Acción Democrática party of Venezuela was more successful, however, governing briefly in the late 1940s and then for all but two presidential terms since 1958. Similarly, the National Liberation party of Costa Rica has held the presidency on five occasions since its creation in 1948. The success of these parties in the late 1950s led some to argue that Latin Americans had finally found the vehicle needed to build democracy throughout the region. Their hopes proved unfounded, however, and democratic government did not spread beyond a handful of countries after 1960.

The second type of democratic reform party is labeled religious because of its identification with Christian democracy, a movement that was begun by Roman Catholics in Europe and later spread to other Catholic countries. Inspired by the political thought of French philosopher Jacques Maritain, the Christian Democrats aspire to a democratic society that is neither socialist nor captialist, but one that combines the former's belief in the common good with the latter's respect for the individual. Though not formally tied to the Roman Catholic church, the party draws heavily on modern Catholic philosophy and the more progressive papal encyclicals for its ideology. Initially quite moderate in their goals and political techniques, the Christian Democrats gradually came to resemble the secular reform parties, expanding their organization to include laborers and peasants and preaching the doctrine of agrarian reform and national planning. Like the secular reformers, they organized parties throughout Latin America; however, they have been successful only in Chile, where they governed in the mid-1960s, and Venezuela, where they held the presidency for two terms in the 1970s. They too were regarded as a major vehicle of democratic rule and reform policy, but with the exception of the two countries mentioned, they have not lived up to their promise.

Last but not least are the revolutionary parties. Revolutionary movements have received much attention of late, but they are certainly not new to the region. There have been essentially two types of revolutionary parties in Latin America, one inspired by Marxist thought and example and the other non-Marxist. Among the first are several Socialist and all Communist parties. Socialists first organized parties in late nineteenth century, primarily under the direction of European immigrants. After the Russian Revolution of 1917, Communist parties were also formed, some of them merging with the Socialists and others becoming rivals because of the Socialists' refusal to accept Soviet leadership of the international revolutionary movement. Thus, at the same time the Radicals were organizing the emerging middle sectors, small Socialist and Communist parties, led by intellectuals and labor leaders, were trying to build a following among the working class. Proletarian revolution and social justice were their causes; strikes, demonstrations, and the education of the masses their weapons. Seldom, however, did they speak with a single voice, for doctrinal disputes and personal rivalries bred divisive factionalism within their ranks. Throughout the 1930s and 1940s most were on the fringes of their nations' politics, often being forced underground or into exile by hostile governments. Moreover, they had to compete with Populists in the 1940s and democratic reformers in the 1950s and 1960s for the support of the proletariat and frequently fared poorly against both movements' more nativist appeal and ability to deliver on promises of moderate social legislation. There have been exceptions, the most notable being Chile, where Marxist parties secured labor support in the 1920s, were admitted to Popular Front governments in the 1930s, and captured the presidency under Salvador Allende in 1970.

The Latin American laboratory of political experience offers three examples of Marxist parties in power. In Communist Cuba we have a decade and a half of societal reconstruction and a notable example of how a Marxist society can be raised on a Latin American foundation. Allende's ill-fated Popular Unity regime in Chile, on the other hand, provides an example of Marxist rule that differed sharply from Castro's in its intent and achievements. And in Nicaragua we find the latest experiment, one led since 1979 by the nationalist Sandinista movement whose leaders espouse their own version of Marxist ideology.

The principal non-Marxist revolutionary party is the Institutional Revolutionary party (PRI) of Mexico. Some dispute whether the ruling party of Mexico is truly "revolutionary." Critics argue that it has been revolutionary in name only, interested more in maintaining political control over the Mexican electorate and promoting industrialization than in social and economic equity. On the other hand, the party's defenders claim that during its first sixty years its government went further toward the elimination of the *latifundio*, the church, and foreign investors than did most Latin American governments. It also implemented significant agrarian reforms long before its neighbors had begun considering the issue. We cannot answer the question of how revolutionary the PRI is without examining its political and economic performance to date. By comparing its record with that of Communist Cuba in later chapters we shall learn not only about Mexico but also about the variety of revolutionary experiences in Latin America.

Finally, it is obvious that we have omitted some parties from this brief introduction. Recent Latin American history is littered, for example, with transitory, personalistic parties. Loyalty to a single leader rather than to a platform holds such parties together. Many rise and fall with a single election, beginning as splinter groups in existing parties or starting from scratch and then withering once their candidates are defeated. Of course, personalism is a factor in nearly all parties from the most conservative to the revolutionary, but some parties are organized to survive the loss of a leader, whereas those we have labeled personalist are not. During the nineteenth and early twentieth centuries one could also find regional parties in Latin America. Their purpose was not to capture the presidency, but to represent a regional point of view in legislatures and force conservative and liberal governments to accept their demands for local autonomy. There have also been Fascist parties of one kind or another. Modeled after the Fascist movements that arose in Italy, Spain, and Germany, they remained on the fringes of national politics in most countries, though they did attain some notoriety in Brazil and Chile and influenced policies and attitudes in wartime Argentina.

The analysis of Latin American party systems would be much simpler if all countries conformed to the history of party development outlined in the foregoing discussion. But they do not. Instead, we find several different patterns throughout the region. Some approximate the course of gradual evolution; in others change has been more abrupt and results dissimilar, such as in the one-party systems of Mexico and Cuba. But regardless of the form each party system takes, parties too are players whose influence on public officials varies with their political resources, skills, and determination. A party supports rules that help its cause and opposes those that do not. Those with widespread support obviously have more to gain from elections than do those without it. Conversely, a party that stands no chance of winning an election might be persuaded that it can gain more from a military coup or insurrection than from an election. But even a party that commands the support of a majority of the electorate may from time to time resort to nonelectoral means to remove a tyrannical government, to block threats from militant opponents, or to create some kind of populist autocracy. Life has not been easy for political parties during the past two decades. They have been attacked by extremists on the Left for being corrupt, self-serving, and intransigent, and by conservatives, especially in the business community, for being demagogic, narrow-minded, and incapable of creating orderly government or achieving steady economic progress. But are political parties really anachronisms, remnants of the liberal democratic state that is in retreat throughout the region? After all, many still survive, taking office again and again as they did in Peru, Ecuador, and Argentina in the 1970s after several years of rule by military officers determined to eradicate them. To settle the issue we will study parties at work in populist, democratic, authoritarian, and revolutionary settings in Part II.

The military

Military involvement in politics is a familiar feature of Latin American life. When not ruling directly, the armed forces exert their influence on civil authorities, affecting the composition of governments, the treatment of political oppositions, and the content of public policy. We need not dwell on the fact of military political participation, for it is obvious; instead we want to understand why it is so deeply involved in politics in the first place. And there is no better place to begin than with the military itself.

Once poorly trained and unsophisticated, most Latin American militaries have become professional organizations led by highly trained officers and armed with modern weapons. Nearly every country has an army, air force, and navy, with the army being by far the largest. Its size varies from 280,000 troops in Brazil to 1,500 in Costa Rica. The Brazilian army is composed of seven divisions, its navy has an aircraft carrier, eight submarines, and fourteen destroyers, and its air force has 160 combat aircraft. As to military expenditures, they ranged in 1979 from a high of $88 per citizen in Chile and $79 in Cuba to virtually nothing in Costa Rica. By way of contrast, it was $6 in India, $27 in Nigeria, $433 in the Soviet Union, and $543 in the United States. When it comes to people in uniform, the number went from 1 per 52 citizens in Cuba to 1 per 424 in Brazil, in comparison with 1 per 110 in the United States. But what does all of this mean for politics? Clearly size, even when measured in relative terms, does not appear to be a critical factor in accounting for the military's role in politics. Large and small alike have been active politically. Once there is a professional officer corps with a few thousand well-armed troops under its command, the armed forces can seize power. To explain why it is so political then, we must turn to other factors.

The military's disciplined, hierarchical organization is one possibility. Without it, coups would be improbable undertakings. To carry out the coup one needs an agreement among the officers in command of major units and decisions about the deployment of troops. Weapons available for the defense of the country can easily be employed to force unarmed civilians from office. But the capacity to carry out a coup is hardly sufficient to explain intervention. It is a capability but not a motive, making the coup possible but not causing it.

What about the social background of officers? Might we not expect that they are most loyal to people of the social class of their origins? Analysts used to argue that officers who came from the *oligarquia* became involved in politics to protect the wealth of their families. This was probably true before 1930, but as an explanation of current military behavior it is quite inadequate. The class background of military officers has changed substantially during the last quarter century. Increasingly, officers are recruited from the middle and lower middle sectors. In place of the offspring of the *latifundistas* one now finds the sons of small-town merchants, skilled laborers, and former military officers. Officers do not yet represent the urban and rural poor to any large degree, but they are more diverse and less tied by blood to traditional elites than ever before. If they intervene in public affairs to protect the elite, it is less because of a need to protect upper-class relatives than other considerations.

An understanding of military education may take us a little closer in our search for motives. Several features of military education merit attention. One is the isolation of young officers. The typical military career begins with admission to a military secondary school at age thirteen or fourteen. After graduation come four years at a service academy, then advanced training in specialty schools, and, before promotion to the rank of general, additional training at a war college of some kind. The result is an educational and professional experience that occurs in relative isolation from civilian society, which gives military officers a strong corporate identity that separates them psychologically from civilian politicians. Equally important is the content of military education. Because he is taken from civilian life at a young age, the officer is heavily influenced by his formal instruction as well as the values he learns from his peers. Most military education concentrates on strategy and tactics, organization and administration, and technical training, especially in engineering. Beyond rudimentary instruction in foreign languages, history, and economics, little attention is given to the social sciences in the officer's education until he enters a war college in midcareer.

After World War II, war colleges were established in several countries to provide advanced training in many nonmilitary as well as military subjects. The curriculum reflects the conviction of the high command that in the future their nations' defense will depend as much on social and economic affairs as on military power. At a war college officers are taught geopolitics, development economics, and advanced management by civilian as well as military instructors. In some countries, such as Brazil, they are joined in the classroom by civilian students from government bureaucracies and private industry.

In recent times the war college curriculum has stressed the mission of the military as the guardian of national security and defense. By security is meant protection not just against foreign enemies but also citizens of the country who challenge the economic and cultural order, most notably anyone who advocates the redistribution of power in society. According to this way of thinking, the military should serve not only as a policeman who occasionally evicts politicians from office, but also as the ultimate authority over the nation, one that has the right to create and enforce the rules whenever officers believe civilians incapable of doing so to their liking. What the officers like is not always clear, however, since they too react to concrete conditions, sometimes disagreeing among themselves over what the military should do. More apparent is what they do not like, namely, the kinds of political conflicts that cause disorder and weaken the strength of the nation, and anything that threatens the power of privileges enjoyed by their own kind.

Military officers also worry a great deal about economic development. Frustrated by repeated failures to achieve sustained economic growth and fearful of popular discontent, they, like civilians, advocate major efforts to increase national production. Officers disagree on the specifics of economic policy, but they are united in the belief that democratic politics can be sacrificed if that is what it takes to promote development. To the order-conscious officer, disputes over political rules, legislative impasses, and social protests are intolerable when they seem to undermine concerted national development efforts.

Military officers have narrow self-interests to protect as well. They learned from the Cuban and Nicaraguan revolutions that they would be the first to go should revolutionary movements succeed in their countries. In both cases the militaries were not only defeated in battle but officers were also tried and convicted of crimes against the nation or were forced to watch as their organizations were replaced by revolutionary armed forces. Informed by these events, their instinct for self-preservation generates a kind of paranoia that leads some officers to attack anyone who they believe has revolutionary intentions. Military self-interest involves more than institutional survival, however. Less spectacular is the preservation of military privileges within the existing system, from their salaries to their management of many state enterprises. The military has been in business for some time in the more industrialized countries, manufacturing iron and steel, communications equipment, and armaments, just to name a few. Officers in Brazil and Argentina, for example, make careers from their employment in these enterprises, and they are the first to resist efforts to deprive them of their positions or to end state subsidization of the firms they command.

Political activism does have its costs, not just to the military as a whole when it invites popular disaffection, but also to individual officers caught in disputes over the governing of the country. The military is organized as a hierarchical command structure in which advancement is supposed to be based on the length of service and individual performance. In practice, of course, personal favoritism and rivalries among officer cliques also influence assignments and promotions. But such intrigues are minor when compared to those that accompany military government. With public office come divisive issues that provoke disputes among officers, which in turn can undermine cohesion within the military. There is no reason to assume that officers will always agree on who among them should serve as president, on whether to trust the free market, on the amount of repression required, or on when to relinquish office. Even where there is consensus within the army, it is often challenged by a navy or air force whose training and professional loyalties have bred rivalries that manifest themselves when the military rules.

No introduction to the military would be complete without mention of foreign influence. Latin American officers are no less subject to foreign influence than civilians. Traditionally, they have secured armaments, advanced training, and technical assistance abroad, primarily from the United States after World War II, except in the case of Cuba, which since 1959 has relied on the Soviet Union. Latin American militaries belong to regional defense organizations and purchase weapons in the United States, England, France, Germany, Israel, and the Soviet Union. With such collaboration often comes the reinforcement of shared political ideologies, such as the anticommunist containment strategy launched by President Harry Truman and sustained by all American presidents since 1947.

It would be a mistake to conclude, however, that the region's militaries are nothing more than the passive instruments of foreigners. A close relationship can develop, but its exact character depends on many things, ranging from how dependent the local military is on foreign support to how determined the foreigner is to make the local military a central part of its strategy. Actually, several countries have been trying to reduce their dependence on any single foreign government by diversifying their sources of armaments. Today the Brazilians, Argentines, and Peruvians rely very little on the United States for their supplies; Brazil and Argentina manufacture many of their small arms and all three buy heavily in Europe. In 1970, for example, all but 100 Latin American military aircraft came from the United States; by 1982, 1,500 had been purchased elsewhere.

Tensions between Latin American militaries and the United States arise occasionally, as happened during the war over the Falkland/Malvinas Islands in 1982 when the Reagan administration sided with the British against Argentina, causing sharp criticism of the United States by officers in several countries. But despite greater independence and continued resentment of American power, there remains an alliance of sorts between the United States military and the Latin American officers who share its fundamental conservatism on hemispheric political matters. Each has been educated in the school of anticommunism, and they are reluctant to abandon each other completely.

In sum, Latin American armed forces are not all exactly the same. Nor is their political behavior caused by a single factor. Yet most officers come to share a way of thinking about society and its governance by the time they reach the senior ranks. Theirs is a bueaucratic culture dependent on hierarchy and command, one that does not cope easily with the unprecedented and the unusual, especially when either appears to threaten their prerogatives. They are happiest when they have a clear mission, one that makes them feel important and causes them to be appreciated by their compatriots, something that still eludes them in most places. Once their mission was confined to protecting conservative oligarchies; today they seek to destroy the militant Left, promote national development, and dominate the state. How they play politics depends as much on their societies and how they assess their condition as on the personal ambitions of service commanders. Their education and military culture filter what they see, causing them to be uncomfortable with the give and take of competitive politics and to fear the political consequences of civil conflict. This does not mean that they never tolerate constitutional government and party politics; obviously they often do. But it does mean that they will try to have things their way, contending daily with the other players, tolerating some while doing all they can to stop others.

Now that we have learned a few of the military's capabilities and motivations, can we predict when and where the next coup will occur? Probably not. An ability to understand military involvement after the fact does not give us the power of prediction. But coups per se are not what should interest us. We will learn little about Latin American politics by viewing the military as an intruder that steps in and out of the game. It is more instructive to see it not as an outsider but as a player much like any other, with its own interests and capabilities. Wishing it were not so will not change the fact of military involvement. As every civilian politician knows, the armed forces will continue to play politics whether anyone else likes it or not.

The Roman Catholic church

One half of the world's Roman Catholics live in Latin America, and 90 percent of the people in the region claim Catholicism as their religion. For more than four centuries the Roman Catholic hierarchy lent its support to the prevailing political order, praying for the souls of the poor while consorting with the rich. Then in the mid-nineteenth century things began to change, starting with an attack on the church by secular authorities determined to deprive it of its wealth and property in an effort to promote private enterprise and to strengthen the state. Thereafter the church was forced to confine itself primarily to its religious mission, leaving economic matters to entrepreneurs and political ones to civil authorities. Nevertheless, the conduct of the Roman Catholic clergy has been the subject of controversy ever since.

Not too long ago the church was attacked by political reformers for conspiring with the oligarchs who exploited the masses, especially in the countryside. By preaching salvation in another life, it was said, the clergy pacified the poor, denying them the motivation needed to improve their condition. In defense, church leaders argued that they had no choice in the matter since their earthly mission was clearly a spiritual and not a materialistic one. Today, in contrast, the criticism of the clergy comes from the opposite extreme, with conservatives accusing a reform-minded clergy of forsaking its spiritual mission in favor of a misguided and dangerous earthly one. Why the sudden change? And why has it come within an institution thought for so long to have been one of the most insulated from the vicissitudes of secular life?

First we need to establish what has and has not actually changed. A hierarchical church led by the Vatican and guided by an essentially conservative theology remains in place. However, within this structure the practices and beliefs of individual clergy are changing. Some of the initiative for change derives from the reformulation of church doctrines by authorities in Rome. But most of it originates below, prompted by the frustrations of priests, nuns, and laity with the condition of the poor.

The doctrinal sources of a revised theology came from two encyclicals, *Mater et Magistra* (1961) and *Pacem in Terris* (1963), which, among other things, stressed the universal right to education, a decent standard of living, and political participation, and from the Second Vatican Council (1965), which established the equality of laity, priests, and bishops. In Latin America the doctrinal reformation was translated to policy by the Latin American Episcopal Conference of Bishops (CELAM) at Medellin, Colombia, in 1968, where Pope Paul VI himself declared that the church "wished to personify the Christ of a poor and hungry people."

Words are one thing, their translation into action something else, of course. Few agreed on how to carry out the new mission. Conservative bishops insisted that the clergy confine themselves to the pulpit, whereas the reformers insisted on pastoral involvement in the mobilization of their poorest congregations for social action. A decade later an attempt was made to settle these differences at the CELAM meetings in Puebla, Mexico; though both sides went away claiming victories, the differences and divisions remained. Conservatives continue to condemn theologies of liberation and the advocacy of social and political action as a violation of church doctrine, whereas reformers remain dedicated to mobilizing the poor for social action.

What are the political consequences of all this? Despite the resistance of church conservatives, the spiritual influence of the church is being used by its clergy and lay leaders to generate social action at the local level. There is no way to measure accurately its effect on national politics, but the fact that it is condemned and attacked violently by the defenders of the status quo throughout Latin America indicates that it has become a real threat to the old way of life. Priests and nuns have become the targets of assassins in Central America and the Andean nations, where local elites fear the effects of their efforts to promote self-help projects and increase the economic independence of the rural poor using the *comunidades de base* (base communities) that they have created in villages and slums throughout the region. Base communities were started a couple of decades ago as a means for overcoming the paucity of priests in the countryside. Laymen were trained to conduct simple services and administer the Eucharist in the absence of priests who had to divide their time among several small parishes. But in teaching Indians and the other *campesinos* to look after their own spiritual affairs the clergy also promoted self-help efforts to alleviate other community problems. As villagers demanded more help and advice, the clergy supplied it. Self-help at the village level threatens local elites and civil authorities who have always taken advantage of the passivity and economic dependence of the poor in order to secure cheap labor and political conformity. One has to appreciate how much farmers, mayors, and merchants have come to take peasant passivity for granted to understand why they are so frightened by self-help projects. What they see is a clergy who are intent on depriving them of their subjects and undermining their way of life.

Another change in the church is its response to authoritarian government. In countries where the military has chosen to rule harshly, using its weapons against civilians who disagree with its wishes, the church has become one of the few institutions able to oppose it and survive. Political parties can be closed, labor unions repressed, and protest movements defeated militarily, but the officers in charge cannot liquidate the entire church hierarchy. To be sure, priests and nuns have been jailed and assassinated, but the hierarchy is too visible nationally and internationally to be treated the same way. Consequently, when they choose, the bishops can denounce government violations of human rights as they have done frequently during the past decade in Brazil, Chile, Nicaragua, and El Salvador.

Lest we rush to conclude that the church has become the source of political revolution, it is important to recognize that revisions in doctrine and grass roots activism have had a greater effect on the church itself than on politics. The clergy are well located to help the poor do more for themselves, but the church is neither organized nor motivated to lead revolutions in Latin America. Moreover, the church continues to be divided over what its earthly mission should be. Life is being changed in many communities, but when it comes to politics the church is just another player in the game, albeit one who has the advantage of being armed with weapons that can work on the minds and spirits of people, yet one without many other advantages over its powerful secular rivals.

Government bureaucrats

Why include bureaucrats as players in the game? Do they not serve the interests of the politicians and military officers who command them? It is tempting to dismiss them as irrelevant to the political contest, but we cannot afford to do so. They do not compete in elections but they do influence policy, and therein rests their importance. Presidents and generals come and go, sometimes quite frequently, but most bureaucrats stay on.

Patronage runs high throughout Latin America, but nevertheless most of those who work for government now make it a career. The majority are charged with routine assignments but many are given immense responsibilities, like supplying the expertise required to run government oil companies, airlines and railways, utilities, development banks, and social security administrations. As government responsibilities have grown, so has the number of technocrats. Today they are educated at the London School of Economics, the Sorbonne, Harvard, MIT, and the University of Chicago, as well as universities within the region. Though short on political skills, they proudly display their technical ones, convinced that their education alone gives them a right to shape their nations' development policies.

The rapid growth of the public sector in Latin America is relatively recent, but it has had an enormous effect on contemporary political life and economic development. During the past fifty years, the Latin American state has gone from regulating domestic and foreign trade to promoting industrialization and executing ambitious development programs. Governments that did little more than build roads and deliver the mail a half century ago now produce a wide range of goods and services, from iron and steel to television programs. This sudden growth has not come without some problems. The Latin American state, despite its immense formal authority, is still quite weak in many areas, especially the enforcement of regulations, and is often hampered by a shortage of financial resources and managerial talent at lower levels. This should not be surprising, for the Latin American state has come very far very fast; its bureaucracies have suddenly been given new responsibilities that require the skilled administration of very complex activities and an unprecedented degree of social engineering.

Frustration with unfulfilled development plans and inefficiently managed state enterprises has become commonplace, prompting a renewed interest in strengthening the state and its bureaucratic capabilities, especially on the part of the military officers and technocrats, who have seized control of many of the region's governments in recent years, promising to halt patronage and reduce corruption and increase efficiency. Most Latin American governments are still a long way from achieving these objectives. Political loyalties still influence appointments, and bribery and other forms of corruption remain almost everywhere. Yet significant strides have been made. The number of trained personnel in key agencies grows each year, and tasks that were left to foreign firms in the past are increasingly being taken over by the state and its newly nationalized enterprises.

It should now be clear why we should regard bureaucrats as players who have their own interests and resources. Whatever their historical experiences or policy beliefs, the managers of the Latin American public sector share many things in common. First, they desire to preserve and expand their influence over public policy. Second, they seek to administer their programs with as little interference from political authorities as possible. And third, they want to dominate those who depend on their goodwill. What they enjoy most is the power they derive from citizens' needs for the goods and services they provide. To a large degree they are the modern patrons of the industrialists, traders, farmers, laborers, and peasants who work in a private sector that depends heavily on the state for licenses, loans, roads, railways, housing, and innumerable regulations and social services. In return they expect deference, tribute, and acceptance of their decisions.

The potential power of bureaucrats is evident when we recognize that no matter how noble a government's goals or how sophisticated its development plans, it accomplishes little without the support of administrators. Bureaucrats are supposed to be the servants of political officials, but political officials often find themselves the captives of their bureaucrats. They rely on them when they design policies as well as when they implement them. If bureaucrats disagree with official policy or find it threatening to their organizational interests, they have recourse to many weapons, which they can use to sabotage the government's effort. Political officials cannot afford to sit back and assume that their programs will succeed simply because they are needed. If they do not closely supervise program implementation, making sure that policy goals are met and services delivered, their best efforts will likely come to naught.

The weakness of political analyses that focus primarily on "politics" rather than "government" is that they miss the impact of administrators in the country's public life and economic development. If we are to understand why some countries do well when they try to solve fundamental development problems and others do not, we cannot halt our analysis after examining legislatures and presidents and their policy choices. Instead, we must go a step further and ask what the state does with its authority and what consequences, if any, it has on the welfare of its citizens.

Foreign interests

Some analysts place foreigners on top when they list the influential, convinced that they are more responsible for the region's condition than Latin Americans themselves. Blaming foreigners for poverty and underdevelopment is nothing new, of course. For a century critics on the Left have argued that the capitalist nations of Europe and North America have prospered by exploiting Africans, Asians, and Latin Americans, reaping huge profits from the extraction of minerals, the purchase of low-priced agricultural commodities, and the export of expensive manufactured goods. For its part the Third World has gained nothing but poverty, economic stagnation, and autocratic government, it is argued.

Even if one disagrees with this view, the fact of foreign influence throughout the region is indisputable, making it impossible to leave foreigners off our growing list of players. Foreign players are citizens of other countries who influence the politics and economic well-being of Latin Americans through direct involvement in the region. They are principally of three types: those who represent other governments, those who work for international agencies, and those employed by private business. Here we will look briefly at a foreign government, the United States, and then at multinational enterprises to illustrate the roles played by foreigners.

Several people represent the United States government in each Latin American nation. Each U.S. embassy, for example, houses officials who work for the State and Defense Departments, the Treasury, the Departments of Commerce and Agriculture, and the Central Intelligence Agency. They are supposed to work together to achieve a coherent set of objectives set by the president of the United States, but the ambiguity and complexity of U.S. government aims in each country leave much room for each agency to pursue its particular aims. Nevertheless, despite variation in the specifics of policy and some change from one president to another, the basic objectives of U.S. policy in the region have varied little over the past forty years.

Since World War II the United States has given highest priority to the exclusion of Communists from the region, fearful that communist government would increase Soviet influence and reduce American power in Latin America. The creation of a communist regime in Cuba followed by the Cuban missile crisis in 1962 reinforced a fear of the Soviet Union gaining strategic advantages over the United States through the creation of anti-American and pro-Soviet regimes like Cuba's. The methods employed to suppress communism are varied, ranging from financing the election campaigns of anticommunist parties to training paramilitary forces to fight guerrillas. Some, like President Jimmy Carter, have even tried to promote economic reform and respect for human rights in order to undermine the political left and win friends for the United States. But whatever the means employed, the anticommunist objective has stayed essentially the same. A second and complementary goal is American access to Latin America's natural resources and markets. Although most U.S. trade is with Europe and Canada, Latin America is an important supplier of essential minerals and a rapidly growing market for American technology. When we put these two objectives together, it is apparent why the United States prefers the status quo to rapid political change in the region, even when it means the existence of autocratic governments alien to American political values.

How does the United States government influence Latin American governments, given the objectives just described? At the diplomatic level it tries to convince host officials of the merits of its case, using logical argument and technical expertise. But logical argument is seldom sufficient to get one's way with officials whose national interests often compete with American ones. Therefore, the United States government also relies heavily on resources that give it advantages over the more dependent and vulnerable Latin American states. On the economic front it takes advantage of Latin American reliance on American markets, investments, and foreign assistance, threatening now and then to reduce the flow if its demands are not met. Similarly, it uses its power within international lending agencies to block funding of projects in nations whose governments threaten American interests.

A second resource, and one that has received much attention of late, is direct intervention through covert action. To secure the kind of government or politics they want, agents of the United States government may enter directly into the political game by giving funds to the players they favor, directing hostile propaganda against those they do not, bribing officials and party leaders, fomenting unrest, and encouraging military intervention. For example, in the early 1980s the Central Intelligence Agency financed guerrillas who sought to overthrow the Sandinista regime in Nicaragua. Even though such techniques frequently fail to achieve their objectives, their availability and the threat of their use may bring a government into line with American wishes.

Finally, there is the threat of American military intervention. Popular at the turn of the century during the era of dollar diplomacy, direct American military intervention in Latin American countries seldom occurs today. Nevertheless, the ability to intervene with troops, especially in the Caribbean, as occurred in 1965 in the Dominican Republic, remains a weapon that can be employed to deter certain undesirable behaviors. More often than not, however, American policy makers are content to use their influence over Latin America's militaries to secure the results they desire.

In sum, what the United States government wants most from Latin America is the region's collaboration with the pursuit of its strategic objectives. The American president has powerful resources at his disposal, but his success is never automatic. The Latin American game is complex and its outcomes are influenced by many things, the efforts of foreign governments being only one, though an important one. And pressure has to be applied skillfully, a requirement not always fulfilled by clumsy foreign governments. Furthermore, as Latin American countries have grown and diversified their markets and sources of capital, they have reduced their vulnerability to any one nation's foreign policy, even one as powerful as the United States. When the United States halted the sale of weapons to Brazil and Argentina in the late 1970s, for example, both countries bought them elsewhere, ignoring the Americans' policy demands.

Foreign governments may receive the most attention in the press, but more foreigners are sent to the region by private corporations than by governments. As the Latin American economies have grown during the past three decades, so has foreign investment, especially in the larger ones like Mexico, Brazil, Argentina, and Venezuela. Mexico, for example, though noted for its nationalism, still relies heavily on foreign investment. Over one-half of the 500 largest U.S. manufacturing firms have operations in Mexico. Moreover, multinationals accounted for as much as 64 percent of Mexico's production of transportation equipment, 51 percent of its chemicals, and 21 percent of its processed food. These figures are significant, for it is not the size of a firm's share of the entire economy that makes it powerful, but its share of particular industries on which a government heavily relies to meet its citizens' needs. The days when one or two foreign firms ran a nation's economy are long gone, but dependence on a few firms for an essential technology or product is quite common.

Not surprisingly, given their importance and influence, multinational firms are one of the most criticized institutions in the region, accused of forcing native entrepreneurs out of business, extracting excessive profits, bribing local officials, and resisting regulation. Criticism has prompted a host of measures designed to reduce their influence, ranging from restrictions on the number of foreigners that firms can employ to the required sharing of ownership with native investors, as in Mexico where foreign firms in some industries are asked to place 51 percent of their operations under Mexican control. And governments can also nationalize foreign firms, which is quite a risky step but one taken successfully by several Latin American governments.

Foreign firms want a favorable investment climate conducive to a high rate of return for as long as possible. More specifically, they want freedom to operate as they wish, an accessible but docile labor force, and the lowest possible cost of operation. And they prefer a government whose actions are predictable, especially in economic affairs. They need to know what the economic rules of the game are and to be assured that they will remain the same in the future. What the multinational firm does not want is a government that is hostile to

foreign investors and that continually harasses them with unanticipated measures that limit their operations and reduce their profits.
Nor does it welcome the kind of economic uncertainty brought on by
inflation and chronic balance-of-payments problems. Foreign firms, of
course, seldom get everything they want. Nevertheless, they have
survived quite well under less than optimal conditions, tolerating
what they cannot change while exerting their influence on government policy makers to secure what advantages they can.

The multinational firm's major sources of influence are the resources and products it contributes to the host country. The more the
local government wants what the firm offers, whether it be the extraction of petroleum or the production of toothpaste, the more vulnerable
it is to the firm's demands. It is Latin America's misfortune (and
conversely the multinational's good fortune) that today the region
finds itself in need of technology and capital, both of which are most
readily supplied by the multinationals. Officials who are in a hurry to
raise the production of goods and services may find the multinationals, with their transferable technologies, capital, and managerial skills,
the swiftest means for achieving their growth objectives. On the other
hand, they know that there is a price to be paid for foreign investment, most notably the absorption of domestic enterprises by the
multinationals and increased foreign economic control.

Not to be overlooked are some of the less advertised ways in which
multinational firms try to influence policy. Bribes are occasionally
given to secure favorable government decisions. Some even cynically
argue that bribes are justified as a kind of informal tax of the rich by
the poor. A more indirect form of influence is the ability of multinational firms to block a country's participation in international markets.
Boycotts of products, embargoes of exports in foreign ports, and the
undermining of confidence in a country's creditworthiness are all
techniques that have been used against Latin American nations in
recent times.

It is worth noting that not everyone in Latin America believes that
relations with multinationals need be unhappy ones. There are many,
including economists, consumers, and industrialists, who are convinced that foreign firms can make important contributions to their
economies. For them, it is not a question of nationals versus foreigners, but rather of how the country can make the best use of the
resources available to it. Labeling these persons "lackeys of imperial-

ism" and the like will not help us understand them or the multinationals' impact. Moreover, throughout the region sophisticated technocrats are designing new approaches to the regulation of foreign firms, including joint ownership, mandatory domestic participation, and foreign marketing arrangements.

In sum, multinational corporations do not compete in elections or fire weapons at politicians, but they do influence the actions of those who do. They have obvious interests to protect and are not reluctant to use their wealth, economic importance to each nation, and personal ties to authorities to protect them. The fact that they operate out of public view does not make them any less important. How well they do and how their actions affect the welfare of Latin Americans are matters that will concern us in Part II.

But before concluding, mention should be made of the role played by foreign banks in Latin America. Borrowing money abroad to finance businesses and government programs has always been a common practice in the region. But recently it has become an obsession. When the Saudis, Kuwaitis, and other OPEC members placed substantial amounts of their new wealth in private European and North American banks, the banks in turn rushed to find customers to whom they could lend the money. Ready and waiting were Mexico and Venezuela who, though oil exporters, needed additional funds to pay for their ambitious development programs, and Brazil, an oil importer also anxious to finance rapid growth. By the early 1980s each had accumulated record debts to the likes of Chase Manhattan, Citibank, the Bank of America, Deutsche Bank, and Barclays. But when the world recession slowed economic growth in the region, the debtors came up short, unable to make payments on their rapidly accumulating foreign debts. Had there not been so many countries in trouble at the same time, the situation might have been handled easily, but with Mexico and Brazil plagued by debts of over $80 billion and Venezuela and Argentina over $20 billion, emergency measures became necessary. Doing nothing to prevent the four countries from being forced to default on their loans would have caused a world financial crisis, not to mention panic among the depositors who had trusted their savings to the suddenly endangered banks.

Putting their heads together, the Latin Americans, bankers, officials from the International Monetary Fund (IMF), and the U.S. government responded as they had to all of the international financial crises that had arisen since 1945. They lent the debtors more money to tide them over in the hope that eventually they would recover. The International Monetary Fund had been created precisely for that purpose after World War II, and for three decades it had served the industrialized nations as a creditor of last resort responsible for preventing the collapse of the international system. It had done the same for Third World countries unable to pay their accounts abroad. But the IMF's assistance did not come without a very high price tag. In exchange for new loans, each Latin American country had to agree to put its own financial house in order, following strict IMF guidelines that required unpopular cuts in expenditures and reduced subsidies to consumers and local businesses. The moral of the story was quite clear: In order to continue to operate within the confines of the international trade system, the Latin Americans once again had to accept the terms dictated by their foreign financiers. Moreover, it did not take much insight to see that in becoming more ambitious in their own development plans some of the Latin American governments had, for the time being, increased their dependence on the foreign powers from whom they were trying to free themselves.

Governments and players

Now that we know something about most of the players in the Latin American game we need to think for a moment about the different ways they participate in the making of public policy in their countries. Players do not participate randomly, even when agreement on a single set of rules is lacking. History teaches us that their involvement is structured either by habit or by design and that the character of the game is heavily influenced by the form their participation takes.

Modes of participation can be divided into four types, each with its own rules about who can play, how they can exert their influence, and where ultimate authority resides. They are pluralism, corporatism, authoritarianism, and communism.

Pluralism involves a process in which many organized private interests compete for influence over public policy. Diversity of interest and bargaining at all levels of government are its dominant traits. For pluralism to work political resources must be widely disbursed, and winners and losers in policy disputes must change from time to time. Though total equality is not essential, a noncumulative pattern of "dispersed inequalities" is required; that is, no group can be allowed to acquire a monopoly of power and influence. Under this arrangement the state governs not by imposing its control on civil society but by serving as a mediator or broker among competing private and bureaucratic interests, making policy by bargaining among them. Pluralism is not a neat arrangement, but a mode of policy making whose openness and competitiveness varies with the distribution of power among players and the willingness of authorities to leave the initiative to others. Thus, the politics of some countries, such as the United States, is more pluralistic than that of others, like Great Britain or West Germany, though all exhibit many pluralist qualities.

Can pluralism work in Latin America where resources have been much more concentrated than in Anglo-America? Doubts exist, as do suspicions that the state has always been too partisan in Latin America to serve effectively as a mediator among contesting interests. Yet, in some societies organized interests are diverse and competition among them for political influence is intense. Whether that makes them examples of pluralism is something we will explore when we examine democratic politics in Chile and Venezuela in Chapter 7.

Corporatism offers another method for organizing player participation. It rejects the notion of open competition and the principle of government neutrality in favor of a more deliberate effort to organize and regulate public–private sector relations. The government assumes responsibility for directing the society, and private economic and social groups become its instruments for doing so. Instead of competing with each other to influence officials, interest groups deal with authorities directly and on the latter's terms, gaining what they can by accepting their place in the government's scheme of things. In its loosest form, corporatism may involve a willing collaboration by interest groups with authorities because they believe that it is to their benefit to work together rather than to compete openly for influence. Such is the case in Scandinavia, where a mild form of corporatism has grown from mutual interests in the management of economic and social policy. At the other extreme is a corporatism where the state dominates labor and business, making them little more than deliverers of government orders to their constituents. Italian fascism was an example of such heavy-handed corporatism. But whatever form it takes, corporatism is attractive to leaders who want to increase their control over public policy and its execution in complex societies where pluralistic competition weakens the state and old-fashioned authoritarianism lacks the means for dealing with dynamic social movements and diverse interests. It seems to offer rulers a way to make labor, business, agriculture, and other groups collaborate with the government as it carries out its plan for the country's development. Nearly all Latin American leaders have been attracted to it at one time or another, and some have actually put corporatist notions to work. The Mexicans adapted corporatist organization to their needs in the 1930s, Argentines and Brazilians to theirs in the 1940s, and military officers to theirs in Peru in 1970s, as we will learn in Part II.

There is a simpler way to handle participation, of course, namely, authoritarianism. Autocrats rule over others instead of ruling with them or through them. Organizationally they are more primitive than corporatists, preferring the monopolization of power by a dictator or small ruling elite and the enforcement of rules by repression rather than the use of interest groups to carry out official policy. Whether authoritarian government can accomplish much more than the maintenance of order in increasingly complex Latin American societies is debatable, though that has not stopped autocrats from trying time and again to run some countries. How well they have done will be the subject of Chapter 8.

Pluralism, corporatism, and authoritarianism are not the only ways that participation and policy making can be organized. Dissatisfaction with all three has led a few Latin Americans to try something very different, namely, communism. Communists do not believe that society has to be divided into separate interests. Instead they want to create a society in which partisan concerns are eliminated by the socialization of the economy, creating a national community united by a single interest in which people as equals devote their energies to the pursuit of the common good rather than to their individual aggrandizement. How one goes about doing this and whether it can be accomplished will preoccupy us in Chapter 10 when we look at Cuban communism.

Further reading

Political parties

Bernard, Jean Pierre, Silas Cerqueira, Hugo Neira, Helene Graillot, Leslie F. Manigat, and Pierre Gilhodes. *Guide to the Political Parties of South America.* Baltimore: Penguin Books, 1973.

Gott, Richard. *Guerrilla Movements in Latin America*. Garden City, N.Y.: Doubleday, 1971.

Kohl, James, and John Litt. *Urban Guerrilla Warfare in Latin America*. Cambridge, Mass.: MIT Press, 1974.

Martz, John. "Dilemmas in the Study of Latin American Political Parties." *Journal of Politics* 26: 509–31, 1964.

"Political Parties in Colombia and Venezuela: Contrasts in Substance and Style." *Western Political Quarterly* 18: 18–33, 1965.

Acción Democrática: Evolution of a Modern Political Party in Venezuela. Princeton, N.J.: Princeton University Press, 1966.

McDonald, Ronald. *Party Systems and Elections in Latin America*. Chicago: Markham, 1971.

Poppino, Rollie. *International Communism in Latin America: A History of the Movement, 1917–1963*. New York: Free Press, 1964.

Ranis, Peter. "A Two-Dimensional Typology of Latin American Parties." *Journal of Politics* 30: 798–832, 1968.

Ratliff, William E. *Castroism and Communism in Latin America, 1959–1976: The Varieties of Marxist-Leninist Experience*. Washington, D.C.: American Enterprise Institute, 1976.

Scott, Robert. "Political Parties and Policy-Making in Latin America," in Joseph LaPalombara and Myron Weiner, eds., *Political Parties and Political Development*. Princeton, N.J.: Princeton University Press, 1966, pp. 331–68.

Williams, Edward J. *Latin American Christian Democratic Parties*. Knoxville: University of Tennessee Press, 1967.

Military

Barber, Willard R., and C. Neale Ronning. *Internal Security and Military Power: Counterinsurgency and Civic Action in Latin America*. Columbus: Ohio State University Press, 1966.

Comblin, José. *The Church and the National Security State*. Maryknoll, N.Y.: Orbis Books, 1979.

Einaudi, Luigi R., and Alfred C. Stepan. *Latin American Institutional Development: Changing Military Perspectives in Peru and Brazil*. Santa Monica, Calif.: Rand, 1971.

Huntington, Samuel. *Political Order in Changing Societies*. New Haven: Yale University Press, 1968, chap. 4.

Jackman, Robert. "Politicians in Uniform: Military Government and Social Change in the Third World." *American Political Science Review* 70: 1078–97, 1976.

Janowitz, Morris. *The Military in the Political Development of New Nations: An Essay in Comparative Analysis*. Chicago: University of Chicago Press, 1964.

Johnson, John. *The Military and Society in Latin America*. Stanford, Calif.: Stanford University Press, 1964.

Lernoux, Penny. *Cry of the People*. Baltimore: Penguin Books, 1982.

Lieuwin, Edwin. *Arms and Politics in Latin America*. New York: Praeger, 1961.

Lowenthal, Abraham F., ed. *Armies and Politics in Latin America*. New York: Holmes & Meier, 1976.

Needler, Martin. "Political Development and Military Intervention in Latin America." *American Political Science Review* 60: 616–26, 1966.

Nordlinger, Eric A. "Soldiers in Mufti: The Impact of Military Rule upon Economic and Social Change in the Non-Western States." *American Political Science Review* 64: 1131–48, 1970.

Nun, José. "A Latin American Phenomenon: The Middle Class Military Coup," in James Petras and Maurice Zeitlin, eds., *Latin America: Reform or Revolution?* Greenwich, Conn.: Fawcett, 1968, pp. 145–85.

O'Donnell, Guillermo A. *Modernization and Bureaucratic-Authoritarianism: Studies in South American Politics*. Institute of International Studies. Berkeley: University of California, 1973.

Putnam, Robert D. "Toward Explaining Military Intervention in Latin American Politics." *World Politics* 20: 83–110, 1967.

Stepan, Alfred C. *The Military in Politics: Changing Patterns in Brazil*. Princeton, N.J.: Princeton University Press, 1971.

Roman Catholic church

Bruneau, Thomas C. *The Political Transformation of the Brazilian Catholic Church*. Cambridge: Cambridge University Press, 1974.

   Religiosity and Politicization in Brazil: The Church in an Authoritarian Regime. Austin: University of Texas Press, 1981.

Gutierrez, Gustavo. *A Theology of Liberation: History, Politics and Salvation*. Maryknoll, N.Y.: Orbis Books, 1973.

Latin American Episcopal Council (CELAM). *The Church in the Present Day Transformation of Latin America in the Light of the Council*. 2 vols. Bogota: General Secretariat of CELAM, 1970.

Lernoux, Penny. *Cry of the People*. Baltimore: Penquin Books, 1982.

Levine, Daniel H., ed. *Churches and Politics in Latin America*. Beverly Hills, Calif.: Sage Publications, 1980.

MacEoin, Gary, and Nivita Riley. *Puebla: A Church Being Born*. New York: Paulist Press, 1980.

Meecham, J. Lloyd. *Church and State in Latin America: A History of Political Ecclesiastical Relations*, 2d ed. rev. Chapel Hill: University of North Carolina Press, 1966.

Smith, Brian. *The Church and Politics in Chile: Challenges to Modern Catholicism*. Princeton, N.J.: Princeton University Press, 1982.

Turner, Frederick C. *Catholicism and Political Development in Latin America*. Chapel Hill: University of North Carolina Press, 1971.

Government bureaucrats

Anderson, Charles W. *Politics and Economic Change in Latin America: The Governing of Restless Nations*. New York: Van Nostrand, 1967, chap. 6.

Daland, Robert. *Brazilian Planning*. Chapel Hill: University of North Carolina Press, 1967.

Dietz, Henry A. "Bureaucratic Demand-Making and Clientelistic Participation in Peru," in James M. Malloy, ed., *Authoritarianism and Corporatism in Latin America*. Pittsburgh: University of Pittsburgh Press, 1977, pp. 413–58.

Graham, Lawrence S. *Civil Service Reform in Brazil: Principles versus Practice*. Austin: University of Texas Press, 1968.

Greenberg, Martin H. *Bureaucracy and Development: A Mexican Case Study*. Lexington, Mass.: Heath, 1970.

Grimes, C. E., and Charles Simmons. "Bureaucracy and Political Control in Mexico: Towards an Assessment." *Public Administration Review* 29: 72–9, 1969.

Grindle, Merilee S. *Bureaucrats, Politicians and Peasants in Mexico*. Berkeley: University of California Press, 1977.

Hopkins, Jack, "Contemporary Research on Public Administration and Bureaucracies in Latin America." *Latin American Research Review* 9: 109–4, 1974.

LaPalombara, Joseph, ed. *Bureaucracy and Political Development*. Princeton, N.J.: Princeton University Press, 1963.

Weaver, Jerry L. "Value Patterns of a Latin American Bureaucracy." *Human Relations* 23: 225–34, 1970.

Wynia, Gary W. *Politics and Planners: Economic Development Policy in Central America*. Madison: University of Wisconsin Press, 1972.

Foreign interests: governments

Agee, Philip. *Inside the Company: CIA Diary*. New York: Stonehill, 1975.

Burr, Robert. *Our Troubled Hemisphere: Perspectives on U.S.-Latin American Relations*. Washington, D.C.: Brookings Institution, 1967.

Cotler, Julio, and Richard Fagen, eds. *Latin America and the United States*. Stanford, Calif.: Stanford University Press, 1974.

Fann, K. T., and Donald Hodges, eds. *Readings in United States Imperialism*. Boston: Porter Sargent, 1971.

Hayter, Teresa. *Aid as Imperialism*. Balitmore: Penguin Books, 1971.

Levinson, Jerome and Juan de Onis. *The Alliance that Lost Its Way*. New York: Quadrangle, 1970.

Linowitz, Sol, ed. *The Americas in a Changing World*. New York: Quadrangle, 1975.

Martin, John Bartlow. *Overtaken by Events: the Dominican Crisis from the Fall of Trujillo to the Civil War*. Garden City, N.Y.: Doubleday, 1966.

Needler, Martin. *The United States and the Latin American Revolution*. Boston: Allyn & Bacon, 1972.

Newfarmer, Richard, ed. *From Gunboats to Diplomacy*. Baltimore: Johns Hopkins University Press, 1983.

Parkinson, F. *Latin America, the Cold War and the World Powers, 1945–1973*. Beverly Hills, Calif.: Sage, 1974.

Pearce, Jenny. *Under the Eagle: U.S. Intervention in Central America and the Caribbean*. Boston: South End Press, 1982.

Schlesinger, Stephen, and Stephen Kinzer. *Bitter Fruit: The Untold Story of the American Coup in Guatemala*. Garden City, N.Y.: Doubleday (Anchor Books), 1983.

Schoultz, Lars. *Human Rights and U.S. Policy Toward Latin America*. Princeton, N.J.: Princeton University Press, 1981.

Theberge, James D. *The Soviet Presence in Latin America.* New York: Crane, Russak, 1974.

Williamson, Robert, William Glade, and Karl Schmitt, eds. *Latin America–United States Economic Interactions: Conflict, Accommodation and Policies for the Future.* Washington, D.C.: American Enterprise Institute, 1974.

Foreign interests: multinational corporations

Baklanoff, Eric N. *Expropriation of U.S. Investments in Cuba, Mexico and Chile.* New York: Praeger, 1975.

Barnet, Richard, and Ronald Muller. *Global Reach: The Power of the Multinational Corporations.* New York: Simon & Schuster, 1974.

Evans, Peter. *Dependent Development: The Alliance of Multinational, State, and Local Capital in Brazil.* Princeton, N.J.: Princeton University Press, 1979.

Fagen, Richard, ed. *Capitalism and the State in U.S.-Latin American Relations.* Stanford, Calif.: Stanford University Press, 1979.

Gunneman, Jon, ed. *The Nation-State and Transnational Corporations in Conflict: With Special Reference to Latin America.* New York: Praeger, 1975.

Ingram, George M. *Expropriation of U.S. Property in South America: Nationalization of Oil and Copper Companies in Peru, Bolivia, and Chile.* New York: Praeger, 1975.

Magdoff, Henry. *The Age of Imperialism.* New York: Monthly Review Press, 1969.

Moran, Theodore. *Multinational Corporations and the Politics of Dependence: Copper in Chile.* Princeton, N.J.: Princeton University Press, 1974.

Petras, James, Morris Morley, and Steven Smith. *The Nationalization of Venezuelan Oil.* New York: Praeger, 1977.

Pinelo, Adalberto. *The Multinational Corporation as a Force in Latin American Politics: A Case Study of the International Petroleum Company in Peru.* New York: Praeger, 1973.

Sigmund, Paul. *Multinationals in Latin America.* Madison: University of Wisconsin Press, 1980.

Sunkel, Osvaldo. "Big Business and 'Dependencia.' " *Foreign Affairs* 50: 517–31, 1972.

Tugwell, Franklin. *The Politics of Oil in Venezuela.* Stanford, Calif.: Stanford University Press, 1975.

Vernon, Raymond. *Sovereignty at Bay.* New York: Basic Books, 1971.

5. The stakes in the game

So far we have confined ourselves to the players and their wants and resources. Now we need to look at governments and what it is they do that interests players so much. Obviously governments do many things: They administer justice, educate citizens, protect the nation against foreign enemies, supervise economies, and provide social services. How they do each is usually a matter of dispute among those they serve. Landlords and *campesinos* disagree over the administration of justice in the countryside, secular and religious authorities dispute the content of education, and nearly everyone finds fault with the ways governments tax their people and spend their money. Conflict over public policy is the rule rather than the exception in Latin America, just as it is everywhere else.

There are many kinds of public policy that we could study in our effort to understand what is at stake in the game. Limits of space prohibit our looking at all of them, however. We will confine ourselves to only one, though one that dominates nearly every policy agenda in the region, namely, economic development policy. Few things stir more conflict or are more important to the well-being of a society than the way its wealth is created and distributed. This is in fact what much of the fighting in Latin America is about today, so in limiting ourselves to economic and social policy we need not worry about straying from the focal point of Latin American public policy.

Politics and economics

Economic affairs are not really all that mysterious. The direction of an economy, be it a socialist or a capitalist one, involves a few fundamental tasks. Imagine yourself a president who is asked to design an economic program for your country. What would you do?

No doubt you would start by determining what you had to work with, beginning with the structure and condition of the nation's economy. You would need to know as much as you can, for example, about the country's human capital: the size of your population, its age distribution, its literacy, skills, and mobility. You would also want to determine the condition of the nation's physical capital, taking into account energy supplies, existing technology, and the adequacy of transportation and telecommunications. If you governed in a country like the one described in Chapter 1, you would learn that half of your rapidly growing population was illiterate, that you were still very dependent on the export of a few commodities, that your physical stock was insufficient to service a larger, more industrialized economy, and that you already relied more than you preferred on foreign banks and multinational corporations to finance your development.

Next you would want to assess current economic conditions. How rapidly is the economy growing, what is the level of employment, what is the rate of inflation, and how is it affecting growth and development? What is the size of your foreign debt and when are your payments due? And what about your crops? Is production as great as you hoped and are prices in world markets what you expected? You cannot predict how each of these conditions will change in the days ahead, but you must try. Of course, no matter how accurate your predictions, you will be forced to adjust to unanticipated events. A doubling of the price of imported petroleum, for example, might require that you spend all of your foreign exchange on energy rather than on projects aimed at promoting economic growth. Or it might force you to borrow much more abroad than you had planned. In other words, no matter how sophisticated and well prepared your plans, you will sooner or later have to adapt them to conditions that you could not anticipate.

Third, and most important, you must design and execute a set of development policies. This requires your selection of concrete objectives, such as rates of economic growth, levels of prices, and the distribution of income, and your choosing the instruments that will achieve them, such as how much to tax and spend, how much currency to allow in circulation, whether to regulate private transactions, and whether to redistribute basic resources, like property, and so on.

In order to match instruments with objectives you need a model of the economy that tells you how it works. Economic models are abstractions that show how economic activities, in theory at least, are related to each other. Like a physical scientist who wants to know how much thrust it takes to send a missile into space, the economist needs to understand how much the government should spend to increase the level of employment. There is no single model for all situations, of course. A model is nothing more than a representation of how you think the economy works based on your experience, observation, and logic. If you are convinced that individual conduct in the marketplace sets prices, then you will create a model based on the logic of market behavior. In contrast, if you believe that the government can control the behavior of producers and consumers, you will design a model based on assumptions of central direction. Whichever you prefer, your model will be your guide when you select instruments to achieve your objectives.

A model does not guarantee success. Economic life is far too complex to be captured perfectly by any intellectual construct of reality. Moreover, people do not always behave as one might expect them to, since they can be affected by unanticipated events and unpredictable states of mind, for example, sudden fears or panic. And the data you need to understand prevailing conditions are seldom readily available in countries like the Latin American ones where elites traditionally have obstructed law enforcement by denying authorities the information they seek. Under such conditions economic policy is at best a mix of economic theory, political calculation, and guesswork.

The result of all of this effort is an economic strategy that will guide specific decisions. One of our goals as analysts of Latin American politics is to identify the strategies chosen by governments, determine their contrasting strengths and weaknesses, and then assess their effects on actual policies. To distinguish among strategies we will focus on four attributes: the theory of development that lies behind the strategy, its specific goals, the policies needed to achieve those goals, and its principal beneficiaries, that is, the players who gain the most from it (see Table 5.1).

First is the matter of development theory. Economic strategies begin with beliefs about the nature of economic development and its causes. Some beliefs are derived from familiar ideologies, for example, capitalism and socialism, and others from recent observation and experience. Such beliefs steer strategists in many directions, depending on their assumptions about the primary agents of economic and social change. For example, one theory might hold that the causes of underdevelopment are found within the nation's culture or natural endowments, whereas another might claim that it is due largely to the poli-

Table 5.1. *The dimensions of economic strategy*

Why:	Causes of underdevelopment
What:	Policy objectives
	Production
	Distribution
	Foreign trade
How:	Policy instruments
	Public–private mix
	National–foreign mix
	Coercion–spontaneity mix
For whom:	Beneficiaries
	Immediate
	Long-range

cies of governments. Obviously, promoting development would be much easier if the second view is correct than if the first is. Another crucial distinction is the importance one's theory places on foreign over domestic forces as determinants of the nation's economic performance. The more important and influential foreign trade, borrowing, and investment are to the nation's development, the less one can achieve with policies directed only at domestic transactions. The critical issue then becomes one of deciding if external forces can be altered at all and at what cost to current economic growth and development. In sum, development theory and economic strategy go hand in hand, and how well one does in achieving development goals will depend in part on how appropriate one's theory is to the situation at hand.

The second attribute involves the concrete objectives of the strategy. Three types of objectives are most prominent. The first involves *production*, or the goods and services desired and the rates at which the production of each should be increased. The second objective is *distribution*, or how products and wealth are to be divided among citizens, which is obviously a matter of controversy and great political importance. Either by accepting the existing distribution of wealth or by trying to change it, the strategist takes a stand on the distribution issue. It cannot be avoided. And third is the objective of *trade*, including the relationships desired with foreign economies. Foreign trade has been crucial to Latin American development until now; yet many Latin American leaders feel that it has not always worked to their advantage and that somehow old practices should be discarded or revised.

Third come the instruments the government employs to achieve its objectives. Governments have at their disposal a wide range of powers that they use to influence economic behavior. They may collect taxes and spend money, regulate the creation and circulation of money, set exchange rates, regulate imports and exports, operate industries, provide services, and control prices, wages, interest rates, and other economic activities. We will focus on three dimensions. First is the mix of *public and private* economic activities. We want to know how much of the economy is owned and operated by the state and how much is left to the private sector. The second dimension is the mix of *foreign and national* participation in the economy. Latin Americans continue to disagree about the appropriate role for foreign capital in their development. They have, however, begun experimenting with innovative ways of handling foreign investors, many of which we will discuss in our examination of individual countries in Part II. The third dimension is the mix of *coercion and spontaneity* permitted by the government. Essentially we want to know the extent to which the government tries to coerce private conduct in order to achieve its objectives.

Once the government decides how much of the economy it will leave to the private sector, it must still determine how free private entrepreneurs should be. Will it, for example, give entrepreneurs free rein within their domains, or will it set the wages they pay, the prices they charge, and the interest rates at which they borrow money? Whether to rely on the market mechanism to promote commerce and investment or to intervene in the marketplace is an unresolved issue that haunts capitalist economics.

Finally, there is the matter of who benefits economically and politically from each strategy. Most development policies greatly favor some players over others. It is important that we determine the effects of development policy not only in terms of its impact on the size of the gross national product or per capita income, but also in terms of its effect on the lives of all people. Players usually try to secure the adoption of policies favorable to them. Conversely, when policies threaten them, they often react, sometimes violently, against the officials responsible. Consequently, when we examine the beneficiaries of development policy we not only want to know what they have gained or lost, but also how they responded to policy politically and how their actions affected the government's ability to achieve its objectives.

Economic development strategies

Latin American leaders did not suddenly discover four or five decades ago that economic development was desirable. Nor did it finally dawn on them that they could actually take steps to promote economic growth. Most of the region's economies have a long history of respectable, if uneven, economic growth. Moreover, governments always made the creation of wealth one of their concerns. What changed after 1930 was not the notion of economic development as a desirable objective, but attitudes about what economic development really meant and the ways to achieve it. Where a single, seldom-questioned strategy had held sway since colonial times, new ideas were introduced after 1930 to challenge the old ways of doing things.

An understanding of the old way is necessary in order to comprehend why new strategies were needed and why they were so fiercely resisted by vested interests. A brief description of the traditional mode of development was given in Chapter 1. It was known as the primary product export strategy. Based on the belief that it was advantageous for Latin Americans to devote themselves to the production and export of agricultural commodities and minerals, the strategy accepted an international division of labor in which Latin America supplied raw materials to Europe and North America in exchange for manufactured goods, and foreign investors financed the construction of power plants, port facilities, and railroads and operated the shipping lines that transported goods to and from the region.

The arrangement brought great wealth to those at the top, and economic growth accelerated after 1880 in most countries as the production of livestock, grain, coffee, sugar, and bananas as well as the extraction of nitrates, copper, gold, silver, and, later, petroleum were increased to meet foreign demand. Meanwhile, populations grew, local commerce increased, and confidence in the system was fortified, at least among the elites. But it was actually a more vulnerable and insecure system than it seemed at the time. Essentially, too many countries relied on too few commodities for their growth. Prices and demand from abroad often rose and fell suddenly, dragging the entire economy up one time and down the next. Moreover, the ability of

Latin Americans to meet demand was undercut now and then by droughts, pests, and other natural disasters. It is no wonder that some people questioned the viability of the system early on. Yet, too much was at stake to hastily abandon it. Powerful players within the region and abroad had invested a great deal in it, and they were not about to give up their investments under the pressure of occasional breakdowns in trade.

When a change did come, it came gradually, induced by the shock of the 1929 world depression and the interruption of trade during World War II. New ideas were plentiful, and eventually they gave birth to three new development strategies that would compete intensely for influence over policy for years to come. Two were capitalist in nature and the third was socialist. Both of the capitalist strategies recognized that the golden years of the primary product export strategy were over. The first of them, "progressive modernization," stressed the need to promote industrialization, combining the efforts of the public and private sectors, and to redistribute property from landowners to *campesinos* in order to bring the poor into a productive modern economy. The second capitalist strategy, called "conservative modernization," was authored by critics of the progressive approach who claimed that the redistribution of wealth and property was incompatible with the stimulation of industrialization in the capitalistic economy; instead they advocated programs that favored investors, both national and foreign, intent on raising production. According to this view, wealth would eventually trickle down to the masses as production and employment rose. The third, or "revolutionary," strategy rejected capitalist economics entirely, convinced that private investors could meet neither the production nor the welfare needs of Latin Americans. Instead of promoting entrepreneurial initiatives, the socialists assigned the state the primary responsibility for allocating the nation's resources and building an egalitarian society.

Progressive modernization

Progressive modernization began in the 1940s as a critique of the primary product export economy and the elitist political system associated with it. Its authors were frustrated by dependence on foreigners, widespread poverty, and economic instability. What began as little more than a depression-inspired desire for more security gradually matured into a new and significant approach to the region's problems. It took its inspiration from many sources, including the Mexican Revolution, the American New Deal, the Catholic social philosophy, but none was more important than the doctrine of "structuralism" popularized by the United Nations Economic Commission for Latin America (ECLA), an organization created in 1949 to promote the region's development.

The structuralists, as their name implies, were concerned with the economic and social structures that impeded the region's development. Foremost in their thinking was the obvious vulnerability of Latin American countries to erratic prices for exports and their victimization by the adverse terms of trade between their primary product exports and the industrial goods they imported from abroad. The structuralists reasoned that Latin Americans had been unfairly treated in their trade relations with the industrial nations and would continue to suffer until their dependence on foreign trade was reduced. They were also disturbed by the maldistribution of income within Latin American societies and how poverty restricted domestic consumption. Surveying their economies in the 1940s and 1950s, they saw a rural sector polarized between a minority of large holdings and millions of excessively small ones, an emerging but weak industrial sector, and a working class that could not afford to consume the goods produced in national factories. The same economic structures that elites had accepted as natural the structuralists saw as obstacles to long-range development and social justice. The only way to progress, they concluded, was to replace the old structures with more productive and equitable new ones.

Progressive modernization contains an important political dimension as well. Only the most naive could ignore the fact that any attempt to reform traditional institutions would be intensely resisted by the well-entrenched elite that had lived off them. Despite their technical sophistication, the proponents of progressive modernization were initially no match for the much more powerful elite. What they needed, they realized, was a larger following and the toleration of the military if they were to win their struggle against the defenders of the status quo. Eventually they turned for support to the only place they could – to laborers and peasants. The cooperation of the former was essential to the expansion of industrial production and consumption; the peasants were needed to improve the rural economy. Moreover, both groups offered progressive modernizers a broad political base that might match the power of the ruling elite and its allies in the military.

In contrast to the traditional elite, which favored production over distribution objectives, those inspired by the structuralist critique of the Latin American condition believed that they could achieve both types of objectives simultaneously. Not only were the two thought to be compatible, but they were absolutely essential to each other. The structuralists were convinced that low rates of growth and excessive vulnerability were caused not just by a shortage of capital, but also by the maldistribution of property and income that had led to inefficient enterprises and insufficient consumption. Therefore, to increase production over the long haul, economic resources had to be redistributed to those who would employ them productively, and the size of the national market had to be expanded by including more citizens, both rural and urban, as consumers in the modern economy.

At the heart of the progressive modernizers' program is rural reform. The traditional system of landownership lies at the root of the region's underdevelopment. In the 1950s there still remained many large landholdings throughout the countryside, as well as millions of small farmers and landless peasants. Not only was rural output inadequate, but there remained intact a rural social structure that prevented the integration of the rural masses into the modern economy. It was imperative, therefore, that the government break up large estates, encourage more efficient land utilization, and bring the rural poor into the marketplace as producers and consumers. This could be done, it seemed clear, through a program of land reform that redistributed property from the larger *latifundios* to peasant farmers and then transformed the latter into efficient producers through education, technical assistance, and the introduction of modern farm practices. Land redistribution without the improvement of production techniques would obviously come to naught, for even though it might satisfy the immediate demands of land-hungry peasants, it would neither increase rural output nor bring peasants into the modern economy. Finally, there was a need to diversify commodity production if the region were to escape its dependence on only a few farm products. As long as its fate was tied to a few crops, stable economic growth would be unattainable; however, through a comprehensive diversification program, greater protection against shifting world prices could be secured and a steady flow of foreign exchange assured.

Rural reform is necessary to economic development, but it is not by itself sufficient, according to the proponents of progressive modernization. Also needed is a comprehensive program of industrialization. Depression and war had taught a generation of Latin Americans that they could no longer rely primarily on the production of commodity exports for their livelihood. The lesson was clear: Instead of selling commodities in order to purchase consumer goods abroad, Latin Americans should manufacture their own goods. Some industrialization had begun spontaneously after the 1929 depression cut off Latin America from its foreign supplies, but that was not enough according to the progressive modernizers. Much more had to be done to build a strong, well-integrated industrial economy.

The third objective of progressive modernization is the reduction of Latin America's dependence on the industrial nations. The region's disadvantageous relationship with its trading partners had originally provoked the structuralist critique of traditionalism. To overcome their excessive dependence they sought to strengthen their bargaining power and increase their margin of choice by diversifying their economies, using industrial development and agricultural modernization. They did not reject the idea of foreign trade but only sought to free themselves from excessive reliance on it.

It is one thing to identify the causes of underdevelopment and set some reformist policy objectives, but quite another to execute them in the face of well-entrenched traditions and vested interests that staunchly defend the status quo. Exceptional skill, determination, and good timing, along with ample technical expertise, are required to make progressive modernization work. The reorganization of rural life, the modernization of farming, and the introduction of new crops cannot be achieved without abandoning habits that have been nurtured for decades. Nor can heavy industries be built without careful planning, substantial managerial talent, and the expenditure of large sums of money. But despite the enormous task they set for themselves, the proponents of progressive modernization were convinced they could devise the instruments they needed to get the job done. By adapting policies that had succeeded in Europe, Mexico, and elsewhere to their local situations, they believed that they could generate solutions to the problems at hand.

The government has to exercise substantial power for progressive modernization to work. No longer can public officials leave economic matters to the private sector alone. Structural change and technological innovation require firm leadership, and the state is the only institution powerful enough to assume that role. Government planners must design development programs and coordinate the activities of private industries through the use of incentives and regulations. To assist in the management of economic affairs, the government must also nationalize public utilities and strategic industries, like minerals, iron, and steel. And in those sectors where private enterprise is permitted the state needs to promote investment using low-interest loans and joint public–private ventures.

In the rural sector the state must redistribute property, but it should do so in an orderly way so as not to upset production. Land can be purchased with cash payments or government bonds at market prices or declared tax value, depending on what the government can afford. Land reform must be accompanied by easy credit and subsidized technology in order to increase production. Moreover, all government policies should be directed at the ultimate objective of redistributing income to the rural and urban poor. Agrarian reform and expanded industrial employment will go a long way toward this end, but the government, through its housing, educational, and health programs, must also do a great deal. A decent wage should be guaranteed all workers, and if necessary, food prices should be subsidized.

In the field of foreign economic relations two important policy innovations are encouraged. One is regional economic integration. It is obvious that national markets are too small in most countries to generate large-scale industries. Mass production is impossible as long as domestic markets include only 20 to 30 percent of the country's population and will increase very gradually even with agrarian reform. Through the missionary efforts of the economists at ECLA, who had closely studied the European Common Market in the 1950s, a way was found to combine national markets into large regional ones able to support major industries. Called "regional economic integration," it required that each country agree to specialize in certain products, reduce its tariffs on goods produced within the region, and coordinate its foreign exchange policies with those of other members.

The second innovation is the use of international commodity agreements to regulate the supply and price of raw product exports. The idea of commodity agreements among producer and consumer nations had circulated for a long time, but it was under the leadership of the proponents of progressive modernization that the idea became an integral part of a Latin American development strategy. Today, agreements apply to many commodities, the most successful being the OPEC (Organization of Petroleum Exporting Countries) agreement on petroleum, which was originally established in the 1960s under the leadership of the Venezuelan minister of petroleum and mines.

The most perplexing issue facing the advocates of progressive modernization is how to mix control with spontaneity in the execution of their programs. As proponents of structural change and economic reform, they know that they must assert their authority over those who would obstruct them. On the other hand, their preference for democratic politics and toleration of private enterprise make them reluctant to use heavy-handed tactics against their enemies. A good example of their ambivalence is their implementation of agrarian reform. Clearly, in order to succeed land reform must confront and overcome the power exercised by the rural elite. The mere passage of legislation, assuming the government progresses that far, does not guarantee compliance with the new reforms. Landowners are skilled at forestalling government attempts to deprive them of their property. Consequently, agrarian reform can seldom be implemented without the use of some force by the state. Yet, extreme measures aimed at repressing reform's opponents risk undermining constitutional processes and provoking violent reactions leading to disorder. There is no easy escape from the coercion–spontaneity dilemma faced by progressive modernizers, for if they fail to use sufficient force, their programs may wither and die, but if they use too much, they may invite violent resistance and disappoint their more democratic followers. Failure to resolve the dilemma swiftly poses one of the biggest threats to the success of progressive modernization.

Who benefits from progressive modernization? In theory, the marginal rural producers and urban laborers stand to gain the most, for they will be freed from oppressive traditional economic institutions. But in practice their benefits will come slowly; agrarian reform, industrialization, and regional integration cannot be achieved overnight, but require sustained effort for several years to spread their benefits widely. During the strategy's initial phase, the state and its many agencies stand to gain most. Regulatory agencies will be increased, new state enterprises added, and planning operations expanded. Next in line come the industrialists who benefit from the state's promotion of industrialization. Labor unions, especially when they are supported by the ruling party, will also gain in power and wealth. So will the professionals in the middle sectors, who stand to profit from economic growth generally as well as from the expansion of the state. Eventually peasants may be incorporated into the mainstream of the nation's economic life, though much more slowly than any other group. Less noticed among the strategy's beneficiaries are the foreign investors who are tolerated under the progressive rules of the game. Though some will lose from nationalization, many others, especially in high-technology fields, stand to gain a great deal as the consumption of their products rises with economic growth. Technically trained military officers are also among the less obvious beneficiaries since they will create their own industries in order to share in the bounties of industrialization or be assigned managerial positions in government enterprises.

The last and most obvious question is: Why, if progressive modernization spreads its benefits so widely, has it not succeeded in transforming the entire region during the past three decades? We will explore this question in Chapter 7 when we assess the strategy's application in Chile and Venezuela. Yet, even before we look to the real world for answers, some problems must be mentioned.

First, there is the question of whether the strategy can work in countries where widespread agreement on the political rules is lacking. Its proponents argue that the redistributive character of the strategy makes it a perfect means for building new faith in government and laying the foundations for authority founded on popular support. But even if this is true in theory, achieving it in the face of well-entrenched opposition is seldom as easy as it seems. Second, progressive modernization carries a very high price, which Latin American governments may not be able to pay on their own. The wealth confiscated from the economic elite is seldom sufficient to cover the costs of the government's development projects. The government must borrow abroad, but that may only lead to a large foreign debt burden and the kind of financial dependence the government had hoped to escape. Last, there is the problem of fulfilling promises to workers and peasants without threatening the well-being of middle-sector supporters. If the government cannot satisfy all of them simultaneously, political conflicts may be provoked that will divide its coalition and undermine its authority.

Conservative modernization

The progressive modernization strategy was heavily criticized from its inception. Naturally, the defenders of the old order denounced it, though seldom to great effect since spontaneous industrialization had already undermined the old order. Eventually another type of critic emerged, one who shared the progressives' desire for industrialization and rural modernization but was opposed to their reformist methods. Instead of making capitalism more productive, these critics argued, social and economic reform had done the opposite by undermining entrepreneurial confidence and misallocating the nation's resources. Moreover, reform had raised popular hopes that it could not satisfy, causing many people to lose faith in it.

Starting from the unexamined premise that capitalist institutions offer the surest route to economic growth, the advocates of conservative modernization believe that the government should do all that it can to stimulate investment and economic modernization. They point out that entrepreneurs are unresponsive in an environment where heavy-handed government control prevails. What is needed instead are policies that encourage private initiative. Investors, industrialists, and commercial farmers must be favored by government policies. Demagogic politics, expensive social programs, and false expectations must give way to strong and stable political rule dedicated first and foremost to restoring the confidence of private entrepreneurs.

The modernity of the strategy lies in its objectives. It has no interest in a retreat to the traditional single-commodity economics of the past, but wants to pursue rapid industrial growth and to increase agricultural exports through the use of large, modern farms. It denies that the redistribution of property and wealth from the rich to the poor is necessary to promote economic development. On the contrary, if economic growth is to be achieved, resources must be concentrated in the hands of investors who will put them to good use in building a modern economy. If there is to be any redistribution, it should be done in the marketplace and not by the deliberate efforts of government bureaucrats. For the time being, social reform should be postponed and income disparities tolerated. Accumulation, not redistribution, is its primary short-term objective because the deliberate transfer of income to the poorer classes drains the economy of its vital resources and hinders productive investment. The benefits of growth will reach the poor, but only gradually, as new workers are absorbed into the expanding industrial economy.

In its choice of policy instruments conservative modernization favors a laissez-faire, market-oriented approach except in those sectors where only the state is capable of promoting development. Where private investment is inadequate or where government leadership is required, such as in the development of energy supplies, utilities, and heavy industry, public enterprises are appropriate. In essence, conservative modernization is a kind of conspiracy between state capitalists and private capitalists, each needing the other in order to achieve their objectives.

Foreign investment is not a pressing issue for conservative modernization. Foreigners are welcome as long as their efforts contribute to growth objectives. Foreign trade must be encouraged and expanded through the diversification of agricultural products and, where possible, the addition of industrial exports. But instead of trying to promote higher rural production by redistributing land to *campesinos*, the government should help finance the investments of modern farmers. Easier credit, guaranteed prices, better storage facilities, and easier marketing arrangements should be used to help farmers who are already prepared to produce on a large scale. If they succeed, the country will reap the foreign exchange it needs to finance its industrialization program without heavy borrowing abroad.

Underlying all conservative modernization's proposals is an important political requirement: To succeed, its unpopular measures need to be enforced by a strong government. Its policies will exact high social costs and provoke discontent. Labor unions, peasant organizations, and mass-based political parties will not stand by idly while the benefits of economic growth are monopolized by entrepreneurial and bureaucratic elites. The proponents of conservative modernization recognize this and are prepared to take harsh actions to deal with resistance. They see an important relationship between political and economic life, but unlike the progressive modernizers, who perceive politics as the means for reforming the economy, conservative modernizers believe politics, especially the competitive variety, is an obstacle to economic progress. It is the intervention of the state in the marketplace in order to bolster the popularity of politicians among urban masses that has distorted the market mechanism and undermined entrepreneurial confidence, they argue. Thus politics, as practiced by many popular Latin American leaders, threatens capitalist economic development. To restore steady growth, competitive politics may have to be suspended and the authority of the state used against recalcitrant labor unions and party politicians.

The immediate beneficiary of conservative modernization is the investor, both foreign and national, in agriculture, commerce, or industry. Obviously the multinational corporation is the best prepared to take advantage of the strategy, though many national investors will gain as well. Less apparent among those it favors is the new generation of technocrats, and, in some places, the military officers, who design and execute development policy. They will be joined in the winner's circle by the professionals and white-collar workers who staff growing public and private enterprises. Left out in the short run are the *campesinos*, who will be confined to their small plots or continue to work as rural laborers on commercial farms, and urban laborers, who will be forced to accept lower income in order to help finance capital investment.

Like all development strategies, conservative modernization raises many unanswered questions about its ability to achieve its objectives. Few would deny that capital must be accumulated in order to promote economic growth. Nor is there much doubt that a government can stimulate entrepreneurial investment by holding down wages and opening doors to multinational corporations. Less certain is how long it can deny well-organized urban laborers the gains they have come to expect in modernizing societies. Sooner or later the government will have to seek working-class acceptance if it is not to survive on repression alone. And when it does, it may have to pay a high price for its past neglect of the masses in the form of wage increases and social expenditures that may undermine the confidence of conservative entrepreneurs. Another question is: How long can the government tolerate increased dependence on foreigners? Even though the immediate economic benefits of foreign investment may be great, the loss of national control over critical economic activities may prove costly, especially if it deprives national authorities of freedom to chart their own course. A third problem concerns the "trickle-down" effect. Critics of conservative modernization argue that it leads to enclave capitalism rather than expanding affluence. With profits being repatriated abroad and social programs in suspension, the benefits of economic growth trickle down to the masses at an appallingly slow rate, if at all,

thereby doing little to alleviate widespread poverty. Finally, there is
the question of legitimizing a government that chooses conservative
modernization. Undoubtedly, the strategy will generate strong support from the 10 to 30 percent of the population that profits immediately from it. But what about those who are left out? How long can
the government survive in the face of their opposition? Force, intimidation, and public apathy will facilitate the government's task, but
they will not eliminate the need to expend much energy and valuable
resources on protecting the government from its subjects.

Revolutionary economics

What do the two strategies we have just examined have in common?
According to their advocates, very little; they are two quite different
ways of solving the development problem. There is, however, a third
school of thought that says that they are not as far apart as they claim.

Despite their disagreements over objectives and instruments, both
progressive and conservative modernization strive to create a society
in which public authorities and private entrepreneurs jointly manage
the economy. They are in essence merely two ways of organizing
the capitalist economic system to meet the needs of Latin Americans.
But what Latin America needs, say the proponents of this third
approach, is not capitalism but revolutionary socialism. Latin American underdevelopment, they claim, is not caused by a shortage of
resources or by misguided policies, but by capitalism itself and the
system of exploitation inherent in it. Neither progressive nor conservative modernization can overcome poverty and underdevelopment
because both try to extend the life of capitalism. Only through a
revolutionary effort to seize public authority and reconstruct society
can Latin America be saved from the dual evils of imperialism and
capitalist exploitation. The revolutionary strategy is dedicated to that
end.

What revolutionaries see when they examine their society is not the
progress evidenced by modern airports, high-rise office buildings, and
cities congested with automobiles and buses, but the dehumanization
and alienation of the Latin American masses. They are victims not
only of traditional institutions like the *latifundio*, but of the modern
factory as well. Modernization, if allowed to take the capitalist form,
will do little to alleviate this condition. Private property, competition,

and the pursuit of narrow self-interests – the motivating forces of capitalism – cannot eliminate poverty and exploitation. Only through the reconstruction of society around the principles of equality and community can underdevelopment and poverty be overcome. Revolutionaries offer their fellow citizens the vision of a world in which the squalid present is replaced by a more just future, one that appeals especially to those who are disillusioned with reform and appalled by the inequities of conservative modernization.

Revolutionaries are more concerned with the distribution of wealth than with its creation, per se. This does not mean that they ignore production, for only the most naive revolutionaries believe that prosperity automatically follows the destruction of capitalism. But once produced, goods must be used to meet the needs of all citizens rather than only some of them. The entire nation should be fed, clothed, and educated in an egalitarian manner. Accordingly, all property has to be socialized and all wages equalized, ending class distinctions once and for all. Once placed in a state of equality, citizens will labor for the good of all rather than personal gain, according to the revolutionary strategy.

The country's external economic relations also have to be changed drastically. Revolutionaries believe that under capitalism resources are siphoned from Latin America by the industrialized nations. The only way to change that is to break the ties that bind the developed and underdeveloped economies together. One should begin with the eviction of the representatives of metropolitan capitalism from the country and the severing of trade relations with those who have exploited the nation in the past. Only after this objective has been achieved can the socialist economy be launched. Naturally there are costs to be paid for the sudden loss of one's trading partners, and the costs are especially high if in the past the country relied heavily on foreign trade and the importation of capital from abroad. But revolutionaries have little choice but to pay it if they are to gain the power of self-determination that they so desperately want.

To create the socialist society, radical instruments are needed. The first is the transformation of the state from the regulator of private economic affairs to the owner of the means of production. Nearly all private property must be expropriated by the state and reallocated to cooperative or state-run production units. The rate of transfer will vary depending on how fast the state can assume its new responsibilities and overcome counterrevolutionary forces. Second, central planning must be instituted to manage the newly nationalized economy. The implementation of development plans is still a matter of some dispute among revolutionaries. Some, especially those who emphasize distribution, favor decentralization and virtual autonomy for local production units; others, most often bureaucrats who place highest priority on the expansion of production, prefer firm central control over all economic processes. And third, during the initial phases of the revolution, a revolutionary elite must assume full control over the nation's economic and political reconstruction. Loyal to the masses they represent, they must make and enforce policies aimed at the fulfillment of revolutionary objectives. They should be guided by revolutionary ideology and their understanding of the needs of the masses rather than by their individual interests or the demands of separate players.

There is no mystery about the means revolutionary socialism uses to free the nation from imperialism. Foreign properties are expropriated and all trade relations reorganized according to principles set down by the new authorities. Of course, to desire economic autonomy is one thing; to achieve it is something else. Few nations possess all the raw materials or produce all the consumer goods they require. Sooner or later they will either trade with other nations in order to meet their needs or do without some basic materials. If revolutionaries choose complete autonomy, they initially must accept a lower standard of living and severe constraints on national development; if they choose to retain ties to some other nations, they must either select trading partners who share their ideology and views of equity or turn once again to the capitalist nations, though hopefully on more favorable terms than before. The same is true when it comes to financial assistance and foreign technology. As much as possible they seek out nations that support their revolution, reasoning that if they must be dependent on anyone, it should at least be an ally in the revolutionary cause rather than someone who desires the restoration of capitalism.

It might at first appear that revolutionaries handle the question of mixing control and spontaneity with ease. Their goal is social reconstruction and they can leave nothing to chance, so whenever necessary they resort to controls without hesitation. Attitudes, institutions, and work habits must be changed, political loyalties transformed, and a new order quickly established. And counterrevolutionaries have to be deterred and made to respect the strength of the new regime. None of these objectives can be accomplished without the use of force. But what happens after the transition to socialism is achieved? Will real power be turned over to the people as promised? There is no simple formula. Revolutionaries live with a dilemma created by their need to use force to create a new society of free people. Their solution often is not to choose between control and spontaneity, but to try to combine them in a special way. The key is the ideological reeducation of the masses. If they can be taught to follow the community ethic of socialism, control will eventually become unnecessary. Individuals will conform not to government power but to their belief in a shared ideology. Spontaneity will be redefined to include all behavior consistent with the ideology. Of course, reeducation of the population, so compelling in theory, is not easily achieved in practice. Values and habits built up and reinforced during centuries of Iberian rule and decades under capitalism do not yield quickly to a new ethic that is centrally imposed. Resistance and counterrevolutionary acts may persist for some time, requiring the constant use of force by central authorities. The greatest danger is that in their determination to transform society revolutionaries will lose sight of their ultimate objectives and never relinquish central control for fear of losing power altogether.

Who benefits from the revolution? Ideally, the peasants and laborers who were exploited under capitalism have the most to gain. The elimination of the *latifundista*, commercial farmer, and factory owner should benefit the masses. So too should their admission to schools and hospitals that previously excluded them. But how rapidly will the condition of the poor be improved under socialism? The rate of redistribution depends primarily on how much of its resources the government allocates to capital accumulation and how much it reserves for social welfare. If it chooses to emphasize capital accumulation, as it has in some socialist nations such as the Soviet Union, the masses will have to wait until substantial economic development has been achieved before their condition can be improved significantly. On the other hand, an emphasis on social services may immediately advance their welfare, but at the expense of rapid economic growth. In either case, however, it is the new revolutionary elite that profits the most at the outset of the socialist revolution. Its members gain status, power, and personal comfort from their positions of leadership. Only gradually, as the economy develops and the supply of goods increases, will the masses gain more access to important though very basic services.

The losers under revolutionism are obvious. Landowners, industrialists, merchants, bankers, foreign investors – all members of the capitalist elite – are deprived of their property and power. Some will survive longer than others depending on how much the revolution temporarily requires their services, but eventually nearly all will go. There is no way their continued existence can be tolerated in a society dedicated to egalitarianism and central direction. Survival of a large private sector means the revolution has failed, so only by eliminating it can revolutionaries demonstrate that they have achieved their objectives. Among the other losers are many in the middle sectors who refuse to live by the socialistic ethic, the prerevolutionary military, and labor leaders who are replaced by others more loyal to the revolutionary elite.

Despite its obvious appeal to anyone frustrated by the failures of other strategies to cure Latin America's ills, revolutionary socialism is no easier to implement than other strategies. In fact, because it is more ambitious it faces enormous obstacles. First, the eviction of foreign and domestic investors exacts a high price in the loss of liquid capital and managerial talent. When the revolutionary regime deprives entrepreneurs of their property, it alienates many of the professionals and technicians who depend on the entrepreneurs for their livelihood; although some join the new regime, many flee in search of better opportunities elsewhere, denying the new government their talents. Second, in executing radical social change, revolutionaries risk making very large mistakes. The sudden transformation of the rural sector, for example, may lead to a breakdown in agricultural production, and new industrial organizations may prove inefficient on a large scale. Revolutionaries must take chances if they are to achieve their objectives, but when they err, they often do so on a grand scale and entire programs may have to be abandoned, setting back the revolution by months or years.

It is also apparent that the creation of a revolutionary regime does not by itself guarantee that the new programs will be implemented. To succeed, the revolution must penetrate deeply into society and transform the attitudes and values of citizens. An elaborate and well-organized bureaucracy must impose its will on areas of life that were previously ignored by public authorities. In the larger Latin American states an immense effort would be needed to reach remote areas and bring their isolated populations under the central government's control. And finally, revolutionaries must continually grapple with the growth–equity dilemma. On the one hand, they wish to spread wealth throughout society in order to achieve equality. On the other, they recognize that they have to concentrate their resources in order to build solid foundations for sustainable economic growth. The problem is especially troublesome for revolutionaries because, unlike conservative modernizers, they are committed, in theory at least, to equality. Seldom, however, can they afford to sacrifice their economic growth objectives to achieve it.

Dependent development

Of all the issues addressed by these strategies none has been a source of more concern and frustration than the matter of dealing with an international economy over which Latin Americans have no control. And few problems have been given more attention and stirred more controversy among scholars in recent times than this international one. Before going on, a closer look at it is merited. As we have seen, Latin America began its economic development as an extension of Spain and Portugal. What the colonies produced and what they received in payment for their goods were determined by authorities in the mother countries. After Independence the region's foreign markets grew and became more diverse, but the reliance of Latin Americans on consumers and investors abroad changed little. Reducing their heavy reliance on primary product exports and foreign investment became an objective of many Latin American governments after World War II. But has Latin America actually gained more economic independence as a result of such efforts, or is the region as subordinate and vulnerable today as it was five decades ago? Answering these questions has been a preoccupation of Latin American social scientists for some time, and their conclusions are especially relevant to understanding the region's plight.

Dissatisfied with the orthodox theory of modernization popular in Europe and the United States after World War II, Latin Americans went on the attack. The orthodox theory assumed that the process of modernization involved a transition from one way of life to another. Essentially, it held that in order to modernize the developing nations had to emulate the experiences of the industrial nations, combining technological modernization with the acquisition of values and beliefs appropriate to operating in an industrial society. As people changed and the use of modern technology grew, production could be expanded and mass consumption eventually achieved. In other words, only by replacing the traditional ways with the rational, acquisitive values of Western industrial society could Latin America modernize.

Latin Americans criticized this view as misconceived and contradicted by their experience. Inspired by several sources, including the work of Raul Prebisch and his colleagues at ECLA, as well as some Marxist thought, they argued that modernization theory ignored conditions that made Latin America very different from the industrialized nations when they began their industrialization. In fact, it was the latter's success and consequent domination of the world economy that made the Latin American condition so different. Rather than stress changes in values as a means to modernity, the student of development should begin with the distribution of power internationally, trying to determine how a nation's place in the international structure has affected its economic development.

This "dependency" view of Latin American development has many authors and it comes in several forms, but it begins with the notion that domestic and international economic structures are inseparable. Consequently, to understand a nation's development one must constantly focus on the relationship between the nation and the international system of which it is a part. If, for example, we examine Latin American development historically, we will not discover a transformation of values leading to affluent societies, but a series of economic changes structurally linked to changes in the international economy. Technological and financial resources have been virtually monopolized by the industrial nations, placing Latin Americans in a subordinate position by making their economies dependent on the capitalist industrialized ones. The incredible foreign debt burdens accumulated by Mexico, Brazil, and Argentina in the early 1980s and the financial crises that arose in each country are recent examples of this condition. This is what one would expect in nations who want to develop rapidly but are part of an international economy that places a high price on the resources they need to do so.

The consequences of dependent development are apparent in a nation's politics as well as its economics, according to the dependency view. Officials who want to develop their nation must create governments that assure that the needs of those who promote development

Table 5.2. *Economic strategies compared*

Strategy	Causes of underdevelopment	Objectives	Instruments	Beneficiaries
Progressive modernization	Concentration of rural land Insufficient industrialization Exclusion of masses from modern economy	Increased rural and industrial production Progressive income redistribution Integration of masses into modern economy Greater economic autonomy	Land reform Industrialization Nationalization of critical enterprises Balance between state power and liberty	State bureaucracy Urban middle sectors Industrialists Organized labor Peasants
Conservative modernization	Misguided nationalism Progressive income-redistribution policies Excessive regulation of private entrepreneurs	Increased rural and industrial production Closer ties to international economy	Assistance for commercial farmers Promotion of large industries Welcome of foreign investors and traders Imposition of firm political order	Foreign investors Industrialists Commercial farmers Exporters Urban middle sectors

Revolutionism	Capitalism Imperialism	Redistribution of political power Redistribution of property and income Increased production	Nationalization of private property Equalization of income Severance of trade with capitalist nations Mass ideology and organization	Revolutionary elite Urban labor Peasants

are met. If the domestic process is subordinated to an international one, then governments must adapt themselves to this condition. Take the case of Brazil. By choosing to promote economic growth with substantial foreign investment by multinational corporations, and according to the rules of the international marketplace, Brazilian officials had to create a state apparatus able to maintain the kind of political order required to assure a stable relationship between multinational enterprises, large domestic industries, and the Brazilian state. When civilians proved incapable of assuring such stability, the military did so in 1964. From this perspective, military rule in Brazil was not the result of the personal ambitions of military officers or animosities between officers and civilians, but simply a logical adjustment to the requirements of the Brazilian type of dependent development.

Of course, there are limits. Advocates of the dependency view admit that not all domestic conditions are the direct products of international ones, nor is domestic change impossible without external changes. The point of the dependency view is simply that in order to understand Latin American economic and political history, we must see it within the larger international structure of which it is a subordinate part.

What then is the significance of the dependency argument? The answer depends, of course, on how you wish to use it. If it is regarded only as another interpretation of history, as many of its authors intended, then it is primarily a matter for academic scrutiny. But if, on the other hand, one wishes to use it to inform policy choices, as some do, then its purpose becomes quite different, for not only is it a way of explaining the Latin American condition but also a possible source of advice about what has to be changed in order to strengthen the region's economies and reorganize their politics. If, for example, one believes that economic dependence retards a country's development, keeps the oligarchy in power, or reinforces a regressive distribution of wealth, then it is the structure of dependence that must be attacked.

In their own elementary way this is what the advocates of the progressive modernization strategy thought they were doing. Sharing some of the same intellectual roots as the dependency view, the strategy's solution to the problem was the narrow economic one of rapid industrialization to reduce reliance on commodity exports and manufactured imports. But, as we shall learn in Part II, instead of reducing dependence significantly, industrialization only altered its form.

The revolutionary socialists not surprisingly claim that the dependency view does not go far enough in portraying the industrial nations' domination over Latin America. They argue that Latin America is the victim of imperialism, a deliberate effort by capitalist nations and multinational corporations to control the economies of the region. The way to deal with imperialism is not with accelerated industrialization, but by withdrawing from the capitalist world economy and, if necessary, reentering it later on one's own terms.

The proponents of conservative modernization, in contrast, do not concern themselves with dependency. Instead, they argue that the dependency notion is irrelevant to policy making. The concept may supply some emotional gratification to frustrated reformers and revolutionaries, but it cannot serve as a guide to policy in today's world. Latin America has no choice but to live by the rules of the international capitalist economy. Self-sufficiency is impossible and increasing one's clout in the international economy is unlikely, except in unusual cases like OPEC. So instead of worrying about dependence, they tell us, Latin Americans have no choice but to play by the existing rules of the international economy regardless of how frustrating it might be.

Clearly the debate over dependency among development strategists is a profound one that cannot be resolved to the satisfaction of all parties. But whatever one's position on matters of strategy, one fact is inescapable, namely, that there is no easy way for Latin America. The region's history, geography, and place in the world economy have denied its nations the opportunity to copy the experiences of the affluent in the industrialized nations of Western Europe and North America. If they are to develop economically, their models will have to be adapted to their own realities.

The population issue

Economic growth is necessary not only to satisfy Latin Americans' desires for a better life, but also to feed future generations, who will be more numerous than their parents and grandparents. Population growth rates accelerated after 1940, reaching a peak in the 1960s. Between 1960 and 1970 the annual average growth rate for the region was 2.8 percent, with highs of 3.8 percent in Mexico and 3.5 percent in El Salvador. During the following decade the rate fell to 2.6 percent, and it appears that it will continue to decline slowly in the

future. Yet because of the relatively large size of the younger populations, the effect of the decline in growth rates will not be felt for some
time. A population growing at a rate of 3.5 percent doubles in twenty
years; one increasing by 2.5 percent annually will double in twenty-
eight years. Assuming that the birthrate continues to decline slowly,
it is estimated that the Latin American population (now at 370 million) will reach 600 million by the year 2000. The effects have been
apparent for some time, especially in the disproportionate 4.2 percent
annual increase in urban populations. Whereas 50 percent of the region's people lived in urban areas in 1960, 66 percent do today. Mexico City alone, one of the fastest growing cities in the world, will be
inhabited by 30 million people by the end of this century.

Long ignored, population growth became a major public policy
issue throughout the region during the 1970s. All governments began
to address it in some fashion, though their dedication to its reduction
varies a great deal. In some countries, like Mexico, clinics were
opened and an estimated 40 percent of Mexican women under the age
of 44 were thought to practice some type of family planning. But
resistance to population policy, or at least some of its methods, remains strong. One of the most entrenched sources of opposition is the
hierarchy of the Roman Catholic church. The church's influence is
much greater among the poor than the more affluent, however. Education and economic self-interest, not the teachings of the church,
seem to guide the behavior of middle-class Latin Americans whose
family size is smaller than the national average.

Another source of opposition is nationalist politicians who, though
not always opposed to family planning per se, suspect the motives of
the population planners sent to their countries by international and
foreign agencies. Foreign advisers come, they insist, because of fear
that a larger Third World population will consume the resources the
industrial nations want for themselves. The redistribution of wealth
and resources from the rich countries to the poorer ones and not
population control is the answer, they claim. However, as it becomes
evident that no one gains from rapid growth, the nationalist argument
has fewer takers than it did a decade ago.

But even if religious and political opposition to birth control were
overcome, other obstacles would persist. The greatest impediment of
all is poverty. In contrast to middle-sector couples, who can gain
economically by limiting the size of their families, many of the poor

believe they benefit from large families. Working children bring in desperately needed income, and once they are adults, they can care for their parents when the latters' working years have ended. It is also among the poor that the Roman Catholic doctrine is most influential. Clearly, if family planning programs are to have any effect in the less affluent Latin American countries, they must begin by changing the attitudes and institutions that have perpetuated poverty and the survival-through-numbers ethic.

In sum, though they would prefer to ignore it, economic strategists are being forced to face the frustrating population growth problem. The achievement of their development objectives depends not only on their expertise and political skill, but also on whether they allow their achievements to be undermined by a failure to keep up with the demands placed on their economies by ever larger numbers of constituents.

Now that we know something of the economic theories that Latin Americans have preferred, it is time to discover how they worked in practice. In Part II we will begin with the Populists, an odd assortment of politicians who were among the first to challenge the primary product export mode of development in Latin America. The governments of Getulio Vargas in Brazil and Juan Perón in Argentina will give us contrasting examples of how populism worked. Next we will turn to the democratic reformers, focusing on political parties in Chile and Venezuela who were guided by the progressive modernization strategy. The military authoritarians follow in Chapter 8, offering examples of how the conservative modernization strategy fared. We will complete our survey with a study of revolutionary economics as it is practiced in Cuba and Nicaragua.

Further reading

Anderson, Charles W. *Politics and Economic Change in Latin America: The Governing of Restless Nations.* New York: Van Nostrand, 1967.

Baran, Paul. *The Political Economy of Growth.* New York: Monthly Review Press, 1957.

Berger, Peter. *Pyramids of Sacrifice: Political Ethics and Social Change.* New York: Basic Books, 1974.

Campos, Roberto de Oliveira. *Reflections on Latin American Development.* Austin: University of Texas Press, 1967.

Farley, Rawle. *The Economics of Latin America: Development Problems in Perspective.* New York: Harper & Row, 1972.

Frank, Andre Gunder. *Latin America: Underdevelopment or Revolution*. New York: Monthly Review Press, 1969.

Furtado, Celso. *Economic Development of Latin America*. Cambridge: Cambridge University Press, 1970.

Obstacles to Development in Latin America. Garden City, N.Y.: Doubleday, 1970.

Glade, William P. *The Latin American Economies*. New York: Van Nostrand Reinhold, 1969.

Gordon, Wendell. *The Political Economy of Latin America*. New York: Columbia University Press, 1965.

Hirschmann, Albert O. *Essays in Trespassing*. Princeton, N.J.: Princeton University Press, 1981.

Latin American Issues: Essays and Comments. New York: Twentieth Century Fund, 1961.

A Bias for Hope. New Haven, Conn.: Yale University Press, 1974.

Loup, Jacques. *Can the Third World Survive?* Baltimore: Johns Hopkins University Press, 1983.

McCoy, Terry L., ed. *The Dynamics of Population Policy in Latin America*. Cambridge, Mass.: Ballinger, 1975.

Mesa-Lago, Carmelo, and Carl Beck. *Comparative Socialist Systems*. Pittsburgh: University of Pittsburgh Press, 1975.

Murdoch, William. *The Poverty of Nations: The Political Economy of Hunger and Population*. Baltimore: Johns Hopkins University Press, 1980.

Powelson, John. *Latin America: Today's Economic and Social Revolution*. New York: McGraw-Hill, 1964.

Prebisch, Raul. *The Economic Development of Latin America and Its Principal Problems*. New York: United Nations, 1950.

Change and Development: Latin America's Great Task. Washington, D.C.: Inter-American Development Bank, 1970.

Roxborough, Ian. *Theories of Underdevelopment*. Atlantic Highlands, N.J.: Humanities Press, 1979.

Tancer, Shoshana Baron. *Economic Nationalism in Latin America: The Quest for Economic Independence*. New York: Praeger, 1976.

Thorp, Rosemary, and Lawrence Whitehead, eds. *Inflation and Stabilization in Latin America*. New York: Holmes and Meier, 1979.

United Nations. *The Economic Development of Latin America in the Post-War Period*. New York, 1964.

The Process of Industrialization in Latin America. New York, 1966.

Warren, Bill. *Imperialism: Pioneer of Capitalism*. London: NLB, 1980.

Part II

The political games of Latin America

6. The populist game

The Populists' achievements were modest, but Latin American politics was never quite the same after them. Not only did they alter the rules in Brazil and Argentina, but they also established a new kind of leadership, Machiavellian in style, nationalist in sentiment, and massive in appeal.

Had the Populists launched well-organized, ideologically coherent movements, studying them would be easy. Unfortunately, coherence and clarity were not among their virtues. Like other rebels who rose from within a tenacious old order, they were absorbed by the immediate struggle for political advantage rather than by a grander crusade to reconstruct the nation in accord with an elaborate ideology. Though radical in their rhetoric, the Populists were moderate in their behavior. Theirs was not the cause of revolution but of the acquisition of political power in order to get a larger piece of the nation's economic pie for themselves and the urban have-nots who believed in them. Getulio Vargas and Juan Perón feared the radicalization of the working class as much as did the Conservatives they displaced; what made them different was their conviction that the labor movement could be handled more effectively by the government's favoring it than by repressing it. Though it seemed a cavalier and risky adventure at the time, it turned out to be a simple task for modern Machiavellians like Vargas and Perón.

The term "Populist" is the source of some confusion. Anyone familiar with North American politics regards a Populist as someone from an agrarian movement that arose at the end of the past century to protest railroad monopolies and government–business collusion. Latin American populism was quite different, for it drew its support from an urban constituency in the midst of industrialization during the 1930s and 1940s in the larger Latin American nations. Second, some confuse populism with fascism because Perón and Vargas used rhetoric and methods resembling those of Franco, Mussolini, and Hitler. But the fascist label distorts more than it helps since the similarities between the two were quite superficial, as we will see. The label is also confusing because Vargas and Perón were not carbon copies of each other. They responded to different national conditions and adjusted their tactics accordingly. Yet, despite all of these limitations, a populist game is distinguishable from the others, identifiable by its policies and their consequences as well as its rules and the behavior they induced. Finally, the study of populism is primarily a study in leadership. Populist movements were leader centered, each heavily dependent for its drive and momentum on the energy of one person. As a result, their strengths and weaknesses were often those of the person in charge.

Populism in Brazil

Getulio Vargas had ruled Brazil for thirteen years – from 1930 to 1943 – before he actually launched his Populist movement. A lawyer from the southern Brazilian state of Rio Grande do Sul and the member of an upper-class ranching family, he began his political career as a federal deputy in 1924, served as finance minister in 1926, and returned to his home state as governor in 1928. After losing the 1930 presidential election – an election rigged by his opponents – Vargas led a heterogeneous coalition of disgruntled civilian politicans and young military officers in an insurrection that deposed the incumbent president. For fifteen years thereafter he personally dominated Brazilian politics as the country's president, employing his exceptional mastery of the rules and norms of Brazilian life and his ability to guide the country through the uncertain times of the post-depression era.

Vargas used nearly every means but direct election to sustain his rule during the 1930s. For four years he played off different influential groups against one another. Then in 1934 he was confirmed as president by a popularly elected constituent assembly. However, just before his term expired in 1938, he drew on the services of the military once again to reconfirm himself as president before new elections could be held. This time he created a new political regime, the Estado Novo (New State), which he modeled loosely after the fascist regimes of Italy and Germany. But the new constitution was little more than window dressing for Vargas's strong but manipulative presidency and his expansion of state power in order to regulate more closely the new economic forces that were emerging in the 1930s. Although he never

seriously challenged the power of the traditional agrarian elite, he did
lead his country into the industrial era by promoting the interests of
industrial entrepreneurs and by turning the Brazilian state into the
patron of organized labor in the 1940s.

Vargas: the early years

Brazil was different from the beginning. It was colonized by the
Portuguese, not the Spaniards. After Independence, when its neighbors were consumed by civil wars among *caudillos* contesting for
power in their new nations, independent Brazil was ruled after 1882
by its own monarch, Emperor Dom Pedro II, a descendant of the
Portuguese royal family. Little changed after Independence except
Brazil's freedom from Lisbon; the monarch, a patriotic and paternalistic but powerful ruler, held the large and ethnically and regionally
diverse nation together for a half century.

Resentment of the power of central authorities plagued the monarchy, but it was some time before regional elites could rebel successfully. Not until 1889 did they succeed in deposing the emperor and
creating a constitutional regime that became a device for the decentralization of real authority into the hands of the political machines that
ran each of the Brazilian states. Thereafter, by agreement the presidency was alternated between the two most powerful states, São
Paulo and Minas Gerais. In 1930, however, the retiring president,
Washington Luis of São Paulo, broke the agreement by selecting
another Paulista to replace him instead of accepting Getulio Vargas,
the nominee of the Minas Gerais and Rio Grande do Sul political
machines. Soon thereafter Vargas led the military-backed opposition
in an insurrection that brought the old republic to an end.

Washington Luis's violation of the electoral agreement was the principal cause of the 1930 insurrection, but not the only one. The 1929
depression and the failure of the Luis government to act decisively to
relieve the crisis undermined the confidence of coffee growers,
bankers, and traders in his administration. Moreover, the military had
grown weary of the old regime and was disturbed by its failure to
accelerate the country's economic development. Increasing professionalization, foreign travel, and greater awareness of Brazil's untouched
economic potential had heightened the concern of younger officers
about the way the country was governed. Once firm supporters of the

Table 6.1. *The Brazil of Getulio Vargas: historical background*

1822	Independence declared by Portuguese Prince Dom Pedro, who is crowned Emperor Pedro I of Brazil
1840	Dom Pedro II, aged fourteen, is declared second emperor of Brazil
1889	Army overthrows emperor and two years later promulgates first constitution of the Republic of the United States of Brazil
1917	Brazil enters World War I on side of Allies
1929	World economic depression strikes Brazilian economy
1930	Military–civilian insurrection led by defeated presidential candidate Getulio Vargas ends Republic
1932	Provisional government of Getulio Vargas puts down constitutionalist revolt in São Paulo
1934	Second republican constitution is adopted, and Congress elects Getulio Vargas president
1937	Just before election of his successor, Vargas leads coup and creates Estado Novo, appointing himself as president with indefinite tenure
1942	Brazil enters World War II on side of Allies
1945	Vargas is forced to resign by military after creating Populist movement drawing heavily on support of organized labor
1950	Vargas wins legitimate presidential election with support of Social Democratic party and Brazilian Labor party, receiving 49 percent of popular vote
1954	President Vargas commits suicide at age seventy-two

regime, they gradually became its strongest critics, convinced that only a new generation of bold leaders could impose on Brazil the kind of moral order needed to achieve the country's full potential.

What the opposition needed was someone bold enough to lead a revolt by politicians, young military officers, businessmen, and professionals who had grown tired of the corrupt old order. Vargas was that person. An experienced and well-known politician aggrieved because he had been denied the presidency after winning it under the old rules, he quickly became the obvious choice. From the outset he assured each of the groups within the coalition that he would serve their particular interests. Some saw him as the long-awaited leader of the march toward a real constitutional order. For others he became the champion of rapid national development, dedicated to the close collaboration between government and business in promoting industrialization in the wake of the world depression. For still others, he seemed the only one capable of bringing the warring local political machines in line by adroitly increasing the authority of the central government.

Gradually Brazilians discovered that Vargas was happier governing as an authoritarian than as a liberal democrat. Of course, this did not disappoint everyone for many wanted a strong government more than they did a constitutional one. The turning point came in 1932, when Vargas invited and defeated a revolt by constitutionalists in the state of São Paulo. The revolt's leaders had accused Vargas of postponing the return to constitutional government so that he could increase the power of the national government at the expense of large states like São Paulo. They were correct, but by launching and losing their confrontation with him, they only enhanced Vargas's stature as a patriot defending the government against unruly, self-interested rebels.

Once comfortably in control, Vargas authorized the election of a constituent assembly in 1933. Less than a year later the assembly drafted a new constitution, converted itself into the Chamber of Deputies and elected Vargas to a four-year term as president. But instead of strengthening the constitutional process, Vargas again dedicated himself to undermining it. Once more he provoked opponents and then used the threats they posed to justify his authoritarian methods. This time he encouraged initiatives by small Communist and Fascist movements, playing each off against the other to make the threat of both to the nation appear much greater than it actually was. The strategy worked, and in 1937, just before an election to replace him, he persuaded the military to overthrow the constitutional regime and appoint him president with indefinite tenure.

An admirer of the powerful fascist regimes in Spain, Portugal, and Italy, Vargas tried to emulate them by creating political institutions resembling theirs. Yet, he never followed through on most of his initiatives. The Estado Novo, as the new order was called, was little more than window dressing to clothe Vargas's expansion of state control over Brazilian life. What he had actually done was join two nineteenth-century Brazilian traditions and adapt them to post-depression conditions. One was the tradition of paternalistic central authority, which was developed during the imperial rule of Emperor Dom Pedro II between 1841 and 1889; the other was the dependence of private economic groups on the Brazilian government. The regional political machines that had governed Brazil between 1889 and 1930 had weakened central authority but had not destroyed popular longing for it. Vargas drew on the need and desire for firm national leadership and transformed the presidency and the national bureaucracy into powerful promoters of the nation's economic development. He also encouraged the development of private interest groups, first among businessmen and later organized labor, but he did so on his own terms, making clear that all such groups were dependent on the state for their rights and privileges. Once these two powerful traditions were merged and adjusted to the needs of an industrializing society, Vargas's reconstruction of the Brazilian political game had begun. Or so it appeared in 1938.

The populist Vargas

The Estado Novo survived only a few years. But not until its end was in sight did Vargas choose the populist path, doing so more for reasons of political strategy than ideological principle. Vargas had always feared the radicalization of Brazilian workers and as early as 1937 had tried to make organized labor the ward of the Brazilian state by including provisions for minimum wages, paid vacations, an eight-hour day, and social security in the Estado Novo's constitution. Thereafter, Vargas portrayed himself as the patron of the country's growing urban working class even though few of his labor programs were actually implemented. Meanwhile, in the early 1940s demands for the restoration of constitutional democracy rose again, coming primarily from democratically inclined politicians, along with military officers who were defending Western European democracies from Fascists in World War II. Always ready to adapt himself to new political realities, Vargas, aware that he needed mass support to defeat opponents at the polls, turned to organized labor for support. At that moment Brazilian populism was launched as a major political force.

Unfortunately for Vargas, his plot came to naught, temporarily at least, for before he could lead his working-class followers to victory the military stepped in. Fearful that Vargas might subvert the constitutional restoration as he had done so adroitly in 1937, they forced him to return to his ranch in southern Brazil to observe the 1945 elections from the sidelines. His retirement was premature, as it turned out, for once constitutional rules had been put into practice Vargas worked his way back into the contest. Mobilizing the Labor party that he had created in 1943 and drawing support from the regional political bosses previously loyal to him, he secured 49 percent of the popular vote and the presidency in 1950.

Once again, Vargas tried to play the role of moderator and unifier, rewarding laborers for their support with patronage and modest social programs while simultaneously trying to promote industry and pacify rural elites. But Brazil had changed a great deal since his first presidency; the urban middle sectors were more numerous, foreign investors more involved in the country, industrialists more demanding, and economic policy issues more complex and hard to resolve to everyone's satisfaction. The techniques that had worked a decade earlier were no longer adequate for controlling the opposition. The National Democratic Union, the principal opposition party, repeatedly refused Vargas's invitations to join his government, preferring a major effort to undermine him. The opposition was also joined by junior military officers who charged Vargas with excessive patronage and corruption and by foreign investors who were disturbed by Vargas's increasingly strident nationalism. As the attacks of the opposition gained momentum in 1954, it became increasingly difficult for Vargas to deter them. The end finally came when the mysterious assassination of an anti-Vargas military officer stirred demands for his resignation. The seventy-two-year-old president responded by shooting himself in his office on August 24, 1954, and leaving the populist cause to his successors.

Populist policy

Brazilian economic policy was dedicated to the achievement of two objectives during the 1950s: industrial development and the distribution of its benefits to the players responsible for it. The first reflected the government's determination to accelerate a process that was well under way by the time Vargas returned to the presidency in 1950; the second was part of a calculated political campaign to integrate industrialists, foreign investors, and labor leaders into the ruling coalition. To be understood, Brazilian policy and the economic development it fostered must be examined against the background of the 1930s and 1940s and the rise of industrialization in Brazil.

When Vargas started his first presidency in 1930 his only choice was to concentrate on protecting Brazil's export economy from the

ravages of the world depression. He began by purchasing coffee and
withholding it from the market in an attempt to propel prices upward.
What he managed, however, was not higher prices – the efforts of
Brazil acting alone could not lift prices significantly – but the preven-
tion of a collapse in domestic demand within Brazil. It was this maintenance of the level of Brazilian consumption coupled with a decline
in imports and repeated currency devaluations that ignited the development of a consumer goods industry within Brazil during the 1930s.

The government's reliance on the stimulation of market forces gave
way to more direct state intervention after the creation of the Estado
Novo in 1937. At the urging of his nationalist military advisers, Vargas accelerated the process of industrialization begun spontaneously
after the depression using investment-promoting taxes, exchange and
credit controls, import quotas, and the development of state-owned
petroleum and steel enterprises. Then came World War II and the
interruption of Brazilian trade with Europe once again. True to form,
Vargas increased state control in order to protect the Brazilian economy from the war's disruptive effects, making his government the
patron and regulator of the country's private entrepreneurs. It was
this recourse to state paternalism that made Brazil's economic development so different from that of early industrializers like Great Britain

and the United States. Where industrial growth was promoted and
managed largely by entrepreneurs in the latter, much greater state
intervention and direction were necessary to accelerate it in a late-
industrializing nation like Brazil.

In addition to the protection of coffee producers and the promotion
of industrial growth, Vargas sought to make the state the patron of
organized labor and labor the loyal servant of the state, as we have
seen. Of course, he reached only the elite of a labor force; most
workers stayed poor and unorganized, especially in the countryside,
but his actions were significant nevertheless.

When Vargas returned to the presidency in 1950, the process of
import-substitution industrialization prompted two decades earlier by
the depression had gathered momentum, but was still far from complete. His initial goal was the acceleration of industrial growth and the
diversification of Brazilian production. His economic advisers recognized that Brazil still suffered from structural bottlenecks and a low
capacity to import because of insufficient returns on its primary product exports. What was needed, they concluded, was the increased

domestic production of consumer goods for local markets. Like most Populists, Vargas cloaked his program in strong nationalist rhetoric, promising to liberate the country from the tyranny of world markets and economic control by foreigners. But his words could not hide the fact that what he prescribed was actually a modest effort to stimulate economic growth by combining rather orthodox international trade policies with state promotion of industrialization using heavy investments in economic infrastructure, the liberal financing of private entrepreneurs, and the expansion of state enterprises involved in the production of iron, steel, petroleum, and other basic materials.

The skills Vargas had used to dominate the Brazilian polity and stimulate its economic growth after the depression were no match for the task of managing a more complex economy and satisfying the more diverse economic interests that had arisen by the 1950s. For example, when the rate of inflation accelerated and the balance-of-payments deficit reached record levels in 1953, Vargas could devise no solution that pleased all the dominant economic forces. Instead, he chose to bow to economic realities and adopt a conventional economic stabilization program that cut public spending, limited imports, and tightened credit – to the displeasure of industrialists, merchants, and union leaders. To make matters worse, stabilization did not immediately rescue the economy or save Vargas from his critics. As conditions worsened, so did his control over his office, until in a moment of desperation he took his own life.

Vargas's elected successor, Juscelino Kubitschek, proved more adept at using economic policy to placate the members of the populist coalition while at the same time promoting rapid economic growth. A student in the Vargas school of politics, he recognized that without the deliberate acceleration of economic growth there was little chance of satisfying industrialists, organized labor, and other economic groups simultaneously. So instead of stressing redistribution, he encouraged investment and industrial expansion by promoting the efforts of domestic and foreign entrepreneurs and supporting them with increased public investments in infrastructure and government enterprises. And to demonstrate that he was a modern leader who would launch Brazil into a new age, Kubitschek also promoted the construction of an ultramodern new capital, Brasilia, in the country's interior.

Bolstered by improving external conditions, Kubitschek achieved impressive results with his program: Industrial production rose 80 percent and the gross national product increased at an annual average rate of 6.1 percent between 1955 and 1961, one of the highest rates in the hemisphere. Equally impressive was Kubitschek's ability to use his policies to satisfy the demands of competing economic groups. He supplied easy credit and tariff protection to industrialists, price supports to farmers, favorable terms to foreign investors, new jobs and rising wages to labor, and pay raises to the military. Only the peasantry and the urban poor – albeit 50 percent of the population – were excluded from the new bounty, but as nonparticipants in the Brazilian game, they could be ignored without serious political repercussions.

The rapid acceleration of economic growth and the simultaneous satisfaction of diverse groups had its costs. For Kubitschek the cost took the form of record budget deficits, which boosted inflation and contributed to balance-of-payments difficulties. But unlike Vargas, who had earlier responded to similar conditions by imposing unpopular stabilization measures, Kubitschek ignored the pleas of foreign creditors and International Monetary Fund advisers, who insisted on cooling off the overheated Brazilian economy. His defiance won him immense popularity within the country, but it only postponed several tough economic policy decisions, many of which were not made until the military seized control and executed a stabilization program with brutal efficiency in the mid-1960s.

Populism in Argentina

Argentina is unlike Brazil in several ways. Brazil was a Portuguese colony and Argentina a Spanish one. Brazil is physically much larger, its population four times greater, more rural, ethnically diverse, and poorer on the average than Argentina's. Yet there arose in Argentina a leader whose politics were, on the surface at least, similar to Vargas's. Like Vargas, General Juan Domingo Perón ruled his nation for nearly a decade and was removed from office only to later return to the presidency and die there. Both men were nationalists, promoted industrialization and social reform, and were popular with the working class. And both were consummate opportunists, skilled at adapting the rules of the game to their political needs. But they also differed in essential ways. Perón gained his popularity by attacking the Argentine oligarchy, whereas Vargas was more moderate and less

Table 6.2. *The Argentina of Juan Perón: historical background*

1816	Independence from Spain declared
1835	Autocrat Juan Manuel Rosas imposes order on strife-ridden country
1852	Rosas overthrown in revolt led by rivals in economic elite
1852	Republican government created under new constitution, and Argentina governed by succession of conservative leaders, who promote immigration from Europe and development of agricultural export economy
1916	Middle-sector-led Radical party wins first election under Hipólito Irigoyen; Radical party again wins presidential elections in 1922 and 1928
1929	World economic depression strikes Argentine economy
1930	Conservative-supported military coup deposes Radical party administration and secures election of conservative presidents in 1932 and 1938
1943	Military takes control of government to prevent election of pro-British conservative president
1944	Colonel Juan Domingo Perón is made vice-president under military President Farrell
1945	After being forced to resign vice-presidency and sent to jail by military colleagues, Perón is released and becomes presidential candidate of Laborista party
1946	Perón elected president for first term
1949	Constituent Assembly promulgates new Peronista constitution
1951	Perón elected president for second term
1952	Perón's wife, Evita, dies
1955	Military insurrection forces Perón to flee into exile
1973	Juan Perón, at age seventy-eight, returns to Argentina and is elected president
1974	President Perón dies of natural causes and is succeeded by his wife and vice-president, Isabel Martinez de Perón, whose administration is overthrown by Argentine military in early 1976

strident. Perón deepened the class divisions and antagonisms in Argentina, creating political conflicts that exist to this day. In so doing, he reinforced the notion that the Argentine state was a partisan instrument to be used by one side against the other. Vargas, though quite partisan, never had the same effect.

Juan Perón enjoys greater fame outside the region than Vargas and is usually cited as the prototype of the populist leader. This is not surprising. Perón began and ended his political career as a Populist, whereas Vargas was many things at different times. Moreover, the urban working class became much more powerful in Argentina than Brazil, making Argentine populism a more durable phenomenon. And Perón ruled for nine years and Vargas only four in his populist phase, leaving behind him a longer list of projects.

Perón dominated Argentine politics from 1946 until 1955, when he was forced from office and into exile. He relied on the support of a working class he had mobilized in 1945, the demagogic appeal and political skill of his wife Evita, the physical and psychological intimidation of his opponents by his followers, and the tacit support of the Argentine military. He was opposed by the rural elite and foreign business, the middle-sector and upper-class political parties he defeated in the 1945 elections, and later the Roman Catholic hierarchy, whom he antagonized with his legalization of divorce. His military colleagues joined the opposition and overthrew him in 1955; but after eighteen years in exile he was allowed back in 1973, elected president, and died in office one year later at age seventy-nine.

The rise of Perón

The agro-exporter elite's monopoly over Argentina's government was first broken by the middle-sector-supported Radical party in 1916. The Radicals opened the political process to their supporters, but they did little to alter the structure of the Argentine economy or to reduce the influence of the elite that ran it. The 1929 depression and declining confidence in the ability of the Radicals to protect the traditional economic order against social protests prompted intervention by the conservative-backed military in 1930. Two years later, a conservative regime was restored and harsh austerity imposed on the depression-ravaged Argentine economy.

In rescuing the Argentine economy from the depression, the Conservatives antagonized Argentine nationalists, who resented the country's heavy dependence on foreign investors and traders. Nationalists condemned conservative leaders for paying too high a price to restore trade with Great Britain, the principal buyer of Argentine beef. Through the Roca-Runciman pact, the Argentine government agreed to guarantee a market for England's manufactured goods in exchange for the latter's purchase of beef, claiming it had no choice but to accept the British terms because there were few other available markets for Argentine commodities. But for a vocal and expanding community of nationalists within the opposition Radical party and the lower ranks of the military the treaty was a distasteful reminder of Argentina's subservience to its trading partners. Their opposition to economic dependence on the English became a resource that Perón later exploited.

The Conservatives also alienated the country's growing working class. Until the 1930s, Argentina's organized laborers had been few in number but militant in spirit under the leadership of Socialists and anarchists. After the 1930 coup working-class militancy was met with harsh repression by a government determined to preserve the old order, and within a few years the labor movement was left impotent by the combined pressures of unemployment and government oppression. Nevertheless, the size of the working class grew rapidly as a result of internal migration from the countryside to the cities, which accompanied the spontaneous industrialization prompted by the shortage of imported consumer goods during the early years of the depression. Consequently, by the early 1940s Argentina had an enlarged industrial work force whose attempts to organize and assert itself were continually frustrated by a hostile government. This gave Perón something to exploit once he was in a position to do so after the military coup of 1943.

Perón's campaign was bolstered by the declining competence of conservative officials. Prior to 1916, the agro-exporter elite had easily dominated Argentine politics through its control over the country's economy. That feat could not be replicated after 1930 in a nation that had changed significantly during the 1920s. Over 1 million European immigrants had entered the country in the interim, bringing its population to nearly 6 million. The middle sectors had asserted themselves and could be excluded from the government only through physical force and electoral fraud. And constant vigilance and repression were needed to contain the aspirations of a growing working class. Nevertheless, the country's conservative rulers held fast to the traditional practices that had served them so well before 1916. But by so doing they not only discredited party politics and constitutional government in the eyes of most Argentines, they also gradually undermined the confidence of the military in their ability to create a stable and durable political order. When President Ramón Castillo tried to secure military support for the reactionary *latifundista* he had nominated as his successor in 1943, the military resisted. And then when

Table 6.3. *Perón's rise to power*

Existing socio-economic conditions →	The opportunity →	Sources of authority for mobilizing support →	Precipitating event →	The seizure of power
Post-depression national humiliation Working–class alienation Elite decay	Military coup of 1943	Under secretary of war (June 1943); minister of war (February 1944) Secretary of labor and social welfare (October 1943) Vice-president (July 1944)	October 17, 1945, demonstration by labor supporters forcing military to tolerate Perón's candidacy	Presidential election of February 1946 56% of popular vote Two-thirds of seats in Chamber of Deputies All but two seats in Senate

officers became dissatisfied with Castillo's vacillating war policies, they joined together long enough to depose him in June 1943.

Colonel Juan Domingo Perón did not lead the coup, but he was an active participant in it as a member of a nationalist, pro-Axis faction of young officers. He was rewarded first with the under secretaryship of war and a few months later added the post of secretary of labor and social welfare. In February 1944, he became secretary of war and in July of the same year was named vice-president.

Perón used his authority as labor minister and war minister to build a large and devoted following. Within the War Ministry he secured the support of young officers whom he promoted in exchange for their political support. From the Labor Secretariat he organized thousands of workers and built a loyal following by rewarding unions that supported him with favorable collective bargaining settlements and social security laws while punishing those who refused to accept his leadership. For Argentine laborers the advantages of the alliance were obvious. After years of being ignored or harassed by a succession of governments and poorly served by socialist and anarchist leaders who could not secure the wages and social services demanded by the rank and file, here at last was a leader who could deliver the goods almost overnight. By the middle of 1945, Perón had converted the General Labor Confederation, the nation's largest labor organization, into one of the strongest political forces in the country.

The last obstacle to Perón's ascendancy was overcome on October 17, 1945. A military faction opposed to him, in a desperate move to block his path to the presidency, persuaded President Farrell to arrest and jail him until after the elections were held. His incarceration came to an abrupt end, however, when his working-class followers, mobilized by loyal labor leaders, marched on the presidential palace and remained there until Perón was released. Four months later he was swept into power in one of Argentina's most honest elections.

Perón in power

To this day Argentines disagree over whether Perón was an autocrat or a democrat. He was elected president under democratic rules and gained control over Congress when his party secured an absolute majority in nearly every province. He was immensely popular with the Argentine masses, as was his wife Evita. An ex-radio actress of lower-class, small-town origin, she became a skilled orator who evoked intense emotional loyalty from the poor, a bond that was reinforced until her early death in 1952 by her distribution of money, food, and clothing to thousands of Argentines. Indisputably, in the beginning the Peróns were the people's choice to rule Argentina.

But the Peróns changed the rules once in power, resorting to some of the same kinds of abuses of constitutional government for which their Conservative predecessors were notorious. With the legislature under his party's control, Perón accomplished his initial policy objectives swiftly. But that was not enough. He and his followers were determined to make the oligarchy pay for its past behavior. Though economic realities prevented Perón from stripping them of their property, he did all he could to intimidate them, especially when they criticized his behavior. Hostility between the Peronistas and their foes quickly intensified, giving Perón, much like Vargas, the excuses he wanted to justify his ignoring their civil liberties.

It is not surprising that Perón feared the opposition. Unwilling to lead a real revolution, Perón knew that the Argentine oligarchy as well as the urban middle sectors had substantial power to use against him, not the least of which were their influence over the economy and their ties to the more conservative factions within the military. Like so many leaders who are unwilling to live within the limits imposed on them by a liberal democratic constitution, Perón tried to stay a step ahead of his opponents, arresting officers suspected of plotting coups, taking over newspapers that became too strident in their criticism, and encouraging his followers to break up mass demonstrations by his opponents. His was not a regime controlled through a highly disciplined political party, but rather one run by a small group of people hastily recruited by Perón from the military, the labor leadership, and young professionals. With their help Perón governed in the manner of the leader of a massive, loosely organized, Mafia-like family whose members trusted their leader to look out for them and in return were prepared to do whatever he asked of them.

Were the Peronistas authoritarians? Clearly they were not the conventional authoritarians who relied on harsh repression to control the entire nation. Yet neither were they classical democrats, respecting their opponents and enforcing justice equally. What mattered most to the Peronistas was not liberty but the power to stand up to those who had previously dominated them. They sought power not by rebuilding the social structure as real revolutionaries might have done, but by picking away at the country's elite, intimidating factory owners, newspaper editors, and opposition politicians whenever they refused to cooperate voluntarily.

Confusion about the character of the Peronista regime is also caused by similarities between Peronism and fascism. Peron had been sympathetic to the Axis powers during World War II. Moreover, like the Fascists, he was nationalistic, believed in strong leadership, and advocated corporatist methods. But on closer inspection, it is clear that Peronism fell short of the fascist ideal. This is especially evident in its failure to build a real corporatist regime.

Corporatism, as we learned in Chapter 4, is a mode of government that stresses central control over society by leaders who exercise their authority through interest organizations representing labor, business, agriculture, and other sectors. It assumes that central direction is better established through functional organizations than through conventional legislatures. In its most extreme form it is very hierarchical and authoritarian, with the executive making decisions alone and then ordering their implementation by the leaders of sectoral associations. More moderate forms involve interest group leaders in decision making, allowing them some influence over the executive's resolution of disputes and design of policy.

The idea of corporatist government was known to Latin Americans long before the Populists arrived. And, as we will discover in later chapters, it has been popular with other governments, from the Mexican one launched in 1917 to the military authoritarian regimes created in Brazil and Peru in the 1960s. It is most attractive to two kinds of authorities: those who seek to dominate potential opponents, preventing their obstruction of policy, and those who believe that economic development requires central direction of producers and laborers. Some, of course, try to use corporatist methods to accomplish both objectives simultaneously.

Clearly Perón, like Vargas, admired the corporatist regimes created in Spain, Portugal, and Italy in the 1920s and 1930s. And he used corporatist rhetoric when it served his needs, emphasizing the importance of the strong leader, the organic society, and the need for the commitment of all private groups to common goals. Yet neither Perón in 1946 nor Vargas in 1950 created a full-scale corporatist regime that converted all private economic groups into instruments of an authoritarian state. Vargas had come close to doing so in 1937 when he launched the Estado Novo and increased the dependence of private groups on the legal and financial support of the state. Yet, even though many economic groups remained heavily dependent on the state after the demise of the Estado Novo, Vargas did not complete the construction of the corporate state when he returned in 1951. Instead, he was forced by the new rules of the game to rely primarily on well-established but informal links with economic and political groups. Unlike Vargas, Perón did not inherit a legacy of interest group dependence on the state when he launched his populist regime in 1946. Industrial and agricultural groups had opposed his election and remained bitter antagonists afterward. They were accustomed to getting their way in the traditional game and resented being ordered about by inexperienced Peronista officials. Perón tried to control industrialists and farmers by forcing them to join a government-subsidized national association, which along with labor, was to assist in the administration of government policy. What he gained, however, was not control over the private sector but increased hostility and a sustained effort to secure his overthrow.

Peronista development policy

At the outset Perón dedicated himself to increasing Argentina's economic independence, convinced that with accelerated industrialization Argentina could become one of the world's economic powers. Simultaneously, he set about improving the welfare of the Argentine working class by adopting social programs and forcing higher wages.

The British had financed much of Argentina's development and in 1945 they owned its railways and, along with other foreign investors, most of the nation's utilities, its meat-packing plants, and grain companies. Ending the country's dependence on the English was an obsession with Perón. Soon after taking over in 1946 he paid off the nation's foreign debts, purchased the railways (at prices favorable to the English), and the national telephone company from the multinational, International Telephone and Telegraph Company. By 1949 his buying spree exhausted the country's abundant gold reserves, but the Peronists claimed a great victory, convinced that they had begun the liberation of their economy from foreign control.

To promote industrialization, the Peronistas relied heavily on high tariffs to protect Argentine manufacturers from foreign competitors and an overvalued exchange rate that encouraged the importation of capital goods. The government also inaugurated the country's first development plan, a loose assortment of projects aimed at improving economic infrastructure. The most important – and most controversial – decision, however, was to create a government monopoly over all agricultural commodity trading, permitting Perón to take the profits from commodity sales abroad and transfer them to industrial and public-sector investors at home. The monopoly was managed by the Argentine Trade Promotion Institute (IAPI), an organization created in 1946 to purchase beef, mutton, and grain from farmers at low official prices; sell them abroad at high postwar prices; and retain the profit to finance government programs. Few things Perón did were more resented by farmers, large and small alike, than his creation of the IAPI. Yet, though the farmers campaigned vigorously throughout Perón's tenure for a return to the free market, they could not dampen his enthusiasm for the scheme.

The Peronistas also tried to redistribute income from the propertied classes to urban workers. By using government authority to force wage settlements favorable to loyal unions, they raised real wages by almost 50 percent between 1946 and 1948. Moreover, they increased the number of jobs available in the public sector by staffing the newly nationalized enterprises like the railways with thousands of laborers, many of them recent migrants to the cities.

Missing from the Peronista program was any commitment to agrarian reform. Perón's goal was the redistribution of rural profits, not rural property. He encouraged the purchase of land by tenant farmers by freezing rents, but he was content to leave cattlemen and farmers alone as long as they supplied the beef, mutton, and grain that would bring high postwar prices in foreign markets and finance the government's development programs. In other words, he left the rural power structure intact because he needed its produce to pay for industrialization. Ironically, at the same time the Peronistas were trying to reduce their economy's dependence on the rural sector, they were forced to rely on it to finance their scheme.

Perón wanted to launch Argentina on a course that would quickly place it among the elite of the world's industrial nations. Its dependence on foreigners was to give way to a new sense of national autonomy as the agrarian export economy was transformed into an industri-

ally self-sufficient one. And workers who in the past had been exploited by an insensitive economic elite were to be given the kind of
social justice they deserved. But prosperity, national autonomy, and
social justice eluded the Peronistas, and by 1955 Argentina, the country they had tried to launch into a new era, had become a sorry
paradox, divided politically and demoralized economically. Between
1945 and 1950, the per capita gross national product had increased at
an annual average rate of 2.8 percent and real income at an impressive
rate of 3.7 percent. But during the next five years, the per capita
product declined at an annual rate of 0.2 percent and real income by
0.5 percent. The quality of the country's economic infrastructure
deteriorated, and rural and industrial entrepreneurs lost confidence in
the country's public authorities. Perón had tried to build a new Argentina, but he had only created a more desperate and discouraged
one.

There are many explanations for the failure of Peronista policy.
Peronistas blame their problems on their enemies, both domestic and
foreign, whom they accuse of subverting them. Their critics point to
economic mismanagement, government corruption, and Perón's failure to heed the warnings of his critics in the private sector. The truth,
as usual, lies somewhere in between.

Several unanticipated external conditions did hurt the Peronistas.
Perón, for example, had counted on the continuation of high commodity prices in European markets to finance investment, but with
the creation of the Marshall Plan and the delivery of millions of tons
of American grain to Europe, Argentine trade prospects declined. To
make matters worse, two of the country's worst droughts came in
1950 and 1951, further limiting production. But the Peronistas must
share some of the blame. They could have used their gold supply
more cautiously to protect themselves against the effects of a sudden
decline in exports. They also underestimated the high cost of industrialization, especially in technology and raw materials. And they contributed to the decapitalization of the private sector with their financial
policies and mismanaged public enterprises, such as the nationalized
railways, which became a source of featherbedding and a cause of
huge fiscal deficits.

Finally, and most important, through his combative, autocratic
style and often arbitrary policy decisions, Perón helped demoralize his
country's rural and industrial entrepreneurs at the very time he
needed their cooperation to execute his programs. Although he made

a valiant effort to reverse many of his policies in 1952 and 1953 by holding labor in check and allowing higher profits for farmers, it was too little and it came too late to either placate his opponents or ignite the Argentine economy.

The durability of Peronism

Peronism's survival clearly distinguishes it from the region's other populist movements. Generally, populism was a transient phenomenon, something that arose during the early phases of industrialization in large urban areas but gave way eventually to more sophisticated reform parties or antipopulist military governments. But it was different with the Peronistas; when they gave way in 1955 they did not disappear.

The military officers who chased Perón from the country in 1955 were determined to rid the nation of Peronism, first by beheading its movement and then by forcing the rank and file to participate through non-Peronista political parties. They tried hard but they failed dismally. Perón deserves much of the credit for their debacle. From the moment of his departure from Argentina he behaved as the leader of a government in exile constantly telling the masses that only if they kept up the struggle could Peronism prevail once again. By adroitly exploiting their hopes as well as their hostility toward the military governments that had repressed them, Perón kept them in line and made it impossible for any other president to govern for long.

Only as the years passed did the magnitude of Perón's achievement become clear. A generation of working-class Argentines, many of them immigrants from abroad and from small towns in the country's interior, had been made to feel part of the nation for the first time between 1946 and 1955. For them Peronism and the Argentine nation were one and the same. To be anti-Peronista was to be disloyal to the nation as they understood it. After 1955, support for their exiled leader seemed their only way of getting their nation back, and for eighteen years they kept up the struggle. Their efforts were not in vain. In 1973 Perón was finally allowed to come home by a frustrated and exhausted military that stood by while Argentines went to the polls and returned him to the presidency one more time.

But the golden age of Peronism was not restored, and the 78-year-old leader died one year later, leaving the presidency to his wife Isabel, a loyal companion but one unprepared to direct the movement or govern the unruly nation. Administrative chaos, intense infighting within the movement, economic crises, and urban terrorism brought the nation almost to a halt, and in early 1976 the military took over once again. The dismal performance of the second Peronista regime delighted the Peronistas' opponents, most of whom hoped that Perón's death and the consequent disaster would undermine the faith of the rank and file once and for all. But nothing changes that quickly or comes that easily in Argentina. Despite the movement's repression by the military after 1976, its loyalists hung on and reasserted themselves when national elections were held in 1983. This time, however, without Perón to lead them, the Peronistas suffered their first defeat ever in free presidential elections. Although they were still supported by nearly one-half of the electorate, they could no longer credibly claim to be the country's only true majority party. The inauguration of Radical Raúl Alfonsín as president in December 1983 gave Argentines a new opportunity to live by the rules of free, competitive politics. Whether they do so will depend on the willingness of the Peronistas and the armed forces to adjust to democracy's requirements.

The populist game in retrospect

What can we conclude about the populist game? Why was it so popular yet so vulnerable to sudden interruption? And what did it accomplish besides raising the hopes of urban masses previously unrepresented in the highest political circles?

Populist movements were the creations of skillful politicians who used their new source of power to put domestic conservatives and foreign investors on the defensive. Yet because they were loosely organized and so dependent on a single leader, they were vulnerable to equally sudden eviction from office through the temporary decapitation of their leadership by the military. And because they were unwilling to deprive entrenched elites of their real power, populist governments were always their hostage, forced to rely on their produce to keep their economies intact. In short, the Populists brought millions of people into national political arenas in Brazil, Argentina, Colombia, Peru, and elsewhere, but they never laid the economic and organizational foundations necessary to keep them there. Instead, the urban masses were left to contend with governments that acted as their patrons one moment only to become their oppressors the next.

Populism was not an exercise in futility, however. It challenged the elite's monopoly of government and forced reassessments of national political purpose. It also ignited a debate over industrialization, its value, and means of promotion that continues today. Most important, the Populists opened the game to many persons who had been disenfranchised in the past. The fact that they did so in a heavy-handed and paternalistic manner rather than an orthodox democratic one does not reduce the importance of their achievement.

Political movements that gain office usually respond to concrete needs. Populism arose where rapid industrialization and urbanization had caused thousands to seek help from above. Where industrialization occurred much later, as in Venezuela, or where other popular parties were already in place as in Mexico, populist movements were less common. But in Argentina and Brazil thousands migrated from the countryside and small towns to Buenos Aires, São Paulo, and Rio de Janeiro looking for work in factories and commerce. The transition from rural to urban life was a shattering experience for many. Consequently, when a new kind of politician appeared with promises of economic security, they responded enthusiastically.

Had the Populists depended only on organized labor to sustain their movements, they would not have survived as long as they did. They also needed the cooperation of the entrepreneurs who managed their nations' commercial and industrial enterprises. The collaboration of such groups did not come easily, especially in Argentina, where the Populists' demagoguery frightened businessmen. Nevertheless, the Populists gained the support of many entrepreneurs, at least temporarily, by promoting the growth of national enterprises.

Also part of the coalition were the people who were given jobs in the populist governments. Until Perón and Vargas, the Brazilian and Argentine bureaucracies had been relatively small by world standards and, like those of most Latin American governments in the early twentieth century, were confined primarily to such rudimentary activities as the maintenance of public order, the provision of roads and postal services, and the management of conservative fiscal and monetary policies. During the 1920s both governments grew, and under Perón and Vargas their expansion was accelerated. Both leaders were motivated by two considerations: a desire to increase state involvement in the promotion of economic growth and the provision of social services and a need to provide patronage for their followers. But in transforming the state into a powerful economic force and public employer, they also added an important new player to the political game in the form of thousands of public employees who would use their bureau-

Table 6.4. *The structure of populist regimes*

Dominant components	Vargas (1950–4)	Perón (1946–55)
Origins of leader	Rural upper class	Small-town middle sector
	Professional politician Authoritarian president 1930–45	Professional soldier Instructor in military history, military attaché in Western Europe, participant in 1943 coup
Means of securing office	Election	Election
Role of political party	Supported by Social Democratic party and Brazilian Labor party, loose federations of local patronage machines, and organized labor	Supported by Peronista party created in 1945 on labor base and dominated by Perón
Role of ideology	Limited to nationalist and populist symbols with little substantive content	Very simple principles, emphasizing ties of leader to masses, nationalism, industrial welfare state
	Almost no impact on policy	Influenced policy only during initial phase, of regime
Treatment of opposition	Co-optation	Verbal and physical harassment
	Manipulation through use of, access to patronage and public purse	Economic discrimination Occasional jail or exile

cratic power to protect themselves and their agencies against anyone who threatened them in later years.

Last there was the military. Like civilians, military officers were divided over populism. Yet, without their collaboration Perón never could have taken office in 1946 and dominated Argentine government for ten years, nor could Vargas have returned in 1951. Initially the young and more nationalistic officers were among their most enthusiastic supporters. For some, it was a matter of personal and institutional pride to support anti-status quo movements that promised to increase the nation's economic strength; others welcomed populism because it opened new opportunities for more direct military involvement in the direction of state enterprises. The support of the military proved a mixed blessing, however. Direct military involvement in the populist game helped protect the government from its opponents; yet, by exposing their administrations to military scrutiny, the Populists could not conceal the excesses and incompetence that often plagued their personalistic rule. Military officers who took pride in the economic achievements of populism were quick to assail the economic crises it provoked and the inefficiencies it encouraged. Moreover, the participation of the officers in the populist game also increased the military's politicization, touching off factionalism and bitter rivalries between officers favored by the president and those not so favored. Eventually, Argentine and Brazilian officers concluded that their countries could no longer afford the demagoguery and waste of populism and took action to bring populist rule to an end.

One player was conspicuously missing from the populist game. The *campesinos* were among neither its loyal supporters nor its active opponents. Although Perón received many votes from Argentina's poor farmers and rural laborers, he never brought them into his ruling coalition or tried to change their condition through agrarian reform. Vargas ignored the plight of the rural poor altogether. In fact, he actively cultivated the support of the landed elite by refraining from threatening the rural power structure. The Populists looked to the urban centers for the salvation of their countries and saw little to be gained, in the short run at least, from meddling with the economic and social structure of the countryside. It was left to their reformist successors to demonstrate that industrialization could not succeed without the modernization of the rural sector as well.

A difference between the populist coalitions formed in Argentina and Brazil was the greater fluidity and diversity of the latter. Few political coalitions have been broader than the one created by Getulio Vargas in the late 1930s and expanded upon his return to office in 1951. It was not really a coalition in any formal sense, but a loose collection of economic groups whose leaders believed there was more to gain by cooperating with Vargas and his bureaucrats than by opposing them. Instead of relying on any single group, Vargas tried to appeal to nearly all, using his authority to reward them for coopera-

Table 6.5. *Populist economic programs*

	Vargas (1950–2)	Perón (1946–8)
Objectives	Industrialization Elimination of trade deficits Moderate improvement of welfare of urban workers	Industrialization National economic autonomy Major improvement of welfare of urban workers
Instruments	High level of investment especially in public enterprises Currency devaluations and import controls Increased wages Mild economic nationalism	State control of banking State control of foreign trade and redistribution of rural profits to public and industrial sectors Nationalization of foreign-owned utilities and payment of foreign debt Increased wages and income transfers to urban workers High level of public investment in infrastructure

tive behavior or deprive them if they opposed him. The more he showered them with favors and regulations, the more dependent each became on the Brazilian state. And the more dependent they were, the easier it was for Vargas to secure their collaboration.

Perón's coalition was narrower than Vargas's and his political style more combative. Where Vargas managed to integrate rural and urban, upper- and lower-class players into his coalition, Perón attacked the agro-exporter elite and limited admission to his movement to organized labor and a new class of small business owners and industrialists. These differences were due in large part to the two men's contrasting development strategies. Perón was convinced that he had to deprive Argentine cattlemen and farmers of their profits in order to finance industrialization. Vargas believed that industrialization could be achieved without making Brazilian landowners and farmers pay for it.

In matters of development policy the Populists were not noted for their contributions to economic theory. They were practitioners who followed their instincts, taking the simple notions of government investment and regulations and applying them to the promotion of industrialization and social welfare. They were less interested in the historical and structural roots of underdevelopment than they were in the selection of a few policies that produced noticeable results. They usually succeeded in the short run only to discover that their gains could not be sustained because of their vulnerability to the forces of the international market, the resistance of elites to their programs, and their own errors.

Populists raised the hopes and expectations of masses in Latin America, not just where they ruled but in other nations as well. Nationalism and public welfare became popular causes throughout the region after World War II. But the Populists were not the only ones to translate popular aspirations into political action after the war. Even more ambitious were the democratic reformers who rose to power in Venezuela, Chile, Peru, and Costa Rica. Joining a belief in constitutional government with a desire to improve the lot of the rural as well as the urban poor in the process of promoting national development, they created mass-based parties of their own, challenged and defeated opponents on the right and on the left at the polls, and earned the right to govern in several nations. How they fared is the subject to which we must now turn.

Further reading

General

Di Tella, Torcuarto. "Populism and Reform in Latin America," in Claudio Veliz, ed., *Obstacles to Change in Latin America*. London: Oxford University Press, 1965, pp. 47–74.
Lipset, Seymour Martin. "Fascism: Left, Right and Center," in Seymour M. Lipset, *Political Man: The Social Bases of Politics*. Garden City, N.Y.: Doubleday (Anchor Books), 1963, pp. 127–82.
van Niekerk, A. E. *Populism and Political Development in Latin America*. Rotterdam University Press, 1974.

Argentina

Alexander, Robert. *The Perón Era*. New York: Columbia University Press, 1971.
Baily, Samuel. *Labor, Nationalism and Politics in Argentina*. New Brunswick, N.J.: Rutgers University Press, 1967.

Blanksten, George. *Perón's Argentina*. Chicago: University of Chicago Press, 1953.

Diaz Alejandro, Carlos F. *Essays on the Economic History of the Argentine Republic*. New Haven, Conn.: Yale University Press, 1970.

Di Tella, Torcuarto. "Stalemate or Coexistence in Argentina," in James Petras and Maurice Zeitlin, eds., *Latin America: Reform or Revolution?* Greenwich, Conn.: Fawcett, 1968, pp. 249–63.

Falcoff, Mark, and Ronald Dokart, eds., *Prelude to Perón*. Berkeley: University of California Press, 1975.

Fraser, Nicholas, and Marysa Navarro. *Eva Perón*. New York: Norton, 1980.

Page, Joseph. *Perón: A Biography*. New York: Random House, 1983.

Potash, Robert A. *The Army and Politics in Argentina, 1928–1945: Irigoyen to Peron*. Stanford, Calif.: Stanford University Press, 1970.

The Army and Politics in Argentina, 1945–1962: Peron to Frondizi. Stanford, Calif.: Stanford University Press, 1979.

Silvert, Kalman H. "The Costs of Anti-Nationalism: Argentina," in K.H. Silvert, ed., *Expectant Peoples: Nationalism and Development*. New York: Random House (Vintage Books), 1963, pp. 347–72.

Smith, Peter. *Argentina and the Failure of Democracy: Conflict Among Political Elites, 1904–1955*. Madison: University of Wisconsin, 1974.

Snow, Peter. *Political Forces in Argentina*. Boston: Allyn & Bacon, 1971.

Turner, Frederick, and José Miguens, eds. *Juan Perón and the Reshaping of Argentina*. Pittsburgh: University of Pittsburgh Press, 1983.

Wynia, Gary. *Argentina in the Postwar Era: Politics and Economic Policy in a Divided Society*. Albuquerque: University of New Mexico Press, 1978.

Brazil

Bello, Jose Maria. *A History of Modern Brazil 1889–1964*. Stanford, Calif.: Stanford University Press, 1966.

Dulles, John W. F. *Vargas of Brazil: A Political Biography*. Austin: University of Texas Press, 1967.

Furtado, Celso. *The Economic Growth of Brazil*. Berkeley: University of California Press, 1963.

Ianni, Octavio. *Crisis in Brazil*. New York: Columbia University Press, 1968.

Jaguaribe, Helio. *Economic and Political Development: A Theoretical Approach and a Brazilian Case Study*. Cambridge, Mass.: Harvard University Press, 1968.

Leff, Nathaniel H. *Economic Policy-Making and Development in Brazil 1947–1964*. New York: Wiley, 1968.

Roett, Riordan. *Brazil: Politics in a Patrimonial Society*. Boston: Allyn & Bacon, 1979.

Schmitter, Phillippe C. *Interest Conflict and Political Change in Brazil*. Stanford, Calif.: Stanford University Press, 1967.

Skidmore, Thomas E. *Politics in Brazil: 1930–1964*. New York: Oxford University Press, 1967.

Stepan, Alfred. *The Military in Politics: Changing Patterns in Brazil*. Princeton, N. J.: Princeton University Press, 1971.

Weffort, Francisco C. "State and Mass in Brazil." *Studies in Comparative International Development* 2: 187–96, 1966.
Wirth, John D. *The Politics of Brazilian Development: 1930–1954.* Stanford University Press, 1970.
Young, Jordon M. *The Brazilian Revolution of 1930 and the Aftermath.* New Brunswick, N.J.: Rutgers University Press, 1967.

7. The democratic reform game

Accepting majority rule is never easy, especially for the powerful few who are accustomed to getting their way through other means. It is even more doubtful when those chosen by the majority are determined to take something from the rich and give it to the poor. Yet that is precisely what the democratic reformers set out to do.

They came originally from the middle sectors, beginning as student activists who refused to assume their places in the old order. Unwilling to try armed revolution, they chose the liberal democratic route, hoping that they could mobilize enough popular support to force open the political process. They recruited laborers and *campesinos*, promising to improve their condition in exchange for their votes. Eventually they were elected to office in several countries, but few of them ruled for long, for their opponents seldom conceded defeat, preferring instead to fight back using nonelectoral means, including military intervention.

The idea of a well-organized, mass-based political party dedicated to improving the condition of the disadvantaged and disenfranchised did not originate in Latin America, of course. There were already models to draw upon, most notably the European Social and Christian Democratic movements; from them and others the Latin Americans took most of their notions of recruitment and constituency organization, though in each case adaptation to national conditions became necessary, and the forms the democratic reform parties eventually took often differed from the models that inspired them.

The democratic reformers tried to do for the rural and urban lower and middle classes in less industrialized nations like Chile, Venezuela, and Costa Rica what the Populists had sought to achieve primarily for organized labor in the more rapidly industrializing ones like Brazil and Argentina, namely, make it possible for their constituents to gain shares of the bounty generated by economic modernization. They were ideologically more sophisticated, better organized, and less reliant on the personal appeal of a single leader than were the Populists.

166

And where populist economics involved quick and often superficial solutions to fundamental development problems, the democratic reformers chose the more sophisticated progressive modernization strategy with its ambitious goals of structural reform in the countryside and government-induced industrial development aimed at increasing and spreading national wealth.

The life of Latin America's democratic reformers was never easy. Unlike reform politicians in the United States, Great Britain, and Scandinavia who take public respect for constitutional rules for granted, most Latin American reformers could never do so; instead it was their task to create constitutional regimes in hostile environments at the same time that they were trying to redistribute wealth and power. They could not assume that democratic rules were in any way normal for their societies; nor should we do so when we analyze them.

Liberal democratic rules are derived from a few beliefs about society and its governance. The first maintains that separate, diverse, and sometimes conflicting interests among individuals and groups are a normal and permanent feature of social and political life. In other words, people by nature and position differ on many things, and, therefore, one must give up any hope of achieving uniformity of interest within society. All that one can do is establish procedures for dealing with the conflicts caused by inevitable differences. Second, these procedures or rules must be agreed upon if they are to be effective. They cannot be changed with each dispute; if they could be, few would have any confidence in them. And third, conditions must be established that guarantee that the winners and losers of political disputes are not known in advance of their resolution. Competition is crucial to motivate everyone to submit disputes for resolution under the agreed-upon rules. The less competitive the game is, the less democratic it becomes, and the less acceptable it will be to all players in the game. Though no democratic game ever achieves perfect competition, it cannot survive for long without substantial amounts of it.

Instead of asking, as we often do, why many Latin Americans choose not to live by the rules of liberal democracy, it is more fruitful to ask why any would want to live by them. After all, democracy is neither easily achieved nor very satisfying to many who try it.

The democratic reformers offer one answer. Pluralists in spirit, they believe in the inherent diversity of interests in society and claim that constitutional democracy is the most flexible means for mediating among competitors. They also prefer democratic rules because they consider them advantageous to their own pursuit of power. Not having the economic resources needed to compete with the rich or the weapons required to defeat the military, these predominantly middle-class politicians believe the selection of authorities in free elections gives them the best opportunity to use their organizational skills to secure public office. Of course, elections alone do not guarantee political triumph. Securing the elite's respect for rules that permit their eviction from office is always problematic. Nor can one assume that the reformer's appeals to the masses will always gain their support. In fact, the poor judge democracy harshly if it fails to meet their material needs regardless of its moral virtues. Democratic reformers are aware of all of this, but are undeterred by it; if anything characterized their past efforts, it was not naivete, but their determination to work tenaciously against very heavy odds. Nowhere is this more apparent than in the achievements and failures of democratic reformers in Chile and Venezuela.

Chile and Venezuela

Chile and Venezuela have much in common. Both have relatively small populations (11 and 15 million, respectively, in 1980), most of their people live in close proximity to each other, both depend heavily on mineral exports for their welfare (copper in Chile and petroleum in Venezuela), and both were governed by sophisticated, well-organized democratic reform parties during the 1960s (Christian Democrats [PDC] in Chile and the Acción Democrática [AD] party in Venezuela).

But there the similarities stop. Their political histories are quite different. Constitutional democracy prevailed in Chile after 1931, giving it one of the region's longest experiences with democratic politics by the time the Christian Democrats took office in the mid-1960s. Venezuela, in contrast, was ruled by autocrats until 1958. The only exception, an abortive three-year try at constitutional democracy after World War II, merely illustrated how strong the Venezuelan elite's hold on politics was. But, paradoxically, once established, democratic reformism has survived much longer in Venezuela than in Chile, where it was brought to an abrupt and brutal halt in 1973 by a military that tightly controlled the nation for over a decade thereafter.

These contrasting histories invite a host of questions. Why, for example, was the democratic game brought to a halt in one country but not in the other? Are the answers found in the strategies of the players, their relative strengths, or the conditions under which the game was played? And what did the democratic reformers actually accomplish in Chile and Venezuela? Did they achieve any of their reform objectives? Finally, what about democracy and reform: Were they compatible given the distribution of economic power in Chile and Venezuela, or was the struggle an unwinnable one from the outset, as critics on the Right and the Left contend? It is to the search for answers to these and similar questions that we shall now turn.

Democratic reform in Chile

Chile escaped the *caudillo* wars that plagued most Latin American countries after Independence because of the unusual unity of its small political elite and the loyalty of the military to it. The strong executive-dominated governments that ruled Chile throughout most of the nineteenth century were replaced in 1891 after a brief civil war by a "parliamentary" regime dominated by an elite-controlled national congress. The latter, torn from the outset by interparty conflict that manifested itself in continual cabinet instability, collapsed in 1924, and after a succession of brief military governments was replaced in 1932 by a constitutional regime that governed Chile without interruption until 1973. Not only did the Chileans enjoy greater political stability than most Latin American countries after 1932, but they did so using an unusually sophisticated multiparty system and a stubborn commitment to competitive electoral politics. It was a system, however, that was controlled effectively by upper-class and middle-sector parties, which tolerated working-class opposition only as long as their interests were not threatened. When working-class parties occasionally did get out of line, they were outlawed, as was the Communist party between 1947 and 1958.

The Christian Democratic party did not have to fight for admission against ruling autocrats as did the Venezuelans and most other reform parties. What they needed at the outset was not a plan of political reconstruction but an election strategy that could generate a large enough following to defeat its conservative, moderate, and radical rivals. Two decades after they commenced their uphill struggle, they succeeded. Under the leadership of Eduardo Frei, they won the presidency in 1964 and spent the next six years implementing their program of economic and social reform.

The Christian Democrats

The rise of Chile's Christian Democrats from a small faction within the Conservative party in the late 1930s to the presidency in 1964 is an impressive, though unspectacular, story. Its origins can be traced back to a group of law students at the Catholic University of Chile in the late 1920s. Sons of conservative families, Eduardo Frei, Radomiro Tomic, Bernardo Leighton, and Rafael Agustín Gumucio took their inspiration from philosophers who had sought to revitalize Roman Catholicism as an agent of social change. They had become disillusioned with conservatism, but they wanted no part of the Marxist or anticlerical Liberal parties then active in Chile. For them social Catholicism offered an alternative to the excessive individualism and economic exploitation fostered by nineteenth-century liberalism and the atheism and collectivism of communism. There was, however, no Chilean party ready to embrace their new ideology during the 1930s. The Conservative and Liberal parties sought only to preserve the power and privileges of urban and rural elites and foreign investors, the middle-sector Radicals were anticlerical and little concerned with social justice in the countryside, and the Socialists and Communists rejected Christian theology. The only option, it became clear in 1937, was to organize a party of their own able to challenge the others.

The conversion of a small, obscure political party into an organization that attracted a majority of the Chilean electorate in the 1964 presidential elections involved a long campaign that did not generate concrete results until the mid-1950s. The young Falangists, as the Christian Democrats were first known, played the game according to the conventional rules of Chilean politics, winning an occasional seat in the legislature and from time to time accepting cabinet posts in coalition governments. Their breakthrough came in 1957 when Eduardo Frei, the party's leader, was elected senator from Santiago, the nation's capital, and a year later polled 21 percent of the popular vote in the national presidential election. From that election it became clear that by doubling their popular support they could win the presidency in a three-way contest with the Socialist-Communist coalition on the

Table 7.1. *Chile: historical background*

1817	Independence from Spain
1830	Autocratic republic created under President Diego Portales
1871	Liberal republic created through efforts of Liberal, Radical, and National parties
1891	Parliamentary republic organized to reduce power of strong executive and give supremacy to Congress
1921	Liberal reformer, Arturo Alessandri, elected president
1924	Military closes Congress and installs Alessandri as president with decree powers to implement constitutional reforms, including proportional representation and strengthening of executive
1927	Colonel Carles Ibañez seizes power and creates personal dictatorship
1931	Colonel Marmaduke Grove creates "socialist republic," which lasts six months
1932	Republican government restored and Arturo Alessandri elected president
1938	Popular Front government of Radicals, Democrats, Communists, and Socialists elected
1952	Carlos Ibañez elected president on populist-type platform
1957	Christian Democratic party created from Falange Nacional (organized in late 1930s) and Social Christian wing of Conservative party
	Communist and Socialist parties form coalition from Frente de Acción Popular (FRAP)
1958	Conservative-Liberal candidate Jorge Alessandri elected president
1964	Christian Democratic leader Eduardo Frei elected president
1965	Christian Democrats win majority in Chamber of Deputies
1970	Socialist leader of Unidad Popular coalition, Salvador Allende, elected president
1973	Unidad Popular government overthrown by military, ending forty-one years of uninterrupted constitutional government
1983	General Augusto Pinochet celebrated his tenth anniversary as supreme ruler of Chile

left and the Conservatives on the right. It was to that objective that they devoted their energies over the next six years.

The Christian Democrats had relied on candidate-based, local constituency organizations during their formative years, but after 1958 they accelerated efforts to build mass organizations to which they recruited the so-called marginals – urban slum dwellers, *campesinos*, and the unemployed who had been effectively excluded from the political process in the past. In doing so they hoped to weaken parties on the Left by denying them their natural constituencies. Chile's Socialist and Communist parties, whose coalition received 30 percent of the vote in 1958, had strong organizations that drew their support primarily from organized labor and intellectuals. In the mid-1950s they became as interested as the Christian Democrats in expanding their ranks by recruiting the rural poor. To neutralize their efforts as well as recruit thousands to its ranks the PDC organized neighborhood associations with the help of the clergy and university students and promoted the creation of *campesino* organizations and farm worker unions.

Especially helpful to the PDC (as well as the Communists and Socialists) were electoral reforms adopted in 1962. In 1932 Chilean Conservatives had designed a constitutional order that restricted participation in elections to middle- and upper-class males. In 1949 they were forced to extend the franchise to women, and finally, in 1962 their congressional opponents secured passage of legislation that extended the vote to nearly all Chileans. Attracting these new voters to their party became the primary objective of the PDC during the next two years.

The support of new voters was, by itself, not enough to catapult the Christian Democrats to victory. They also needed the votes of thousands of citizens who had opposed them in 1958. As we can see from Table 7.2, only 21 percent of the electorate had voted for the Christian Democrats in 1958, whereas almost 30 percent had supported the Socialist-Communist coalition, FRAP, led by Socialist Senator Salvador Allende. The likelihood of the Christian Democrats' taking votes from the Left was remote, for the Marxist parties had, since the 1920s, developed a hard core of supporters, especially in the labor movement. This dictated that the PDC seek some support among those who had supported the Conservatives or Liberals in 1958.

But how does a political party that campaigns on a platform of social and economic reform attract conservative and middle-sector voters? It does so, Frei and his colleagues decided, by convincing Conservatives that the Christian Democrats offered them their only hope for preventing a dreaded Marxist victory in the 1964 elections. The logic of their argument was simple. In 1964 Chileans were locked in a three-way electoral battle involving parties of the Left, Center, and Right, with each standing a chance of victory. Thus, if the con-

Table 7.2. *Chilean presidential elections, 1958 and 1964 (%)*

Party	1958	Party	1964
Conservative-Liberal parties		Democratic Front	5
Jorge Alessandri	31.6		
Christian Democratic party		Christian Democratic party	
(PDC)		(PDC)	
Eduardo Frei	20.7	Eduardo Frei	55.7
Popular Action Front (FRAP)		Popular Action Front (FRAP)	
Salvador Allende	28.9	Salvador Allende	38.6
Others	18.9		

servatives, Liberals, and Christian Democrats competed with each other, dividing slightly less than two-thirds of the electorate equally among them, they would make possible the election of Marxist Salvador Allende. To avert such a fate, the Conservatives should throw their support to the Christian Democrats, according to this logic. If the Christian Democrats needed some assistance in persuading Conservatives to support their candidates, they received it in March 1964, six months before the presidential election, when a Conservative was upset by the FRAP candidate in a special congressional election for a minor rural seat. They also received it from the United States government, which helped finance the PDC campaign and worked hard to persuade Conservatives to join in the PDC's anti-Marxist coalition, arguing that without it a FRAP victory was certain. Consequently, the threat of a Marxist victory suddenly seemed likely, and, exploiting it to the fullest, Christian Democratic candidate Eduardo Frei secured enough Conservative and Liberal party support at the last minute to block Salvador Allende's path to the presidency. With the assistance of his allies on the Right, Frei, who had received only 21 percent in 1958, polled an amazing 56 percent of the popular vote in the September 1964 election. Thus, playing by the Chilean rules and turning them to his personal advantage, Eduardo Frei concluded a thirty-five-year uphill struggle with one of Chile's most impressive presidential victories.

Reform politics

Election victories open the door to public office, but they give the winner no assurance of success in governing the nation, as reformist presidents everywhere will testify. Exceptional skill and substantial good fortune are required to prevail in democratic societies. Unlike the authoritarian who can command obedience, securing compliance using force, the democratic leader must always deal with competitors whom the rules allow substantial latitude for obstruction.

Chile's Christian Democrats worked hard to make democratic reform work despite the odds against them. Once in office a rhetoric developed during three decades in the opposition was not enough. Suddenly they had to deliver on their promises of agrarian reform, increased national control over the nation's resources, improved social welfare, and accelerated industrial development. Unfortunately for Frei, Chile's was not a parliamentary system in which party victory meant control over the government but a presidential one in which Frei faced a legislature controlled by the opposition. Consequently, like other presidents his success depended, at a minimum, on his ability to do three things: create and maintain effective legislative coalitions, keep his own party united, and help his party win subsequent congressional and presidential elections.

First came the need for a coalition supportive of reform legislation. Frei had won the 1964 election by attracting conservative voters to his party. But once the Conservatives had accomplished their objective of denying Socialist Salvador Allende the presidency, the coalition dissolved. Consequently, until congresssional elections were held in March 1965, Frei could count only on the support of his own party which held 23 of 147 House and 4 of 45 Senate seats, hardly enough to secure the passage of his program against the combined opposition of Communist, Socialist, Radical, Conservative, and Liberal party legislators. So instead of seeking a coalition with one of these parties, the Christian Democrats put all their effort into the 1965 elections, asking Chileans to sustain the mandate they had given in September 1964. The strategy was in large part successful, for the PDC increased its hold on the House by taking 81 seats; however, it gained only 13 seats in a Senate election in which only half the seats were contested. Consequently, throughout the remainder of his term Frei had to work with a divided Congress in which the parties of the Left and the Right could unite to block PDC measures in the Senate.

Frei also faced serious divisions within his own party. Throughout his presidency the PDC was divided into three factions: one that supported Frei's moderate course, a second that demanded a more socialistic program, and a third that sought a compromise between the other two. Disputes over the government's program were common, but serious conflicts were initially avoided through the distribution of cabinet posts among members of all three factions. Gradually, however, frustration with the slow rate of reform increased, and disputes among the three wings of the party became more intense, especially during the 1967 party conference. Just as Frei was preparing to introduce austerity measures to deal with rising inflation, he was met with demands for the acceleration of reform through the adoption of the Plan Chonchol, a proposal prepared by agrarian reform minister Jacques Chonchol, advocating greater state control over the economy and more rapid land expropriation. The battle was eventually won by Frei and his supporters in the moderate faction, but their victory came at the expense of the loss of Chonchol and his followers, who left the PDC in 1969 to form their own party, the United Popular Action Movement (MAPU), which allied itself with the Marxist coalition that supported the candidacy of Salvador Allende in the 1970 election.

The real test of the Christian Democrats' political power came in the 1970 presidential elections. Since Frei was prohibited by Chilean law from succeeding himself, the party nominated Radomiro Tomic, a long-time party leader to the left of Frei ideologically. Like the previous one, the 1970 election was a three-way contest among the National party (formed by the merger of the Conservative and Liberal parties in 1966), which nominated elder statesman Jorge Alessandri who had been president between 1958 and 1964, the Christian Democrats led by Tomic; and a coalition on the Left, led again by Socialist Salvador Allende, this time called Popular Unity (UP). Alessandri promised to halt the reformism begun by the PDC, Tomic offered a more radical reformist program than Frei's, and Allende proposed a peaceful socialist revolution. The Conservatives once again held the trump card, for if they supported the PDC, it would undoubtedly win, but if they supported Alessandri, the election would be close, with any one of the three the possible winner.

This time both the National party and the Christian Democrats chose to gamble for victory by going it alone. National party leaders were convinced they stood to gain little from the accelerated reformism of another PDC administration. Bolstered by preelection polls that predicted Alessandri's victory, they fully expected to win a three-way race. Tomic believed that another alliance with the Conservatives would retard reform and make a mockery of his promise of radical change. Yet, because the leadership of the PDC refused to allow him to pursue a coalition with the Marxist parties, as he desired, he was forced to adopt an electoral strategy that sought to undercut Allende's support by appealing again to the urban and rural poor as well as to the middle sectors.

When the ballots were counted, Salvador Allende the Socialist, not Tomic or Alessandri, had won. In the weeks that followed the National and Christian Democratic parties had to make some of the hardest strategic decisions ever to face Chilean party leaders. Because Salvador Allende had received less than a majority of the popular vote (36.6 percent), he could not be inaugurated without confirmation by the majority of the Congress. And for that he needed the support of parties outside his coalition because they still controlled two-thirds of the seats.

Few judgments could have been more troublesome for a democratic reform party than the one made by the Christian Democrats in December 1970. If they confirmed Allende's election, they were gambling that he would respect the country's democratic traditions long enough to allow the PDC to regain the presidency in the 1976 elections. If they voted against confirmation, they would break the rules and invite others to do likewise, eventually perhaps undermining the whole system. Thus, in the face of clandestine efforts by the United States government and Chilean conservatives to prevent Allende's inauguration, the PDC legislators confirmed Allende's victory and their own electoral defeat, thereby upholding the democratic rules of the Chilean game.

Reform policy

Frei intended to use popular reform policies to attract the masses to the PDC, making it strong enough electorally to withstand future competition with Conservative and Marxist parties. But the party's constituency changed little under Frei, and in 1970 no more than one-third of the Chilean electorate preferred it to its rivals. What Frei did achieve with his reform politics, however, was the alienation of the Conservatives who had supported him over Allende in 1964. Thus, like so many who start from a position between the two extremes, Frei succeeded in hardening their opposition without drawing many constituents from either one.

The government's development program combined tax and regula-

tory measures aimed at increasing mass consumption and national production with agrarian reform. Frei's progressive tax reforms and liberal
wage policies raised consumption as intended, but with rising demand
for goods came the threat of rising inflation. When revenues from the
new taxes and foreign credits leveled off in 1967 and unions became
more militant in their wage demands, Frei was forced to cut back on his
popular expansionary measures. The decision was an especially bitter
pill for his party to swallow, for not only did it threaten its chances in
the forthcoming national elections, but it also raised concern within the
party about the ability of its leaders to overcome the nation's production and inflation problems. In their own defense, party leaders
claimed that the fault was not theirs but belonged to their opponents
who delayed their programs in Congress and obstructed their implementation using their influence within an unresponsive bureaucracy
and the labor movement. But whatever the cause, the result was the
same: Few Chileans were convinced that the Christian Democrats had
solutions to the nation's fundamental problems.

Reform involves much more than new solutions to inflation and
production problems, of course. At the heart of the progressive modernization strategy is agrarian reform. Even though it was blessed
with fertile lands, Chile had to import substantial food. In the 1950s,
moreover, it suffered from a constant exodus of the rural poor to
already overcrowded cities because of the impossibility of economic
survival on the land. The causes of low production and rural-to-urban
migration were the same: the maldistribution of property and its inefficient use by landowners. By the time Frei had come to power,
Chile's rural economies had been extensively analyzed and their defi-
ciencies were well known. The only question that remained was
whether the government could do anything about them.

Frei was not the first Chilean president to sign an agrarian reform
bill, but he was the first to implement one. In 1962, under the pressure of his coalition partners in the Radical party, Conservative President Jorge Alessandri had secured the passage of a weak agrarian
reform law. But like so many other agrarian measures adopted
throughout the hemisphere at the time, it had very limited application, having defined eligible property as only that which had been
abandoned or was used inefficiently. It is no wonder, then, that Frei
made agrarian reform a campaign issue in 1964 and a central part of
his legislative program in 1965. Nevertheless, despite its compelling

nature, Frei's bill did not become law until 1967 because of the opposition of Conservative and Marxist legislators, the former because they stood to lose property and power under the law and the latter because they did not want the Christian Democrats to be credited with alleviating the land tenure problem through their modest reforms.

The new law contained several innovative measures. First, size rather than use would determine expropriation. Large estates, regardless of how they were farmed, would be broken up. Second, the land would be purchased by the government at its declared tax value rather than its current market value. Because Chilean landowners habitually underdeclared their land value at tax time, this approach would penalize them for such practices as well as save government funds by lowering the cost of expropriation. Third, the landowner would be paid only 10 percent of the price in cash with the other 90 percent in twenty-five-year bonds. Finally, the expropriated estate would be turned over to the peasants who had worked it or lived in the immediate area and then organized into an *asentamiento* under the direction of an elected peasant committee and experts from CORA, the government agrarian reform agency. The actual administration varied from one *asentamiento* to another, with some dividing property into private plots, others formed into cooperatives, and a few farmed collectively. Frei's rural reforms were not, however, limited to the reallocation of property. He also encouraged the organization of farm workers' unions and their use to raise rural wages. At the same time, new incentives were given to farmers to raise production, and self-help projects were encouraged in rural villages to build schools, roads, and health care facilities.

Throughout his campaign and during his first year as president, Frei had promised to transfer land to 100,000 of the country's approximately 200,000 landless peasant families. It was a promise he could not complete. In fact, only 21,000 peasant families had received land by the time Frei left office in 1970. Legislative opposition, bureaucratic delays, technical problems, and obstruction by landowners turned a noble promise into a bitter disappointment and give Marxist opponents a campaign issue they could use to attract peasant support in 1970. The Frei government did raise the income of rural workers by an estimated 70 percent and increased rural production by an average of 3.8 percent a year, but it became clear in 1970 that despite their bold initiatives, the Christian Democrats had not solved their country's rural problems. They had made a beginning, but in the process they had raised hopes they could not fulfill and alienated a conservative elite that was prepared to risk defeat by the Marxists rather than lend further support to the Christian Democrats in 1970.

The "Chileanization" of the foreign-owned copper industry was more easily achieved. Like most Latin American countries, Chile was heavily dependent on the export of a single commodity to finance its development. When copper prices dropped, so did the performance of the nation's economy. Naturally Chileans resented their vulnerability; what made it worse was that foreigners, not Chileans, owned and operated most of the mines. The Christian Democrats and the Marxists had responded to popular sentiments in their presidential campaigns, promising to put the mines under national control. But whereas Allende called for their complete nationalization, Frei proposed a less drastic solution, one he labeled "Chileanization." Rather than evict the Braden, Anaconda, and Kennicott corporations, the Chileanization law, which gained legislative approval with Conservative party support, only authorized the Chilean government's purchase of 51 percent of the shares in the largest mine (owned by the Braden Company). The deal, which was supported by moderates within the PDC and tolerated by foreign investors, was severely criticized by Socialists and Communists as a sellout to foreign interests. Frei nevertheless held firm to his moderate course, arguing that anything more radical would drive foreign investors from the country and severely damage the economy. The issue became one of the most controversial the Christian Democrats faced during Frei's tenure because it forced them to confront directly the costs of compromising with the foreigners whose control over the Chilean economy they were trying to reduce. It divided the party during the 1970 presidential campaign and gave the Marxists another popular issue to use against the PDC.

The limits of democracy: the Allende years

Under what condition does the democratic game work in Latin America? And under what conditions does it fail? Clearly we are better able to answer the second question than the first, since experience with failures is much greater than with successes. In most instances the democratic game is insecure from the outset because some players simply refuse to live by its rules. But there have been some outstanding exceptions, and none greater than Chile, where for forty years all players seemed to tolerate each other and abide by constitutional rules. But even the Chilean democracy did not endure, as the world discovered one September day in 1973 when the Chilean military seized control.

We are left to speculate about why the constitutional rules were broken in Chile. Was it because constitutional government and Socialist politics were incompatible, as some contend? Should they be? After all, Socialists have governed recently in Greece, Spain, and France without meeting the Chilean fate. And what about foreign involvement? Was the United States government responsible for Allende's downfall, adding him to its list of deposed leftists it found intolerable? Clearly, the abrupt termination of constitutional democracy in Chile raises a host of challenging questions about the nature of class conflict, foreign intervention, and the strength of democratic institutions. It also offers insights into political tolerance and how it is shaped by economic and political self-interest.

Salvador Allende was not supposed to win the 1970 elections. In fact, his Marxist coalition barely made it to the polls. Many Socialists wanted to boycott the elections to protest Chile's bourgeois democracy, which they claimed had always been rigged against them. Only when half of the members of the Socialist party's central committee agreed to abstain from its endorsement vote did Allende secure the party's nomination. But even then their Popular Unity coalition of Socialists, Communists, and three minor parties had no chance of victory if the Conservatives agreed to support the Christian Democratic candidate as they had done in 1964. Of course, they did not support the PDC in 1970, but ran their own candidate and in doing so gave the UP the opportunity it needed.

Once in office Allende still faced divisions within his own ranks. The collaboration of the Socialists and the Communists had been motivated more by political necessity than mutual affection. The Socialists were the most doctrinaire of the two, eager to achieve the immediate creation of a socialist economy, whereas the Communists were pragmatic, more willing to compromise with opponents in order to avoid provoking military intervention. Although the two parties agreed on most of their ultimate goals, their debates over legislative strategy, economic policy, and the mobilization of the masses placed

Table 7.3. *Chilean presidential election, 1970*

Party	Male voters	Female voters	Total	Percent
National party (PN) Jorge Alessandri	479,104	557,174	1,036,278	35.3
Christian Democratic party (PDC) Radomiro Tomic	392,736	432,113	824,849	28.1
Popular Unity party (UP) Salvador Allende	631,863	443,753	1,075,616	36.6

constraints on Allende that would never have been tolerated by Marxists like Fidel Castro in Cuba.

Instead of viewing Salvador Allende as the leader of a typical Marxist party-state, we should see him for what he was: an elected president who was plagued by problems common to the leaders of minority coalitions who face stiff legislative opposition. The radical character of his program merely made his job harder by threatening Chilean entrepreneurs and causing the United States government to do what it could to prevent Chile from becoming a Marxist success.

As a political strategist, Allende was actually quite cautious. He knew that his electoral triumph had been slim and that he lacked majority support in Congress. Although he was eager to achieve his economic revolution, he did not want to antagonize his Christian Democratic opponents. Consequently, he sought to deprive the economic elite of its wealth and power without harming the middle sectors. In practice, this meant a gradual nationalization of large enterprises accompanied by a prohibition on measures that might deprive the middle sectors of their wealth and property. Separating the two sets of interests proved quite difficult in practice, however, since most professionals, technicians, and white-collar workers depended on private enterprise for their livelihood. As Allende's critics within his own coalition warned him, nationalization, even if carried out in a gradual manner, would sooner or later threaten all members of the Chilean bourgeoisie, making the cultivation of their support a hopeless and self-defeating endeavor. Nevertheless, Allende held firm to his original strategy, guided by the belief that his revolution would be achieved only if he avoided a direct confrontation with potential middle-sector opponents.

Allende's development program had two primary goals: the gradual socialization of the means of production and an immediate increase in mass consumption to build a working-class–middle-sector alliance. The first was essential if the state was to reallocate society's resources in a more equitable manner; the second was prompted by Allende's determination to secure a majority of the popular vote in future elections as well as protect his government from its upper-class and foreign enemies.

During 1971 and 1972, the government moved swiftly toward the socialization of Chile's capitalist economy. Its immediate objective was the creation of a mixed economy that included three sectors: one controlled entirely by the state, another composed of mixed public-private enterprises where the state was dependent on the private sector's supply of technology, and a third consisting of small private firms involved in retail sales. The government requisitioned some private firms without compensation, using an old law that permitted the seizure of firms that refused to produce at capacity. The local plants of multinational enterprises like Ford, General Motors, and Dow Chemical were among those taken in this manner. Others – for example, all banks, Coca-Cola, Dupont, and Bethlehem Steel – were purchased at book value. And a few, most notably the Kennicott, Braden, and Anaconda copper mines, were nationalized with congressional approval but denied compensation because, according to Popular Unity officials, they were guilty of extracting excess profits and therefore had already taken their compensation. Many foreign firms, however, were left untouched in the initial round because they provided essential goods and services; among these were IBM, Xerox, Mobil, Texaco, Exxon, and RCA. In fact, Allende never went as far with nationalization as his more militant supporters would have preferred or his enemies had feared. Nevertheless, the nationalizations eventually alienated many Christian Democrats who were initially disposed to cooperate with the government; equally important, they also imposed an immense fiscal burden on the Chilean state that heavily taxed its limited resources.

As a Marxist Allende believed that the proletariat would continue to be exploited as long as it was denied control over the means of production. And as an experienced campaigner and party leader, who had received less than 40 percent of the popular vote in 1970, he knew his hope of electoral victory in the March 1973 congressional elections rested with the mobilization of the urban and rural poor and many in the middle sectors. Accordingly, he decreed across-the-board wage increases during 1971, expanded public works programs giving jobs to the unemployed, and to the distribution of scarce foodstuffs to retail outlets that served the urban poor. As a consequence, 1971 was a boom year for Chilean workers, whose real income rose by an average of 40 percent during that year alone.

Popular Unity also had a plan for rural development. The Marxists had blamed Chile's failure to feed itself on the inefficient use of farmland by *latifundistas*. Moreover, the plight of the Chilean poor could be traced, they argued, to the antiquated class structure that prevailed in the countryside. Accordingly, Allende pledged himself to the speedy completion of Frei's agrarian reform program to improve the lot of the *campesinos* and foster a higher level of production. Prompted by a wave of land seizures by impatient *campesinos*, Allende moved fast, expropriating and redistributing twice as much land in his first two years as Frei had done in his last three. In 1965, 55 percent of Chile's farmland was held by owners of farms that exceeded 200 acres in size, but by the end of 1972 only 2.9 percent was still left in such large privately owned units. Expropriated lands were reorganized in several different ways, with some turned into agrarian reform centers or large production units controlled by the *campesinos* who worked them, and others, especially those of a more agro-industrial type such as cattle breeding, run as state farms by government administrators.

Four conditions had to be met for Allende's economic program to succeed. First, economic expansion had to be sustained in order to satisfy the demands of working-class and middle-sector consumers simultaneously. If it was not, shortages would develop, inflation increase, social tensions rise, and support for the government, especially among the middle sectors, decline. Second, the government had to gain enough control over the economy through its nationalizations to capture industrial and financial profits for the treasury and pay for its expansion of public works and other job-creating programs. Without substantially increased revenues, it would be forced to borrow heavily abroad or resort to inflationary Central Bank financing of the deficit. Third, exports, especially high foreign exchange producers like copper, had to be increased to pay for capital and consumer goods imports. This was especially important because Chile could expect little financial assistance from capitalist nations and international agencies who opposed its economic revolution. Finally, a rapid decline in agricultural production due to land expropriation had to be avoided. A drop in food production at a time of rising consumption would lead either to food shortages or increased imports to cover the deficit, neither of which Allende could afford. Obviously, the Allende program was plagued by hazards. If any one of these conditions was not met, serious problems could arise that might undermine the entire effort. Moreover, any failure could be easily exploited by enemies in the elite or from abroad who were determined to stop Allende's socialist revolution.

At first the program did quite well. In 1971 unemployment was reduced to nearly zero, the gross national product grew by nearly 9 percent, and prices rose by only 20 percent, slightly below the annual average of the Frei years. Despite expropriation and the controversy it caused, copper production also rose slightly. By taking a pragmatic approach to the Chilean economy rather than the more doctrinaire one recommended by radicals within his coalition, Allende had, it seemed, achieved the kind of economic growth and reallocation of income that would boost his political fortunes without inducing a violent reaction from his opponents.

But Allende's policies, it soon became apparent, were neither as bountiful nor as moderate as they first seemed. Cracks in his economic edifice, which began to appear in 1972, widened rapidly during the first half of 1973. Some were of his own making; others were helped by his foreign and domestic opponents. Hidden from view in 1971 were several disturbing facts. Although consumption rose, gross domestic investment declined by 5 percent as private firms responded negatively to the threat of expropriation, and the state, already heavily involved in spending to increase consumption, did little investing. Moreover, the fiscal and monetary policies followed at the end of 1971 differed substantially from those proposed by Allende after his inauguration. First, public revenues were much less than intended (owing in part to the refusal of opponents in Congress to authorize tax increases), and expenditures were much greater. This forced Allende to increase the money supply by 100 percent to cover a fiscal deficit that was 71 percent larger than planned. Second, the balance of payments took a turn for the worse, accumulating a $315 million deficit in 1971

Table 7.4. *Chilean economic performance, 1971–3 (annual growth rates)*

	1971	1972	1973	1960–73
Gross national product at constant prices	8.9	1.0	−5.0	3.5
Gross domestic investment at constant prices	−5.0	1.6	−5.5	3.6
Retail price index	20.0	77.5	353.5	43.5

Source: World Bank, *World Tables 1976*. Washington, D.C., 1976, pp. 74–5.

after a $91 million surplus in 1970. An overvalued exchange rate, increased imports to meet consumer demand, the accelerated flight of financial capital, and a 30 percent drop in copper prices all contributed to the deficit. To make matters worse on the supply side, agricultural production began to fall during the 1972–3 harvest as the effects of low prices, a lack of seed and fertilizer, and administrative bottlenecks began to be felt. Finally, although the government managed to contain the inflationary effects of its programs in 1971 with price controls, prices began to rise rapidly in late 1972 and continued into 1973, increasing 190 percent during the first nine months of the year alone.

Inflation and shortages were not new to Chile, and governments had survived such conditions in the past. What made Allende's situation different was both the serverity of the economic problems he faced in 1973 and the determination of his enemies to exploit them. Prominent among the latter were the United States government and the multinational firms with investments in Chile.

The administration of Richard Nixon was opposed to Chile's Marxist government and was determined to secure its demise through any means short of direct military intervention. One tactic was to limit the flow of financial assistance to Chile. Allende had been careful to make payments on Chile's foreign debt in order to keep his country's good credit rating. The United States government was, however, determined to undermine that rating by cutting off new credit to Chile and forcing Allende to request moratoriums on the payment of Chile's debt, something he reluctantly did in late 1971. As part of its campaign to isolate Chile financially, the United States disbursed only $15.5 million in previously authorized loans in 1971, while Chile was

Table 7.5. *Distribution of seats in Chilean Chamber of Deputies and Senate before and after 1973 elections*

Party	Chamber	Senate
Before 1973 elections		
CODE (PDC-PN alliance)	93	32
UP (Socialists, Communists, Radicals, et al.)	57	18
After 1973 elections		
CODE	87	30
UP	63	20

repaying $51.3 million in old debts. At the same time, the United States maintained a generous program of aid to the Chilean military as well as an estimated $8 million in covert assistance to several opposition groups. Pressure was also exerted by the American-owned copper companies, which, displeased with Allende's refusal to compensate them for their expropriated enterprises, tried to block the delivery of Chilean copper in United States and European ports. The Chileans succeeded in bypassing some of the foreign embargoes and locating other sources of credit; nevertheless, the American blockade reduced Allende's policy options considerably.

The Popular Unity government might have survived the impediments placed in its path by President Nixon, but it could not overcome those imposed by an increasingly intractable and effective opposition within Chile that went to the streets to stop Allende. In September 1973, almost three years to the day after his election, they succeeded, but only after sacrificing Chile's democratic government to military wolves.

Allende had hoped to fortify his government by winning congressional elections in March 1973. As we can see from Table 7.5 the UP needed to gain nineteen seats in the Chamber of Deputies and eight in the Senate to gain majority control. Socialist and Communist party organizers had worked hard after Allende's inauguration to enlist new voters, hoping that his initial populistic wage and price policies would attract many to their ranks. Recognizing this, the Conservatives and the Christian Democrats joined ranks once again, merging their congressional campaigns to maximize their gains and prevent a UP victory in 1973. When the votes were counted it was apparent that Allende had been blocked once again, for the UP had secured only 44 percent of the popular vote and was still short of a majority in either house.

Elections were only one means of the opposition attack. Even more effective in the long run was their mobilization of protests that virtually shut down the Chilean economy in mid-1973. After searching for vulnerable points in Allende's armor, the PDC and Conservatives, with financial help from the United States and Christian Democrats in Europe, decided to concentrate on the copper and trucking industries.

In April 1973, miners and technicians at the El Teniente copper mine went on strike. Despite their ideological sympathy for the Popular Unity Government, they initially refused to accept its decision to reduce the amount of a promised wage increase to fight inflation. A month later a settlement was reached and most of the miners returned to work. However, a hard core of white-collar workers and technicians, encouraged by the PDC, remained on strike until July and did substantial damage to the production of copper. But the critical blow was struck by the trucking industry from June through August. Chile's truckers, most of whom are small, independent operators, had gone on strike once before in October 1972 to protest a government proposal to absorb them into a state trucking company. Backed by a sympathy strike of retailers, they had forced Allende to declare a state of siege, admit military officers to his cabinet, and eventually withdraw the proposal. When they went on strike again in June 1973 they were acting as part of a well-conceived opposition campaign to force the government to halt its program of nationalization, admit Christian Democrats to the cabinet, and chart a more gradual course. There is general agreement that the truckers' strike, which lasted until the coup of September 11, was the single most important factor in paralyzing the Chilean economy and fomenting political chaos during July and August 1973.

In the end, it was the military, emboldened by Conservative and Christian Democratic protests and provoked by rising civil strife and economic chaos, that abruptly brought Chile's brief socialist experiment to a close. The Chilean military, known since the 1930s for its restraint in political matters, had been divided in its assessment of the Popular Unity government and its program since Allende's inauguration. Some officers were willing to give the government their support as long as it carried out its revolution in a constitutional manner; members of this group, whose support Allende deliberately cultivated and whom he trusted until the day of the coup, went so far as to join Allende's cabinet in order to help him deal with the civil violence encouraged by his opponents. Others in the military opposed Allende and his attack on Chilean capitalism from the outset, but did not undertake to overthrow him until 1973, when increasing civil unrest and the encouragement of the Christian Democrats gave them the political support they wanted. By then, Allende's frantic last-minute efforts to deal with his collapsing economy and work out a compromise with his opponents were not enough to stop officers determined not only to evict Marxists from the government but also to end constitutional democracy in Chile.

What can we learn from the Chilean tragedy? First, it reminds us of the tentative and precarious nature of the democratic game. As we learned at the beginning of this chapter, there is no way of guaranteeing that democracy will work, for its survival hinges on the willingness of society's most powerful citizens to live by its rules. Although minor lawbreakers can be punished by the democratic state, the defiance of the mighty will always undermine it. Liberal democratic politics is, to be sure, sustained by something more than the narrow self-interests of players. Constitutional rules are also derived from beliefs in values like liberty and legality. But there is always tension between the maintenance of these values for society as a whole and individual self-interests, and Chile serves to remind us how vulnerable the former is when the vital interests of powerful players are seriously threatened.

Democracy works best when the stakes in the game are not great. The less one stands to lose, the less threatened one is by possible defeat. Conversely, the greater the stakes, the greater the threat and the harder it becomes to achieve peaceful conflict resolution. Political conflicts had always been intense in Chile's democracy but their resolution had exacted few sacrifices by the powerful until the 1960s. The middle sectors and the elite of organized labor gradually gained admission to the game after 1930 and, in exchange for their moderation, were given some of the spoils. The Christian Democrats raised the stakes somewhat in 1964 when they tried to reduce foreign control over the Chilean economy, increase workers' rights, and redistribute some rural property. That is why the Conservatives decided to fight back in the 1970 elections. Then Allende and the UP raised the stakes even more when they attacked the resources on which the Chilean bourgeoisie and its foreign allies had relied for their power and its maintenance.

Rather than ask why Chilean democracy failed to withstand this kind of test, a more appropriate question is why anyone should have expected it to survive. Should not Allende have understood the impossibility of his task at the outset, given the apparent incompatibility between liberal democracy and radical socialism? Perhaps, but it was not hard for Allende to convince himself that Chile would be different. He was, after all, an experienced politician who knew his country and its politics intimately. And by living by its rules all of his life he was rewarded with an opportunity to govern the nation. Allende had rejected armed insurrection as a political strategy long before, eschewing violence in favor of the democratic rules of the game. Consequently, when blocked by the opposition, he relied on what he knew best: political dexterity and the authority of his office, neither of which was enough.

Today Allende's former colleagues, most of whom still live in exile, continue to debate the wisdom of his strategy. Some insist that arming the masses was the only way to preserve the regime. The fact that Allende did not do so and was overthrown convinces them of the merit of their position. Others argue that such second guessing ignores realities of power and political practice within Chile at the time; arming the masses would have only provoked a coup earlier. The only real option he had, they argue, was moderation. Where he went wrong was not in his failure to engage the military in conflict, but his excessive populism, which damaged the economy by raising consumption too rapidly, causing rampant inflation and shortages, both of which gave the opposition the issues it needed to mobilize the middle sectors, truckers, copper workers, and other consumers against the regime.

No doubt disputes will persist as we continue to study the Allende experience. But if it teaches us anything it is the vulnerability of the democratic game to the intensification of conflict, especially over fundamental issues of economic development and the distribution of wealth. Tolerance is a fragile thing, and seldom does it survive anywhere when elites find themselves under assault by the masses.

Democratic reform in Venezuela

There was nothing in Venezuela's history that would have caused one
to predict its governance by a democratic regime in the mid-twentieth
century. On the contrary, torn by regionalism and civil war during
the nineteenth century and ruled by an old-fashioned dictator until
1935, Venezuela seemed doomed to autocratic politics. Escaping such
a fate was a major achievement, one that was made possible by Venezuelans' possession of a valuable resource – petroleum – which generated the income needed to finance development without threatening
the wealthy, and by the emergence of a class of politicians who
proved exceptionally skilled at creating mass organizations, placating
the armed forces, and securing agreements among contending players
that laid a foundation for constitutional rule.

Acción Democrática

Until 1935 the Venezuelan game was a traditional, dictatorial one.
Between 1908 and 1935 the country was governed by Juan Vicente
Gomez, a heavy-handed *caudillo* who modeled his rule after that of his
nineteenth-century predecessors. Among the few who protested his
brutality was a group of university students who came to be known as
the "Generation of 1928," for the year in which they started their
campaign for democratic government. It was from this nucleus that
the Acción Democrática party was formed a decade later.

Gomez died in 1935, and the Venezuelan oligarchy was quick to
replace him with officials who were no more eager to democratize the
nation's politics than they were. They ran the nation with little serious opposition, and those who did protest were jailed, exiled, or
forced underground. Nevertheless, quietly but diligently the future
leaders of the AD party spent a decade roaming the country, clandestinely recruiting *campesino* leaders and organized laborers into their
party, laying the foundation for a broadly based, national political
organization. They reasoned that if they were to rule the nation one
day, their chance would come only after they had secured enough
popular support to force the ruling conservatives to compete with
them in open elections.

The AD eventually made it, but when it did the door was opened
unexpectedly by the military and not through negotiated concessions

from the ruling elite. To this day Acción Democrática leaders deny that they conspired with the young officers who were responsible for the 1945 coup, arguing that to have done so would have made a mockery of their claims of being different from those who had ruled the nation using military might. Whether or not they actually did conspire, it is clear that with the exception of guerrilla warfare, which the democratically inclined AD leaders had rejected from the start, the coup was the only means available for dislodging the oligarchs at the time.

True to their word, Acción Democrática leaders persuaded the military to hold free elections of delegates to a constituent assembly, which wrote a new constitution in 1947. To no one's surprise, AD polled 78.8 percent of the Assembly vote, and a few months later won the presidency with 74.4 percent and captured two-thirds of the seats in the new Congress. The magnitude of its victory bore witness to the success of the mass organization strategy, which by 1948 had brought 300,000 urban workers into the AD-controlled Venezuelan Workers Confederation (CTV) and 43,000 peasants into its Venezuelan-Campesino Federation (FCV).

Venezuela's new democracy was short-lived, however. In 1948 the conservative opposition struck back with its own military coup, sending AD leaders back into exile, and disbanding all labor and peasant organizations. Massive electoral victories and a new constitution had not been enough to ensure that all players would conform to the new rules of the Venezuelan game. Acción Democrática's success had been too swift and its break with the past too sharp for the Venezuelan elite. When the government tried to use its mandate to execute a sweeping agrarian reform and revise the petroleum law, Conservatives responded with the coup. AD leaders spent the next ten years in exile reassessing their past campaigns and planning future ones. They came away from their deliberations chastened and less radical, convinced that more caution was required in their relations with Venezuela's agricultural and commercial elite and that more attention had to be given to creating a new role for the military in the democratic game. Despite the immense popularity of democratic government, it was still vulnerable to the economic power and military strength of its opponents. If reform measures were to succeed, it was concluded, they would have to be implemented slowly and carefully, avoiding direct attacks on those who were capable of striking back.

After a decade of exile AD leaders returned to try once again when officers, annoyed by the abuses of dictator Marcos Perez Jimenez, removed him in 1958 and called for elections. This time Romulo Betancourt, Raul Leoni, and their AD colleagues rejected their original vote maximization strategy in favor of alliances and preelection agreements with opposition parties and economic interest groups. Confident that they would capture the presidency, they concentrated on sharing power in order to secure the acceptance of the constitutional rules by their competitors. They pledged themselves to consultation when formulating reform policy and to dividing government patronage with coalition partners. They insisted that agrarian reform, government promotion of industrialization, and greater national control over petroleum resources remain government policy objectives, but promised moderation in the pursuit of each. And, equally important, they gained the support of the Venezuelan armed forces by offering them a large piece of the new government's budget for use in the modernization of weapons and the professionalization of officers.

The AD strategy succeeded in reducing partisanship and in reassuring those most threatened by reform policy. But it carried a high price, for to meet his obligations, Betancourt had to moderate the party's original platform substantially. Instead of redistributing wealth and property, he was forced to draw heavily on government revenues from petroleum sales to finance increased social services and to use public lands to satisfy the demands of the landless.

AD's primary concern when Venezuelans went to the polls in 1959 was not its possible defeat – for it was confident of victory – but the size of the newly created democratic opposition with which it would have to deal in the years ahead. Opposing the AD this time were the Christian Democratic party (COPEI), formed a decade before by Conservatives and Catholic reformers, and the Republican Democratic Union (URD), a party dedicated primarily to the candidacy of Jovito Villalba, a member of the Generation of 1928 who had abandoned his colleagues several years before. Both cut into Acción Democrática's base of support for Betancourt received only 49.2 percent of the popular vote, compared with the URD's Jovito Villalba's 34.6 percent, and COPEI's Rafael Caldera's 16.2 percent. AD's strength, as before, was in the countryside, where it received 66 percent of the rural vote. Of greater concern for furture elections was its failure to gain more than 13 percent of the vote in the cities.

Table 7.6. *Venezuela: historical background*

1821	Independence from Spain
1859	Federal (civil) War lasting four years, killing 40,000, and leaving country in economic ruin
1870	Eighteen-year dictatorship of Liberal Antonio Guzman Blanco begins
1908	Dictatorship of Juan Vicente Gomez begins
1921	Export of petroleum commences
1935	Juan Vicente Gomez dies
	Generation of 1928 student leaders, led by Romulo Betancourt, create Movimiento de Organizacion Venezolana (ORVE, later renamed Partido Democrata Nacional), predecessor of Acción Democrática party (AD)
1945	Union Patriotica Militar, organized by young officers and supported by Acción Democrática, overthrows conservative government of General Isaias Medina Angarita
1947	Under new constitution Acción Democrática wins presidential election and congressional majority
1948	Acción Democrática grovernment overthrown by military, which creates ten-year dictatorship of General Marcos Perez Jimenez
1958	Military overthrows Perez Jimenez government
1959	Romulo Betancourt, leader of Acción Democrática, elected president
1963	Raul Leoni, of Acción Democrática, elected president
1968	Rafael Caldera, of Christian Democratic party (COOPEI), elected president
1973	Acción Democrática regains presidency with election of Carlos Andres Perez
1976	All foreign petroleum and iron-mining firms nationalized
1978	Luis Herrera Campins, of Christian Democratic Party (COPEI), elected president
1983	Jaime Lusinchi, of Acción Democrática, elected president

Party government

Once elected Betancourt invited the Christian Democrats and the URD parties to join in the formation of a coalition government, and together they secured swift legislative passage of the programs they had agreed upon before the election. Subsequently the coalition crumbled, with the departure of the URD in 1960 and the COPEI in 1963. But by then it had served its purpose by reinforcing an ethic of peaceful competition and legislative cooperation among the country's principal parties. Clearly the Venezuelan experience indicates the utility of some kind of collusion among competing parties during the formative stage of constitutional government in countries where a tradition of intense conflict and distrust prevails. Though hardly sufficient by itself, it does seem to be a necessary condition for launching a competitive political process. Competition is quite risky for most participants, especially those who do not enjoy an immediate electoral advantage; only by assuring them that their competitors are trustworthy can one expect them to play by the new rules.

Dealing with its opponents is thought to be the primary problem facing the victorious party, but equally crucial is its ability to avoid divisions within its own ranks. Few things have cost Acción Democrática more than the inability of its activists to stay together. From the outset the left wing of the party opposed its conciliatory strategy and policy moderation, and in April 1960 a pro-Castro faction gave up and left the party. A second split occurred in early 1962 when a group of middle-level party leaders broke with Betancourt and the old guard, forming a small party of their own. In 1967 the AD split once again over the selection of the party's presidential candidate. Although the first two splits did little damage, the third one cost it a presidential election. Led by the party president Luis Beltran Prieto Figueroa, whom a large minority of the party members supported for president in 1968, the rebels formed their own party when the dominant faction, guided by Betancourt, insisted on the nomination of Interior Minister Gonzalos Barrios. The result, as we can see in Table 7.7, was the unexpected victory of Christian Democrat Rafael Caldera in 1968.

This brings us to the third condition that affects the survival of democratic reform parties: their ability to win elections. As we can see from Table 7.7, despite its failure to secure a majority of the vote, Acción Democrática won reelection in 1963, but went down in defeat in 1968. The COPEI victory in 1968 was not, however, as great a threat to AD and its reform program as first appeared. By the time of its election, COPEI had already adopted much of AD's platform and during its campaign had promised to retain most of the reforms already implemented. Consequently, AD's leaders were called upon to do little more than tolerate a familiar and trusted rival whose legislative program was virtually a carbon copy of their own. The primary threat posed by COPEI was not its possible maltreatment of the AD but its exploitation of its newly acquired power to increase its

Table 7.7. *Venezuelan presidential elections (%)*

Party	1958	1963	1968	1973	1978
Acción Democrática (AD)	<u>49.2</u>	<u>32.7</u>	28.3	<u>44.3</u>	43.3
Christian Democrats (COPEI)	16.2	20.2	<u>29.1</u>	30.3	<u>46.6</u>
Republican Democratic Union (URD)	34.6	17.5	12.0	3.2	–
Peoples' Electoral Movement (MEP)	–	–	19.3	5.1	1.1
Others	–	29.6	2.3	17.1	9.0

Note: The winner's percentage of the vote is underlined. Dashes indicate party noninvolvement.

popular support, thereby keeping the AD from recapturing the nation's highest office in 1973. But that seemed unlikely given AD's strong, if somewhat diminished, appeal to the Venezuelan masses. Consequently AD leaders stepped aside, proudly boasting that their electoral defeat marked a major triumph for democracy, giving the nation its first peaceful transfer of power from the leader of one party to the democratically elected leader of another.

AD self-confidence proved justified, for after the reunification of the party AD candidate Carlos Andres Perez gained 44.3 percent of the popular vote and the presidency in 1973. But the AD comeback proved to be only temporary; in 1978 the electorate turned to COPEI, electing Luis Herrera Campins president in a very close contest. Then in 1983 they brought Acción Democrática back, electing Jaime Lusinchi president in a landslide. Clearly something remarkable was happening: Not only had Venezuelan democracy survived for two decades, but for the fourth time in a row the party of the incumbent president was defeated at the polls. Equally significant, the country's multiparty system had become essentially a two-party one in which the electorate seemed as comfortable with the COPEI as it was with the AD.

How do we account for this unusual development? Part of the explanation lies in public acceptance of both parties as the principal founders of the country's constitutional order, which gives them a legitimacy and respect not available to parties created after 1959. It is also caused by their ideological convergence. Previously more conservative than the AD, the COPEI was forced by electoral realities to accept AD's agrarian, social, and petroleum policies. Moreover, after the initial reforms had been put into effect in the 1960s, both parties came to share in the defense of the new order, each relying on the other to protect the privileges of the country's new ruling elite.

Equally important is the wealth each party has at its disposal for campaigning. Wealthy Venezuelans, labor unions, and government bureaucrats want to be on the winning side and are eager to help both of the likely winners by donating to their campaign chests. In 1978, for example, AD and COPEI candidates spent an estimated $125 million (or $8 per capita) to discredit their opponents. Moreover, each presidential candidate was advised by a noted North American consultant; the victor, COPEI's Luis Herrera, a rather aloof politician, was converted by media expert David Garth into a folksy, tireless friend of the common people who claimed to stand with them against the upper class created by AD policies. For two months prior to the election radio and television stations broadcast hundreds of party ads. The more AD spends on its campaigns the more COPEI spends to keep up with it, making Venezuela's democracy one of the most expensive in the world.

Criticism of Venezuela's new Tweedledee-Tweedledum, mass media politics is common today, especially from those on the political left. What AD and COPEI have created, they argue, is not a popular democracy dedicated to social justice but a powerful state directed by a new elite drawn from the upper middle class who are more interested in their own aggrandizement through the use of patronage to manipulate the masses than in elevating the nation's poor. In rebuttal, AD and COPEI leaders argue that political order is necessary for industrialization, and order through a two-party democracy is preferable to either military authoritarianism or one-party socialism.

Reform policy

Few Latin Americans embraced the progressive modernization strategy more enthusiastically than Romulo Betancourt and Acción Democrática. No wonder, since they were among its original authors. Exiled by the military coup that installed autocrat Marcos Perez Jimenez in 1948, they took their notions of agrarian reform, industrialization, and social policy with them to the United Nations Economic Commission for Latin America in Santiago, Chile, and to Mexico City where they refined them in dialogues with foreign colleagues who shared their reformist objectives. These collective efforts, along with the lessons that were learned from the policy experiments of the Mexicans in the 1930s and 1940s, gave birth to the progressive modernization approach to development.

The Venezuelans have one advantage over other reformers in the hemisphere, namely, their possession of a means for financing reformist programs. The sale of petroleum has paid most of the government's bills since the 1920s. Its actual value to Venezuela has varied, depending on the price it brought on the world market and how much of the companies' profits the Venezuelan government took from the multinational firms that extracted, transported, refined, and marketed it. As long as there was a large surplus of petroleum on the world market, prices were low and revenues inadequate to finance the AD's ambitious development programs. Moreover, the smaller Venezuela's share of the profits, the less Venezuelans could take advantage of their wealth when prices rose. Therefore, action was necessary on both fronts.

This is why Betancourt placed so much stress on the development of a coherent, nationalistic petroleum policy from the earliest days of the AD party. His proposals consisted of two parts: One was to gradually increase the country's share of the revenues from sales abroad, and the other was to work in collaboration with other petroleum-producing nations to gain more control over the world supply and, therefore, over the world price, with the aim of raising the price as high as possible.

Nationalization of the foreign holdings would obviously have accomplished the first objective but the Venezuelan government was unprepared to manage the industry on its own when the AD first came to power in 1946. What they wanted was a strategy for increasing their take without alienating the firms whose technology and marketing networks were needed to extract and sell petroleum. Their solution was to gradually increase the nation's share, always leaving enough to keep the firms producing. In 1946 they increased Venezuela's portion from 30 to 50 percent, and then, when they returned in 1959, they raised it to 70 percent where it remained until 1976 when the industry was finally nationalized.

Nationalization had been contemplated for some time, but it was not until the AD lost the presidency to the COPEI and needed a popular campaign issue that AD candidate Carlos Andres Perez promised nationalization if elected in 1973. Equally important was that it was finally feasible, for by than several thousand Venezuelans had learned how to manage the facilities. Moreover, the Venezuelan government had accumulated the financing necessary to purchase the installations, thereby avoiding the more risky alternative of confiscating them without compensation to the powerful multinationals. With near unanimous congressional support the nationalization bill was approved in 1975 and implemented successfully in 1976. To assure the stability of the industry, many foreign technicians were hired by PETROVEN, the newly created government corporation, and the original foreign firms were granted the right to market the product as they had done before.

The AD's second objective – securing a high price on the world market – was harder to achieve since most of the forces that determined the price were out of its control. But here too the Venezuelans were patient, persistent, clever, and successful. Under the leadership of Betancourt's minister of petroleum and mines, Juan Pablo Perez Alonso, the organization of Petroleum Exporting Countries (OPEC) was formed by Third World petroleum producers in 1960. Not until the early 1970s, however, when world demand for petroleum had risen to record levels, were the OPEC nations able to take advantage of their cartel. Exploiting the industrial nations' need for abundant supplies of imported fuel, they raised the price from $4.60 a barrel in 1973 to more than $12.00 two years later. The economic impact was immense: The Venezuelan balance-of-payments surplus which was at a respectable $372 million in 1972, rose to $4.3 billion (American billion) in 1974.

Venezuela's petroleum policies, with their gradual but deliberate assertion of national control, are regarded by many as one of the highest achievements of reformism in contemporary Latin America. It was an impressive feat. Yet before one holds it up as a model for others, it should be noted that Venezuela enjoyed several advantages over its neighbors. Petroleum was a unique commodity during the 1970s, for none other, except perhaps gold, enjoyed such inelastic demand. Moreover, because of petroleum's international visibility and because Venezuela's democratic regime was held in such high esteem in Europe and the United States, political retaliation against Venezuela was out of the question. To their credit the Venezuelans exploited these advantages adroitly, but they were fortunate to have them to exploit.

Agrarian reform was equally vital to the AD program. Not only were reforms needed to bolster the nation's agriculture and improve the condition of the rural poor, but the AD was also compelled to deliver on its promises to the many *campesinos* who joined the party years before through the Venezuelan Campesino Confederation and supplied most of its votes in 1959. The agrarian reform law was the product of interparty bargaining prior to Betancourt's election. Moderate in design, it required the government to purchase land at market prices, rather than declared tax value as in Chile, a concession aimed at placating landowners that few countries other than oil-rich Venezuela could have afforded. It authorized the expropriation of private property not in production, grazing lands, and properties occupied but not owned by tenant farmers and sharecroppers. In fact, most of the land distributed was taken from government reserves rather than private holdings, lowering the program's cost and reducing opposition to it. Of the estimated 300,000 families who needed land, approximately 100,000 received it between 1960 and 1970, a major accomplishment in comparison with the performance of most agrarian reform programs in Latin America, though nevertheless one that fell short of government objectives.

The law was intended not only to improve the condition of *campesinos* but also to promote the more productive use of privately owned land. And here it was even more successful. Under threat of expropriation, farm production increased dramatically after 1960, rising in value by 58 percent in ten years and making Venezuela self-sufficient in most commodities. Nevertheless, in the 1970s the agrarian reform program was still a matter of controversy in Venezuela, though in contrast to the early years, the criticism came increasingly from the Left rather than the Right, with the former claiming that agrarian reform had done more for the large commercial farmer than for the rural poor, leaving the country with a rural proletariat that was migrating to the cities in greater numbers than ever before.

The nationalization of oil and agrarian reform laid the foundation needed to accomplish a third objective: the industrialization of the Venezuelan economy. Without industry, AD leaders argued, economic growth would collapse once the nation's mineral resources were exhausted. The Betancourt administration dedicated itself to a program of centrally planned development that included the creation of a large and diverse universal sector to reduce the country's dependence on petroleum exports. Industrial development objectives were set in successive five-year economic plans drawn up by CORDI-PLAN, the national planning agency, and supervised by the Ministry of Development and the autonomous Venezuelan Development Corporation. The private sector was to assume the largest burden for plan implementation, but the most spectacular achievements were those of public enterprises like the Venezuelan Guayana Corporation, an organization created to supervise one of the most ambitious regional development projects in Latin America. Located in the basin of the Orinoco River, the project included hydroelectric facilities, iron ore mines, steel and aluminum industries, and several petrochemical enterprises. The Venezuelan Development Corporation has financed many other public and private ventures; after specializing in import substitution industries for six years, it switched to intermediate and capital goods enterprises in 1966. Largely because of these efforts the value of manufacturing in constant dollars was 240 percent greater in 1980 than it was in 1960. Though still heavily dependent on its petroleum industry, Venezuela finally began to construct an industrial base intended to sustain the economy once petroleum resources were exhausted.

What went wrong

Prosperity is not assured by the discovery of petroleum, even in the age of OPEC, as the Iranians, Nigerians, and Mexicans will testify. So will the Venezuelans. Twenty years ago they appeared to be more fortunate than the others, for not only were their mineral resources abundant, but their population was also quite small (only 7.4 million in 1960). Moreover, they were governed by a constitutional regime whose leaders shared a commitment to economic development and social reform. Nevertheless it did not turn out the way it had been planned.

The Venezuelans had become accustomed to steady economic growth only to be shocked when it stopped in 1979. After averaging 5.7 percent annually between 1960 and 1975, the GDP was increased by only 0.9 percent in 1979 and then declined by 1.6 percent in 1980, (see Table 7.8). Simultaneously, the nation's debts to foreign banks suddenly rose, reaching an unprecedented $32 billion in 1982, one of the highest on a per capita basis of any nation in the world. Why the

Table 7.8. *Venezuela: economic growth rates (at market prices)*

	1979	1980	1981
Total gross domestic product	0.9	−1.6	1.0
Mining	10.4	−6.2	−3.0
Construction	−9.7	−16.5	−2.6
Manufacturing	4.2	2.5	0.5

Source: Inter-American Development Bank, *Economic and Social Progress in Latin America 1982 Report*. Washington, D.C., 1982, p. 333.

swift change? The answer lies in the very nature of petroleum-induced development.

In the 1970s petroleum gave some Third World nations unprecedented development opportunities, but like all opportunities it carried some risks. The possession and export of a valuable commodity encourage officials to hope that its sale will finance the kind of economic development that leads to the reduction of the nation's dependence on foreign finance and trade over the long haul. The vision is compelling, but on the way to making it reality the nation must become heavily dependent on the sale of a single, if lucrative, mineral. Thus, ironically, an increase in short-term dependence is necessary to achieve what one hopes will be greater economic independence. So it was in Venezuela. If one measures a nation's dependence on trade by the ratio of total imports and exports of goods and services to the gross domestic product, it increased from 45 percent in 1970, when oil prices and imports by Venezuela were modest, to 108 percent in 1980 after the oil boom, making it the most trade-dependent nation in South America (in contrast, the ratio was 80 in Chile, 51 in Argentina, and 23 in Brazil). Of course, Venezuela was richer than before, but in becoming so it also became much more vulnerable.

AD leaders rapidly accelerated economic modernization after 1973, basing their investment decisions on estimates of future income from petroleum exports, convinced that it would rise through the efforts of OPEC to control its supply internationally. If their revenue estimates proved correct, as they hoped, all would go well; but if they were incorrect, they would face a new problem, namely, insufficient income to pay for the expensive investments they had made. If that happened, they would have little choice but to borrow heavily abroad to pay their bills, thereby increasing their dependence on foreign banks, or close down their projects, which would undoubtedly pro-voke hostile reactions from the contractors, national businessmen, and consumers who were counting on them. Unfortunately for the Vene-zuelans their optimism did prove unfounded and, consequently, they faced an unprecedented crisis in 1979.

President Carlos Andres Perez had borrowed heavily abroad to pay for the AD projects, anticipating that oil revenues would rise fast enough to handle the nation's debts as payments came due. But he guesed wrong. Energy conservation in the industrial nations, a world recession, and rising interest rates in 1980 cut world consumption of petroleum and with it Venezuelan income. Perez's successor, Chris-tian Democrat Luis Herrera, a candidate who had exploited the "mis-management" issue during the 1978 campaign, had no choice but to impose an austerity program, causing a generation of Venezuelans to discover for the first time that their nation's economic growth could not be taken for granted.

The world economy was not the only culprit, however; the demo-cratic politicians' ambition also bears some of the blame. One of the virtues of democratic government is said to be its responsiveness to the wants and needs of the electorate. Yet, wants are unlimited, whereas government resources are quite finite. Governments can and do increase their resources through borrowing, but the amount they acquire depends on how much others will lend. This is where the oil producer has an advantage. Mineral wealth builds lender confidence and brings substantial short-term financing from foreign banks, mak-ing it possible for vote-seeking politicians to live beyond their means.

Perez tried to fortify his party's hold on the electorate and pay off his debts to party activists and Venezuelan businessmen by going on a spending binge and nearly doubling the number of public employees in just five years. When he stepped down in 1978, an estimated 25 percent of the country's work force was employed by the Venezuelan government and its many state corporations. To make matters worse, most of his projects proved to be much more expensive than originally planned, creating an even greater drain on revenues.

No doubt Venezuela will overcome its financial troubles, though the replication of its high growth rates is doubtful for some time to come. But there remains the issue of how much the Venezuelan state can and should do to satisfy citizens, rich and poor alike. Moreover, what will happen to public confidence in constitutional democracy if the nation's leaders reduce patronage, social services, and long-term investments? Should we anticipate the kind of social conflicts and disruptive politics that have led to military interventions in the Southern Cone nations?

Critics of the Venezuelan democracy on the Left claim that the recent crises have exposed the system for what it really is: an experiment in capitalist development that is doomed by the contradictions inherent in dependent capitalism. Despite its natural wealth, its growth cannot help but be sporadic and the reaction of the Venezuelan masses increasingly hostile given the country's vulnerability to economic forces beyond its borders. In contrast, AD and COPEI leaders are, as one would expect, less pessimistic, for they are convinced that they have been quite successful in absorbing elite and working-class interest groups into the state apparatus that they supervise, making them too dependent on the current system, whatever its faults, to ever abandon the current rules of the game. Whether or not they are correct will be determined by their compatriots as they cope with their fickle source of prosperity in the years ahead.

Democratic reformism: lessons learned

Eduardo Frei, Romulo Betancourt, and their colleagues were practical politicians who stubbornly refused to give up their quests for political power until they had succeeded. They came from the middle sectors but knew that they needed the support of those outside their social class if they were to triumph. So they organized *campesinos* and laborers where they could, giving them the hope of long-sought access to authority in exchange for their trust and their defense of the reformist cause. That they succeeded in their political quests within systems ruled by elites determined to block their path is testimony to their skill and persistence. It also lays to rest antiquated notions about the incapacity of Latin Americans for democratic politics. Clearly, the frequent interruptions of democratic government in Latin America are not caused by an inability to understand what democracy requires; on the contrary, it is because they comprehend its implications that some choose to undermine it.

Democratic reformism teaches us much about coalition politics. It was as coalition builders that the democratic reformers' skills were

most notable. Even though no coalition, no matter how well conceived, could guarantee security from sabotage and military intervention, without one they knew that they stood little chance of securing
office and passing reform legislation. But coalition maintenance was
no simple task; not only did it require the constant attention of politicians who would have preferred fewer political obligations, but it also
demanded the adoption of programs able to accomplish the nearly
impossible task of satisfying partners whose demands were incompatible or, when added together, too expensive.

Conspicuously missing from the democratic reform coalition, yet
essential to its survival, was the military. Unless the military is neu-
tralized or won over to the government's cause, it poses a serious
threat to the government's survival, as the Venezuelan military demonstrated when it overthrew the AD government in 1948. When the
constitutional regime was restored to Venezuela in 1958 AD leaders
were careful to cultivate military support by lavishly financing military budgets, turning the military loose against occasional insurgents,
and refraining from direct confrontations with the military's friends
within the economic elite. In return, the Venezuelan military respected the norms of democratic politics. Chilean democratic reformers were more fortunate. After a coup in the late 1920s, the
Chilean armed forces left politics to civilians. As long as the Christian
Democrats maintained public order, respected the military's institutional integrity, and did not permit the radicalization of Chilean politics, they too were not challenged by military leaders.

Also important was the United States government, which became
an important ally of democratic reform governments throughout the
hemisphere during the 1960s. Actually, Fidel Castro can take most of
the credit for the creation of this alliance, for it was the U.S. government's fear of more rebels like him that drove it to assist reform efforts
in Chile, Venezuela, and elsewhere. In addition to substantial economic assistance, it gave nearly $3 million to the Christian Democrats
to finance their campaign in 1964 in Chile. And in Venezuela Romulo
Betancourt delighted in playing the role of the democratic answer to
Fidel Castro, whom he personally despised and blamed for an assassination attempt on his life in 1962. He and Frei were held up as
models for the kind of reformism that the Kennedy and Johnson
administrations believed to be the most tolerable alternative to communism within the hemisphere. They were democratic in spirit, stri-

dently anticommunist, and, though nationalistic, quite tolerant of foreign investment, which they believed to be essential to the achievement of their development objectives. The democratic reformers would have survived politically without U.S. support and assistance, but it did fortify them when they began to govern and it helped reduce the reformer's normal concern about the always present threat of American intervention to protect its vested interests.

The democratic reform coalition, though adroitly conceived, was never as secure as its creators intended. Disputes over the substance and pace of reform haunted it and led to frequent defections, especially by labor and party factions who thought presidents were too willing to compromise with their conservative opponents. Reformers were also plagued by the problem of holding together a coalition that sought to unite peasants with urban workers and both of them with the middle sectors. As long as resources were plentiful the coalition could be held together, but when the competition for scarce resources intensified, as it did frequently in Latin America, each coalition member tended to go its own way in the struggle for survival.

Reform policy was always easy game for critics. Much of the criticism was deserved. To be sure, the reformers did achieve a great deal: the redistribution of rural property, industrialization, and the nationalization of some enterprises. And they increased government responsibilities for the social welfare of their people and improved the condition of many. But they never achieved as much reform as they had promised.

As the Populists discovered before them, import-substitution industrialization did not secure the kind of national independence and self-sustaining development that was desired. Nor did agrarian reform eliminate rural poverty or substantially improve the welfare of those who were given property, even if it did reduce their discontent somewhat. And the expansion of the public sector turned out to be more expensive and less productive than expected. The reasons for these shortcomings are many, most important being the enormity of the reformers' task and the resistance of elites to the redistribution of real power.

To begin with, reformers had to cope with two practical problems, one technical and the other political. They knew what to do, but they were not very experienced with agrarian reforms, national development plans, and regional economic integration. Consequently, they were often forced to become incrementalists, slowing down their efforts and abandoning some of their more ambitious schemes when they encountered unexpected technical problems.

Incrementalism was also forced on reformers by the political obstacles they faced. As we have learned repeatedly, democratic rules afford one's opponents abundant opportunities for halting reform. In Chile, it will be recalled, agrarian reform legislation was delayed for two years by a coalition of Conservatives and Marxists. But it does not stop with the passage of legislation. As elsewhere, bureaucrats were amenable to bribes and other means of opposition influence, and judges often intervened to protect the rights of defenders of the status quo, slowing government programs and disappointing their intended beneficiaries.

Much of the democratic reformers' political frustration also stems from the trap they create for themselves by advocating programs that threaten vested interests on both the Left and the Right. If they concede to their opponents, they must sacrifice much of what they hope to achieve. But if, on the other hand, they go after their opponents, intending to deliberately strip them of their power, they risk eviction from office, as Salvador Allende discovered. Is there no escape from the trap? Maybe not, but that never deters democratic reformers. For them politics does not involve choosing between acquiring enough power to impose one's will on society and resigning oneself to political immobility; rather it requires living with hosts of dilemmas and accepting imperfect solutions. To demand that it be otherwise is to ignore the nature of the democratic game. This is why they are so much less disturbed by the paucity of their economic achievements than are their opponents on the Left who are less dedicated to liberal notions of civil liberty and political competition.

Lest we blame all of the democratic reformers' shortcomings on politics, we should recall that they operate in the same economic world as all other Latin American leaders, one that treats the highly dependent Latin American economies quite harshly. Import-substitution industrialization and agrarian reform did not free Chile and Venezuela from their need to import a great deal. As their production of consumer goods rose, so did their demand for imported capital goods and financial capital, forcing them to rely as before on the export of primary products to secure the foreign exchange needed to finance their imports. How well they did economically depended as much on growth

and inflation in the industrial nations as it did on their own policies.
Ambitious development programs, like those undertaken in Chile and
Venezuela, make a nation even more vulnerable to external forces by
increasing the costs of incorrect calculations about the future price of its
exports and the cost of its imports. Reformers are optimists who accept
short-term risks in order to achieve long-term objectives, but because
they take such risks, they are easily undermined when things do not go
according to plan. Such was the case in Venezuela in the late 1970s. No
nation seemed better prepared for rapid development, yet in few instances have a government's ambitious programs been reversed so
quickly in order to avert financial disaster. But the Venezuelans were
not alone in their plight, for it was the same throughout the region. The
cause of their problem was not the government's reform politics but the
simple fact of the region's economic dependence on others richer than
themselves. If reformers are to be criticized then, it should not be for
their goals but for their inability to reduce their nations' vulnerability to
forces beyond their direct control.

Further reading

General

Anderson, Charles W. *Politics and Economic Change in Latin America: The Gov-
erning of Restless Nations*. New York: Van Nostrand, 1967.
Hirschman, Albert O. *Journeys Toward Progress*. New York: Twentieth Cen-
tury Fund, 1963.
Prebisch, Raul. *The Economic Development of Latin America and Its Principal
Problems*. New York: United Nations, 1950.
Wiarda, Howard, ed. *The Continuing Struggle for Democracy in Latin America*.
Boulder, Colo.: Westview Press, 1980.
Williams, Edward J. *Latin American Christian Democratic Parties*. Knoxville:
University of Tennessee Press, 1967.

Chile

Allende Gossens, Salvador. *Chile's Road to Socialism*, ed. Joan Garces. Balti-
more: Penguin Books, 1973.
Boorstein, Edward. *Allende's Chile: An Inside View*. New York: International
Publishers, 1977.
Debray, Regis. *The Chilean Revolution: Conversations with Allende*. New York:
Pantheon Books, 1971.
De Vylder, Stefan. *Allende's Chile: The Political Economy of the Rise and Fall of
Unidad Popular*. New York: Cambridge University Press, 1976.
Feinberg, Richard E. *The Triumph of Allende: Chile's Legal Revolution*. New
York: New American Library (Mentor Books), 1972.

Francis, Michael J. *The Allende Victory: An Analysis of the 1970 Chilean Presidential Election.* Tucson: University of Arizona Press, 1973.

Gil, Federico. *The Political System of Chile.* Boston: Houghton Mifflin, 1966.

Gross, Leonard. *The Last Best Hope: Eduardo Frei and Chilean Democracy.* New York: Random House, 1967.

Kaufman, Robert. *The Politics of Land Reform in Chile 1950–1970: Public Policy, Political Institutions, and Social Change.* Cambridge, Mass.: Harvard University Press, 1972.

Loveman, Brian. *Chile: The Legacy of Hispanic Capitalism.* New York: Oxford University Press, 1979.

North, Lisa. "The Military in Chilean Politics." *Studies in Comparative International Development* 11: 73–106, 1976.

Operations and Policy Research, Inc. *The Chilean Presidential Election of September 4, 1964.* Washington, D.C., 1965.

Petras, James. *Politics and Social Forces in Chilean Development.* Berkeley: University of California Press, 1969.

Petras, James, and Morris Morley. *The United States and Chile: Imperialism and the Overthrow of the Allende Government.* New York: Monthly Review Press, 1975.

Roxborough, Ian, Phil O'Brien, and Jackie Roddick. *Chile: The State and Revolution.* London: Macmillan Press, 1977.

Sigmund, Paul. *The Overthrow of Allende and the Politics of Chile 1964–1976.* Pittsburgh: University of Pittsburgh Press, 1978.

Smith, Brian H. *The Church and Politics in Chile: Challenges to Modern Catholicism.* Princeton, N.J.: Princeton University Press, 1982.

Sweezy, Paul M., and Harry Magdoff, eds. *Revolution and Counter-Revolution in Chile.* New York: Monthly Review Press, 1974.

United States Congress, House, Committee on Foreign Affairs, Subcommittee on Inter-American Affairs. United States and Chile During the Allende Years, 1970–1973. 94th Congress, 1st Session, 1975, pp. 1–677.

United States Senate, Select Committee to Study Governmental Operations with Respect to Intelligence Activities. *Covert Action in Chile, 1963–1973.* 94th Congress, 1st Session, 1975, pp. 1–62.

Valenzuela, Arturo. *The Breakdown of Democratic Regimes: Chile.* Baltimore: Johns Hopkins University Press, 1978.

Valenzuela, Arturo, and J. Samuel Valenzuela, eds. *Chile: Politics and Society.* New Brunswick, N.J.: Transaction Books, 1976.

Venezuela

Alexander, Robert J. *The Venezuelan Democratic Revolution: A Profile of the Regime of Romulo Betancourt.* New Brunswick: N.J.: Rutgers University Press, 1964.

Baloyra, Enrique A., and John D. Martz. *Political Attitudes in Venezuela: Societal Cleavages and Public Opinion.* Austin: University of Texas Press, 1979.

Blank, David Eugene. *Politics in Venezuela.* Boston: Little, Brown, 1973.

Bonilla, Frank, and Joseph Silva Michelena, eds. *The Politics of Change in Venezuela,* vol. 1. Cambridge, Mass.: MIT Press, 1967.

Farley, Rawle. "The Economics of Realism: A Case Study of Economic

Change in Venezuela," in Rawle Farley, *The Economics of Latin America*. New York: Harper & Row, 1972, pp. 279–303.

Freidmann, John. *Venezuela: From Doctrine to Dialogue*. Syracuse, N.Y.: Syracuse University Press, 1965.

Levine, Daniel H. *Religion and Politics in Latin America: The Catholic Church in Venezuela and Colombia*. Princeton, N.J.: Princeton University Press, 1981.

Martz, John. *Accion Democratica: Evolution of a Modern Political Party in Venezuela*. Princeton, N.J.: Princeton University Press, 1965.

Martz, John, and David Myers, eds. *Venezuela: The Democratic Experience*. New York: Praeger, 1977.

Penniman, Howard, ed. *Venezuela at the Polls: The National Elections of 1978*. Washington: American Enterprise Institute, 1980.

Petras, James, Morris Morley, and Steven Smith. *The Nationalization of Venezuelan Oil*. New York: Praeger, 1977.

Powell, John Duncan. *Political Mobilization of the Venezuelan Peasant*. Cambridge, Mass.: Harvard University Press, 1971.

Tugwell, Franklin. *The Politics of Oil in Venezuela*. Stanford, Calif.: Stanford University Press, 1973.

8. The military authoritarian game

Why militaries rule

Not long ago it was believed that military involvement in Latin American politics was caused primarily by the region's economic and social backwardness. Plagued by widespread poverty and illiteracy, Latin American nations could not help becoming breeding grounds for violence and dictatorial politics. But once they developed economically and became more educated and urbanized, military coups would become a thing of the past. Or so it was hoped. Actually, it did not turn out that way. Instead, the more the region developed, the more deeply involved the military became.

What happened? We can begin by recalling that disagreements over political rules and economic strategies are an integral part of the region's modern history. Military officers have always joined in these disputes, though usually on the side of the defenders of the status quo. That they are still involved today should not be all that surprising. If anything has changed during the past twenty years, it is not military politics per se, but the form it has taken recently. Where they were once content to remove some civilians from office in order to protect others, the militaries of several countries decided to step in and govern themselves, ignoring the requests of civilians to return to their bases once the coup had been carried out. More and more they came to blame politics itself for their nations' problems and, accordingly, set out to eliminate it altogether while they reconstructed their nations as they wished.

To understand this change in mission we need to look beyond the armed forces to Latin American society and the many things that happened to it before the military authoritarians came along in the 1960s. We know that post-1930 economic development did not foster the growth of liberal democracy in countries like Brazil and Argentina. Instead, as we discovered in Chapter 6, new social conflicts and politi-

210

cal alliances accompanied industrialization. New players appeared while old ones held on and the simultaneous satisfaction of both became difficult if not impossible in some cases. Industrialists demanded protection and subsidization and the repression of organized labor. The middle sectors, who themselves had advocated reforms at the turn of the century, became fearful of the reforms advocated in the 1950s by those below them in the class structure. Laborers who were aroused by populist politicians refused to retreat voluntarily to the sidelines, having tasted the fruits of political power; instead they demanded ever larger pieces of the national economic pie for themselves. And the many multinational corporations who entered the region after 1950 insisted that their interests be given priority over all others in exchange for the capital and technology they supplied nations desperately in need of both. Had economic growth been rapid and steady, governments might have dealt with these disparate interests in an orderly and mutually satisfactory way. But growth, though at times rapid, was never steady. Instead, spurts of growth were often followed by deep recessions that stripped governments of the resources they needed to compensate interests hurt by economic decline. Farmers always balked at sacrificing their income to help industry; industrialists resented making concessions to their workers; and the middle sectors felt victimized by inflation and recession. Something had to give and civilian politicians often found it difficult to agree on what it should be and, once decided, to enforce their decisions.

Conflicts over scarce economic resources do not always provoke military intervention, obviously. Much depends on how deeply civilians are divided, how fearful each faction becomes of the other, and how tolerant the military is of the consequences of their disputes. What changed most in the more industrialized Latin American countries in the 1960s was the depth of the conflict between the upper and middle classes on one side and the working class on the other. Simply put, the propertied classes, both domestic and foreign, became convinced that their world could no longer be preserved without military government. The demands and expectations of the popular classes had become too great and civilian governments too unreliable to tolerate any longer. The only solution left for them was the termination of open competitive politics in favor of the concentration of power in the hands of a government able to impose its will on society regardless of popular objection.

It did not take much to convince military officers that something had gone wrong. They saw politicians bicker, workers protest, and economies deteriorate. They heard businessmen complain about politicians and multinational corporation executives warn of economic decline. And they also noticed radicals on the Left, inspired by Fidel Castro's triumph in Cuba, organize for the purpose of rising up against the military and its many civilian friends. As the military's fears increased so did their conviction that only they could assure the kind of political order that guaranteed their own survival and that of the institutions in which they believed. When the time came to decide, they acted, first in Brazil in 1964, then Argentina in 1966, Peru in 1968, and Chile and Uruguay in 1973.

To bolster their sense of mission the armed forces created a new ideology. Labeled the National Security Doctrine, it was invented originally by Brazilian officers in the cold war atmosphere of the 1950s and was taught in military academies and war colleges throughout the region thereafter. The doctrine, which draws heavily on notions of "geopolitics" popular among European nationalists during the nineteenth century, places the interest of the nation above that of the individual. It argues that citizens are obligated to do whatever is required of them to protect the nation against other nations and against people within its borders intent on weakening it by undermining the existing social order. Thus, in contrast to liberal democratic thinking, which argues for individualism, diversity, and competition, the National Security Doctrine stresses conformity to a single set of values. Its view of human nature is decidedly Hobbesian, convinced of the passionate character of human beings, creatures whose aggressiveness cannot be restrained by reason alone. Some people must control the rest, preventing them from destroying each other and the fabric of the community. Equally important is the reinforcement of authority using values that touch the emotional needs of the people; in Latin America conservative Catholicism with its emphasis on hierarchical authority, spiritualism, and discipline starting with the male-dominated family, could, it was hoped, be made to serve that purpose.

The doctrine reminds one of the fascist ideology popular in Italy and Spain between the wars. Like Italian fascism it is designed to mold national character and unite a people behind its leaders. It wants citizens who are devoted to their nation and its accumulation of power, people who will make personal sacrifices when called upon to do so. Like fascism it detests liberalism, multiparty democracy, and the free press, and makes little room for reasoned argument. Yet, despite these similarities in substance, the doctrine has differed from fascism in one important regard. Mussolini turned fascism into a popular doctrine, one embraced by millions of Italians as a source of emotional security and national salvation. Latin Americans, in contrast, have never taken the National Security Doctrine all that seriously. Conditioned by a history of partisan military rule, they responded to the military's patriotic proclamations quite cynically, usually accepting them as little more than rationalizations for its attempt to preserve the existing socioeconomic order.

The fact that many more countries merit study than we can fit into one chapter indicates how common military authoritarianism has become in the region. Not considered here are the kinds of military regimes that rule in Central America; though as repressive as those found in South America, their origins and purposes are different, as is their mode of operation to some extent. We will limit ourselves to Brazil, Argentina, and Peru. In our study of each we want to know what their armed forces sought to do and how well they achieved it. Equally important is the nature of the game they created: how it operated, how durable it became, and who gained and lost from its policies. And last is the matter of their ultimate fate. Some of the military authoritarians who took over before 1975 eventually returned the reins of authority to the very civilians they had removed a decade before. Is this evidence of success or failure?

Brazil: the new authoritarianism

Size matters in Brazil. Over one-third of all Latin Americans live there, and one of its states, São Paulo, is larger with its 40 million people than all Latin American countries but Mexico. And two-thirds of the region's largest public and private corporations are located there. But size alone tells us little about the country today. There are really two Brazils now. Within one, several million businessmen, professionals, commercial farmers, public servants, and skilled laborers live in relative comfort. Most of them reside in the rapidly developing southern third of the country and have great confidence in Brazil's future. The other two-thirds of the population live in another Brazil, one characterized by illiteracy, subsistence agriculture, urban unemployment, and insecurity, one that the more affluent Brazil seems too busy to deal with. Some will escape their poverty as did others before them or will see their children do so, but most will not. They are heavily concentrated in the poverty-stricken northeastern part of the country but can be found everywhere.

Much had changed between Vargas's coup in 1930 and the one that launched military authoritarianism in 1964. Industrialization and the growth of the Brazilian state had allowed some to become wealthy and many to become part of a large urban middle class. But the new order was a precarious one, made possible by spurts of rapid economic growth and the skill of politicians like Vargas and Kubitschek who achieved substantial development without depriving the propertied classes of their wealth or allowing the emerging working class to get out of line. But it could not last. Aspirations rose too fast and economic growth too slowly to maintain the old harmony of interests. Conflicts grew, economic disappointments increased, and the military and the country's elected officials took to squabbling about how to respond.

The 1964 coup

Traditionally the Brazilian military had acted as a moderating force in national politics, intervening from time to time to restore an equilibrium among the country's contending political forces. Since the fall of the emperor and the creation of the republic in 1889, the Brazilian political game had been characterized by its reliance on a balance of power among the most influential players. Before 1930 regional political machines held the game together by regularly exchanging public offices and policy favors. After 1930, as we saw in Chapter 6, Getulio Vargas expanded the power of the central government at the expense of the state machines. Under Vargas, new players were admitted to the game as long as they did not seriously threaten those already involved. Thanks to his efforts, industrialists, urban professionals, bureaucrats, foreign investors, and organized labor were added to the political process, and a new equilibrium was created and maintained by the powerful Brazilian state. With the inauguration of a constitutional regime in 1945 came the addition of political parties. But they too took on uniquely Brazilian characteristics, eschewing ideology and mass mobilization in favor of regional electoral organizations dedicated primarily to capturing the presidency and seats in the legislature.

Essential to the governance of Brazil between 1945 and 1964 was the maintenance of a balance among its dominant players through the state's promotion of a growing industrial economy. This required the execution of policies that satisfied some of the demands of each player without seriously offending anyone who mattered. Few Brazilian presidents directed this system more skillfully than Juscelino Kubitschek did between 1955 and 1960. His successors, however, proved less adept at making it work.

The first was Jânio Quadros, who had promised to purge Brazilian politics of patronage, corruption, and political balancing acts – all legacies of the Vargas years that had been perpetuated by Kubitschek. What made Quadros unusual was his determination to operate independently of the ruling coalition that had been held together and expanded by presidents since 1930. Instead of acquiring power by becoming an indispensable mediator among coalition members, he sought to secure it through the mobilization of popular support for his political purification campaign. It was a bold innovation, but one that failed. In less than a year Quadros had alienated the party politicians, who had thrived on patronage, and the bureaucrats, who had lived on corruption; antagonized industrialists with an antiinflationary, tight credit policy; prompted labor opposition with wage controls; and upset the military with a neutralist foreign policy. When Quadros suddenly resigned in August 1961 in an attempt to generate an outpouring of popular support that he hoped to use against his opponents, few Brazilians responded, and his leave of absence became permanent retirement.

Vice-President João Goulart, who succeeded Quadros, also upset the traditional equilibrium. Goulart, a former protégé of Getulio Vargas and labor minister in his last administration, initially tried to replicate the development program employed by Kubitschek. He was haunted, however, by his reputation as an opportunistic and unreliable labor operative deeply distrusted by the military.

To make matters worse, the Brazilian economy deteriorated rapidly in 1962 and 1963. Kubitschek's acceleration of growth in the late 1950s had left Quadros and Goulart with rising inflation and a slowdown in production followed by a decline in investor confidence. Goulart tried several conventional solutions to the inflation problem, but when none worked and opposition to him grew, he turned in desperation back to populism, this time radicalizing it somewhat to

Table 8.1. *Postwar Brazil: historical background*

1950	Getulio Vargas elected president with support of Social Democratic Party and Brazilian Labor party, receiving 49 percent of popular vote
1954	President Vargas commits suicide at age seventy-two
1955	Juscelino Kubitschek, candidate of Social Democratic party and Brazilian Labor party, elected president with 36 percent of popular vote.
1960	Jânio Quadros, candidate of National Democratic Union party elected president with 48 percent of popular vote
1961	President Quadros resigns and is succeeded by Vice-President João Goulart; military allows Goulart to become president after imposing parliamentary system to reduce his powers
1963	Presidential system restored by national plebiscite
1964	On March 31 military overthrows Goulart and creates authoritarian regime under Marshal Humberto Castelo Branco, who is elected president by Congress
1967	Marshal Artur Costa e Silva selected as president
1969	President Costa e Silva forced to resign because of ill health and is replaced by General Emilio Garrastazú Médici
1974	General Ernesto Geisel selected as president; opposition outpolls government in congressional elections
1979	General João Baptista Figueiredo selected president
1982	Local, state, legislative, gubernatorial, and congressional elections held; opposition wins majority of popular vote

attract mass support. In early 1964 he announced a modest land reform, nationalized some private oil refineries, gave illiterates the right to vote, and, most disturbing to the armed forces, took the side of enlisted men in a public protest against their commanders. What Goulart had done, of course, was break two basic rules of the traditional Brazilian game: one forbidding the state to redistribute property from one player to another, and one prohibiting the mobilization of the masses against their bosses.

Before 1964 the military had tried everything but a coup to slow Goulart. But the more they pressed the more recalcitrant he became, making the coup ever more likely. If the armed forces needed any encouragement, there was plenty available, especially from the United States government, which had always feared Goulart's nationalism at a time when American firms were heavily involved in Brazil, and from the Brazilian upper and middle class, who were upset by the deterioration of the economy as well as by Goulart's flirtation with the masses. When the coup finally did come in April few were surprised.

The authoritarian state

Military officers are not trained to design political systems, but that is precisely what they set out to do in Brazil in 1964. Understandably they began with a clearer idea of what they wanted to destroy than about what they would construct in its place. Moreover, within the military itself there were differences of opinion about what to do. Moderates wanted only to restore economic growth and purge the system of those who championed popular causes, leaving the rest of the civilian politicians to function under temporary military supervision. Hardliners, on the other hand, sought much more, starting with the burial of liberal democratic politics and ending with the creation of a permanent authoritarian state run by the military.

Gradually the foundations of the new state were laid through compromises between both factions. Several thousand political activists were jailed, all political parties, labor movements, and student organizations were outlawed and a security network went to work identifying and jailing any who opposed the new leadership. But once purged the legislature continued to operate, though with little real authority, evidencing the moderates' desire for some continuity with the past. Two new political parties were formed hastily, one composed of politicians loyal to the military, called the National Renovating Alliance (ARENA), and the other of opposition politicians, known as the Brazilian Democratic Movement (MDB). Neither, however, was given the right to interfere with presidential rule.

Authoritarian government was not unfamiliar to Brazilians. The country had been ruled by a monarch, Emperor Dom Pedro II, during the nineteenth century and by Getulio Vargas after the depression. Under both the government had acted as the nation's commander and patron, supervising its development and seeing to it that everyone relied on the state for most rights and privileges. Some sectors, such as organized labor, were formally incorporated into the state apparatus by Vargas, whereas others were regulated by central authorities determined to maintain order. Experiments with electoral democracy between 1946 and 1964 did not change this basic structure, so it was not hard for the military to step in and put the state to work as the supervisor of the nation's development.

New regulations were announced by the government in a series of Institutional Acts decreed between 1964 and 1969. The result was a hierarchical order that gave the president almost total control over the nation's political life. If he wished, he could jail anyone, close any newspaper, and dismiss any public official. As one might expect, the presidency became the center of attention and the selection of its occupant the most important decision made by the high command. Brazilian generals and admirals were determined to create a regime in which they, as leaders of the armed forces, would govern the nation rather than turn it over to a single officer who would become a one-man dictator as had occasionally happened in the past. Nevertheless, they still had to allow one from their ranks to act as chief executive in order to operate in an orderly manner and make it clear to the Brazilian public that someone was in charge. Consequently, they were forced to select one person to serve a fixed term, doing so after intense, secret negotiations among a few hundred of the highest ranking officers of the three services. Civilians were given no say whatsoever. Divisions within the military over candidates were always present, but service commanders proved skillful at limiting public knowledge of their internal disputes and giving the appearance of knowing what they were doing.

The president's power was great but certainly not unlimited. First, when making decisions he had to take the opinions of other officers into account. Second, in matters of economic policy, he was heavily dependent on the bureaucrats who ran state corporations and on the Brazilian entrepreneurs and multinational firms who managed the private sector. The president could not command them to invest or produce more, but had to induce their cooperation using conventional tax, monetary, price, and wage measures, much like his peers in democratic systems. When his and their interests coincided, as they often did, cooperation was easy, but it was never guaranteed since few economic policies could satisfy all business interests simultaneously.

Economic miracles: real and imagined

We should not forget that the principal aim of the Brazilian military was economic, not political. Politics was primarily a means to the end of economic modernization through the use of state, foreign, and domestic private capital. From the beginning the armed forces were more confident of their ability to find solutions to the nation's economic problems than they were its political ones. Their civilian advisers, most of them internationally known economists, were ready with answers to every question the officers asked about what it would take to halt inflation and restore investor confidence in Brazil, but offered little advice on political reform. Consequently, it was to the economy that the government turned its attention, confining politics to the two-party charade in a powerless legislature during its first decade in power.

Economic policy began with a conventional austerity program aimed at getting rampant inflation under control. To the surprise of skeptics, including some within the military, it gradually succeeded. Not only did the government bring stability to the economy, but rapid growth followed as Brazil achieved some of the highest rates of growth in the nation's history, causing the generals to boast of having worked a miracle by taking the country from economic chaos to record growth in only five years. There is some evidence to support the claim, as we can see from Table 8.2. After a few years of economic stabilization, the Brazilian economy suddenly accelerated, growing at a record pace between 1968 and 1973. At the same time, inflation, which reached nearly 100 percent in 1963, was reduced to an annual average of 23 percent after 1965, business confidence rose and foreign investment accelerated. However, claims of a miracle are a bit exaggerated. The government did not so much rebuild the economy as it did consolidate and expand a process of industrial development that had begun in the late 1940s but had become stalled in the early 1960s because of erratic policies.

The Brazilian economy grew steadily after World War II largely because of a policy of import substitution encouraged by high tariffs and favorable exchange rates. But unlike Peronist Argentina, where foreign investment was discouraged until the early 1960s, the Brazilians welcomed capital-intensive foreign enterprises, especially between 1955 and 1960. With the help of foreign capital and imported business practices, the production of consumer durables, machinery, and transportation equipment increased by approximately 50 percent between 1949 and 1964. By 1964, approximately one-third of Brazil's manufacturing industries were owned by foreigners. Equally impor-

Table 8.2. *Brazilian economic performance, 1950–73*
(average annual real growth rates)

	1950–60	1960–5	1965–73
Gross domestic product			
per capita	3.1	1.2	6.0
Agricultural product			
per capita	1.5	1.5	1.6
Industrial product			
per capita	6.0	0.8	8.1
Retail price index	–	54.0	23.3

Note: Dash indicates information not given.
Source: World Bank, *World Tables 1976*. Washington, D.C., 1976, p. 396.

tant, after World War II the government increased its production of goods and services by expanding the operations of public enterprises in banking, transportation, petroleum and petrochemicals, steel, and public utilities. It was primarily the combination of foreign and state investment, supplemented by domestic private efforts in agriculture and commerce, that launched Brazil along the path of rapid economic growth. It was accompanied, however, by rapidly rising public expenditures and wages, which contributed to an annual average inflation rate of 52 percent between 1959 and 1963. Uncertainty grew and the per capita growth rate fell to less than 0.5 percent in 1962 and 1963; soon thereafter the military stepped in, blaming the populist demagoguery and managerial incompetence of President João Goulart for the sudden decline.

The new government's solution to the country's economic malaise was the adoption of something resembling the "conservative moderation strategy" described in Chapter 5. It involved the immediate reduction of inflation through a harsh austerity program backed by authoritarian rule. With the assistance of civilian economist Roberto Campos, President Castelo Branco launched a program that combined several conventional austerity measures with a system of built-in adjustments to inflation using index linking of the exchange rate, interest rates, taxes, incomes, and prices. The theory was that all variables would move at the same speed and that production and employment would rapidly and efficiently adjust to sharp changes in domestic and external economic conditions. But even with indexation, real wages fell and wealth became even more concentrated in the hands of the wealthy.

To the government's relief, the program bore significant results after 1968. The flow of foreign investment grew rapidly, and the Brazilian stock market, with the encouragement of government tax incentives, increased by an impressive annual average of 7.0 percent between 1968 and 1973. And with the help of government subsidization Brazil raised its exports of manufactured goods, which helped to diversify its trade.

The principal beneficiaries of the military's development program are not hard to identify. Most of them were concentrated in the southern third of the country where most industry and commercial agriculture are located. Multinational corporations from the United States, Western Europe, and Japan took full advantage of the new opportunities opened to them in Brazil, as did domestic industrialists, bankers, and retailers. Commercial farmers who shifted from traditional to new export crops (e.g., from black beans to soybeans), as well as the producers of coffee, grain, and other commodities, also did well under the new regime. Even the landed elites of the northeast survived with most of their economic resources undiminished. Urban professionals, bureaucrats, white-collar workers, and others associated with public and private enterprises also profited from the new prosperity. Less fortunate were the factory workers and unskilled laborers, who saw their real wages decline until the early 1970s, when the government began compensating them for past losses. But their condition was still better than the estimated 50 percent of the population that survived on the fringes of the modern economy. The plight of the peasant was as ignored by the military regime as it was by previous Brazilian governments. And though significant strides were made in literacy and basic education, little of the country's increased wealth trickled down to the masses. As a result, income disparities between the middle sectors and the masses increased.

Not surprisingly, Brazil was held up as an example of what the conservative modernization strategy could do in Latin America. Using authoritarian methods to impose harsh austerity and then encourage domestic and foreign investments in industry and commercial agriculture, the Brazilians did achieve one of the highest rates of economic growth in the hemisphere before 1973. But Brazil has also been heavily criticized. By worshiping at the altar of growth the Brazilians

Table 8.3. *Brazil: shares of national wealth (%)*

	1960	1970	1976
Active population			
Poorest 50%	17.7	14.9	11.8
Next 30%	27.9	22.8	21.2
Next 15%	26.7	27.4	28.0
Richest 5%	27.7	34.9	39.0

Source: Getulio Vargas Foundation (cited in *Comercio Exterior de Mexico*, March 1979, p. 104).

postponed efforts to solve the critical social problems that still plague the country. While they were expanding the modern sector for one-half the population, the other half languished at or just above the subsistence level. In 1976 the poorest 50 percent of the population still received only 11.8 percent of the national income, whereas the wealthiest 5 percent received 39 percent (see Table 8.3).

On balance, how do we assess the authoritarians' economic record? Clearly their initial effort was impressive. No other Latin American nation matched Brazil's spectacular growth during those years. But before declaring it a success, four things should be considered. First, what the military regime demonstrated was not the unqualified success of the conservative modernization strategy, but only its ability to promote rapid industrial growth in a country that already enjoyed an established industrial base. Post-1964 governments did not start from scratch, but only reinforced, albeit quite skillfully, a growth process well underway.

Second, Brazil's performance before 1973 was attributable not so much to free-market capitalism as to the efforts of the Brazilian government and large multinational enterprises. By 1979 the government owned 560 enterprises employing 1.3 million people. And, 60 percent of the investments made during the boom years 1967–73 came from the public sector. Moreover, between 1970 and 1973 investments by multinational firms in Brazil increased sevenfold, and between 1973 and 1979 Brazil received $10.8 billion in foreign investments, over half of the total foreign investment made in Latin America. Together the nation's bureaucrats and corporate executives made the Brazilian economy work as they wished.

Third, Brazil's economic boom cooled off some after 1973, with

Table 8.4. *The twenty largest corporations in Brazil, 1981 (all figures in billion cruzeiros)*

Conglomerate	Control of Capital	Sales
Petrobrás	State	2,178.8
Shell	Foreign (UK/Neth.)	400.0
Siderbrás	State	327.0
Exxon Brazil	Foreign (U.S.)	319.8
Souza Cruz	Foreign (UK)	280.4
Electrobrás	State	269.9
Telebrás	State	248.7
Ipiranga	Braz. private	211.3
Eletropaulo	State	200.0
Copersucar	Braz. private	196.6
Atlantic	Foreign (U.S.)	184.0
Volkswagen	Foreign (W. German)	180.0
Ford-Philco	Foreign (U.S.)	179.0
Texaco	Foreign (U.S.)	177.4
Pau de Acucar	Braz. private	167.5
Votorantim	Braz. private	154.1
Bung & Born	Foreign (U.S.)	144.0
Vale do Rio Doce	State	128.6
Mercedes-Benz	Foreign (W. German)	127.1
General Motors	Foreign (U.S.)	126.1

Note: Average exchange rate for 1981: U.S. $1.00 = Cr$92.2.
Source: Exame magazine, July 1982.

GDP growth averaging 6.8 percent annually from 1976 to 1980. Especially disruptive was the OPEC nations' increase in oil prices in 1973 since Brazil imports 75 percent of its petroleum. Indexing could not hold down inflation and by 1981 it had risen to an annual rate of over 100 percent. Moreover, Brazilians were forced to borrow heavily abroad, even more so after petroleum prices were raised again in 1979, causing their indebtedness to rise astronomically, reaching $80 billion in 1982, 75 percent of which it owed to private banks in the industrial nations. When the prices of its exports fell during a world recession in 1981 and 1982, making it impossible for Brazil to earn enough to pay the interest on its loans, the government turned in desperation to the International Monetary Fund for emergency assistance and to its creditors for the postponement of its payments. Since they could not risk losing interest payments most creditors complied. Thus, Brazil bought some time, but its fundamental problems remained unsolved.

An end to authoritarianism?

Moderates and hardliners within the armed forces had always disa-
greed over the ultimate political purpose of authoritarianism. But
from 1974 onward the moderates had the upper hand, and both president Ernesto Geisel (1974–9) and his successor General João Figueiredo promised to lead the nation toward constitutional government.
Geisel relaxed many restrictions on civil liberties, but it was up to
Figueiredo to design the new rules of the game. Demands for free
elections grew rapidly after 1979 as did labor activism, with strikes
directed as much at government repression of labor organizations as at
wage issues. In response the government followed two paths simultaneously, one involving the harassment of labor leaders not amenable
to negotiation and the other the incremental design of electoral rules
that would regulate national elections in November 1982.

How to open the political process became a strategic matter com-
manding presidential attention for nearly three years. The most obvious solution to the problem was simply to elect a constitutional convention, write a new constitution, and then hold elections creating a
new government. But the Brazilian officers were not ready for that,
since they still wanted a say in the form that new regime would take
and in its operation. Thus, from the outset they were faced with a
basic dilemma: They sought to convince Brazilians that the new regime would be democratic while at the same time limiting the power
of those whom the public selected to lead them. In other words, the
military wanted to retain its veto without alienating the civilians it
would allow into office, and it tried to do so by cleverly manipulating
election rules and representation to assure that it would get its way
without provoking public abstention from the rigged contest.

It began with the government's announcement of its intention to
create its own party to compete with the others. The military's
ARENA party was renamed the Democratic Social party and its
civilian activists were put to work mobilizing voters in regions where
the military had always been strong, namely, the northeast and other
rural areas. But, it was quite apparent from the start that the Democratic Social party, though strong, lacked majority support. Consequently, to retain control, something more was required.

First, it was decided that the presidency would be excluded from
the national elections and would be filled two years later through

Table 8.5. *Brazilian economic crisis, 1979–81*

	1979	1980	1981
Gross domestic product growth rate	6.8	7.9	−1.9
Inflation rate	52.7	82.8	105.5
Debt to foreign banks ($ billions)	$38	$48	$50

Source: Inter-American Development Bank, *Economic and Social Progress in Latin America 1982 Report.* Washington, D.C., 1982, p. 208.

indirect election by an electoral college composed of national and state legislators. Second, the government encouraged the creation of more than one opposition party in an attempt to divide the opposition at the polls. And third, and most important, congressional districts were designed so that the Democratic Social party could secure a majority of the seats with less than a majority of the popular vote.

The government's calculations proved quite accurate and its precautions most wise. It received only 39.4 percent of the popular vote but retained a majority of the Senate (only one-third of whose seats were contested) and held on to a strong plurality in the Chamber of Deputies. Most important, last-minute changes in the rules used to elect delegates to the electoral college left it under military control. The electoral college is composed of all senators and deputies and some representatives from state legislatures. Almost unnoticed, in July 1982 Figueiredo had amended the electoral college to allow just six legislators from each state rather than one per 1 million people as was originally planned; moreover, he raised the size of the Chamber of Deputies from 420 to 479. Had he not done both the opposition would have gained a slight majority in the electoral college as a result of its gains in the 1982 elections and selected the next president; instead the government ended up with a majority of the college seats. Machiavelli would have been impressed.

Of course, the message of the elections was not good for the military despite the party's holding onto the Senate and the presidency. It was won by the Brazilian Democratic Movement, an urban-based party that had attracted people from all social classes who were united in their determination to evict the military (see Table 8.6). Moreover, the opposition won the governorships and legislative control in all of

Table 8.6. *Brazilian national election: 1982*

		Number of Seats	
	% of Votes	Senate	Chamber
Brazilian Democratic Movement (PMDB)	44.1	21	200
Democratic Social party (PDS)	39.4	46	235
Democratic Labor party (PDT)	6.7	1	24
Brazilian Labor party (PTB)	5.5	1	14
Workers' party (PT)	4.3	0	6

Note: Each citizen voted for one party list of candidates for local office, governorships, and the two houses of Congress
Source: The Economist, November 27, 1982, p. 60.

the powerful south-central states where 75 percent of the nation's gross national product is produced, including São Paulo, Rio de Janeiro, and Minas Gerais, leaving the military with a precarious hold over the new constitutional regime.

Argentine authoritarians

Argentina, like Brazil, started the twentieth century as a major exporter of primary products and a land of opportunity for European immigrants. Industrialization began in earnest during the 1930s and accelerated after World War II in both countries, and with it came urbanization, the growth of an urban working class, and the populist politics of Juan Perón in Argentina and Getulio Vargas in Brazil. And when the Brazilians launched their new military regime in 1964, the Argentine armed forces followed suit in 1966. But there the similarity stops. Unlike the Brazilian military, which ruled without interruption for over twenty years, the Argentines lasted only seven years during their first try (1966–1973) and seven more during a second effort (1976–83), each time giving up without completing the job they had set out to do.

Why was the Argentine experience so different? And what does it tell us about the nature of military authoritarianism that we did not learn in our study of Brazil?

In order to answer the first question we need to review what we learned about the two countries in Chapter 6. They did share similar economic histories during the twentieth century, causing like structural problems and social conflicts that led to the advent of military authoritarianism in the 1960s. Yet they were quite different in important ways, especially in their politics and the manner in which the state dealt with class and sectoral conflicts. Recall the ways Juan Perón and Getulio Vargas governed their nations. When Perón rose to power on the shoulders of the working class he provoked intense middle- and upper-class opposition; Vargas, in contrast, was entrenched in the presidency long before urban workers became assertive and was able to bring them under the control of the Brazilian state without offending economic elites. Consequently, Peronist workers came to see the oligarchy as their enemy, whereas Brazilian labor was diverted from similar antagonisms by their presidential patron.

Second, political tensions ran deeper in Argentina than in Brazil. One might have expected the opposite given the greater poverty and disparity of wealth in Brazil; but poverty, by itself, seldom generates political antagonism. Hostility between Argentine oligarchs and the working class had existed since the turn of the century, but not until Perón did the Argentine masses secure admittance to the government. Peronism became their vehicle to the top and the means for temporarily expelling the country's upper class from office. Rather than looking to government as the patron that dispenses some rewards to all contending players simultaneously, as was attempted in Brazil, Argentines came to see the presidency as something to be held exclusively either by Peronistas or by their opponents. The Argentine military reinforced this when it prohibited Peronists from running for public office in 1958 and 1973. To rule Argentina then, the military could not pretend that it was merely a moderator among competing players as the Brazilians tried to do; instead they faced a well-organized mass movement whose members considered the military the instrument of their middle- and upper-class oppressors. Any attempt to reconstruct the nation's political game had to deal in some way with this reality. Repression might bring temporary peace, but it could not guarantee the Peronistas' eventual acceptance of a new order that excluded their party from power.

Table 8.7. *Postwar Argentina: historical background*

1955	In September President Juan Perón is overthrown by military insurrection known as Revolución Libertadora. After brief interlude under General Eduardo Lonardi, General Pedro Aramburu becomes president
1958	Constitution of 1852 restored, and Arturo Frondizi, candidate of Intransigent Radical party (UCRI), elected president
1962	Frondizi overthrown by military after Peronista candidates in March 1962 gubernatorial and congressional elections are victorious in several provinces
1963	Arturo Illia, candidate of People's Radical party (UCRP), elected president with 26 percent of popular vote
1965	Peronistas win plurality in March congressional elections
1966	In June military overthrows Illia government and creates new regime under General Juan Carlos Ongania
1970	In June commanders replace President Ongania with General Roberto Levingston
1971	In March Levingston is replaced by General Alejandro Lanusse
1973	Peronista candidate, Héctor Cámpora, wins presidential election in March, and Peronistas win majority of seats in Congress
	Cámpora resigns and Juan Domingo Perón is elected president in September
1974	Perón dies and is replaced by his wife, Vice-President Isabel Martinez de Perón
1976	Military overthrows Peronista government in March and creates new military regime under General Jorge Videla
1981	General Roberto Viola selected by junta to replace Videla at end of his term
	General Leopoldo Galtieri deposes Viola seven months later
1982	On April 2 Argentina invades Falklands/Malvinas Islands; in June British expeditionary force defeats and evicts Argentine forces
	Galtieri deposed; General Renaldo Bignone made president in July
1983	Radical party candidate, Raúl Alfonsín, defeats Peronista Italo Luder in presidential election

Military authoritarianism I: 1966–73

The government headed by General Juan Carlos Ongania was simpler than the one started in Brazil two years before. Instead of reorganizing the legislature as the Brazilians had done, Ongania simply closed it. Nor did he bother with rigged elections, preferring instead a simple form of autocratic rule. To his fellow Argentines he promised political order, social discipline, and economic stability if they joined in implementing his plan. It was to begin with a campaign against inflation and economic stagnation and end with the restoration of constitutional government within a decade or so. But Ongania never made it beyond the first stage; economic growth was achieved but political reform was not.

Ongania delegated immense authority to his minister of economy and promised to back him until inflation was under control and business confidence restored. Simultaneously he repressed the national labor movement, jailing its leaders and using force to block its protests. Assuming an almost regal posture, he insulated himself from interest group leaders and ignored politicians. His approach to government was more that of the technocrat than the politician, one of command rather than bargaining and compromise, of long-term economic management rather than piecemeal problem solving.

Adalbert Krieger Vasena, the minister of economy, believed that Argentina's industrialization could not be completed as long as the economy was plagued by high rates of inflation and a large fiscal deficit caused by bloated publc enterprises and patronage-ridden bureaucracies. The fundamental problem, he argued, was inefficiency in both the public and private sectors caused by subsidized industry, undisciplined workers, overextended welfare programs, and politicians unwilling to tighten their belts in hard times. A strong government dedicated to the implementation of a coherent set of efficiency-promoting policies was needed to deal with such problems, and Ongania and Krieger Vasena believed they had created one in 1966.

Initially they did quite well. Wages were held down, inflation was reduced to its lowest level in three decades, investment rose, and organized labor's defiance of authority ceased. But appearances were deceiving, especially in Argentina where temporary docility is easily mistaken for conformity with the will of the authoritarian state. Riots suddenly broke out in Cordoba, an industrial center in Argentina's interior, in May 1969. The week-long protests – which had to be repressed by the military when local police proved inadequate – never threatened military rule directly, but they made a mockery of Ongania's claim that he had subdued the Argentine masses and transformed them into compliant citizens. In the days that followed the military could not hide disagreements among officers about how to deal with the growing militancy of an emboldened working class. Ongania favored harsh repression, convinced that labor had to be subdued and that eventually the government would triumph. At the other extreme were officers who believed that the Peronistas were unconquerable and, therefore, had to be accommodated. Most officers, however, were in the middle, opposed to the sustained physical repression of millions of workers, yet unwilling to yield to the protestors. Disturbed by Ongania's rigidity and refusal to change course after the Cordoba riots, officers from this middle group removed him in 1970, and after a year of indecision, reluctantly decided to pull out after supervising the election of a civilian government.

If Argentines learned anything from Ongania's departure it was the impossibility of replicating the Brazilian experience in their country. Accustomed to ruling for themselves, the country's political parties never gave up hope of forcing the military out and resuming their old positions as active combatants in the nation's political arena. Nor did the economic interest groups representing agriculture, industry, commerce, and labor accept their exclusion from the inner circles of government, even when benefiting from its policies. Together they confined Ongania's revolution to the economy until he was forced to give up his crusade in 1970.

Military authoritarianism II: 1976–83

Argentines learned much from Ongania's experiment in authoritarian government, but typically they did not all draw the same conclusions. His failure convinced some officers that their National Security Doctrine objectives were unattainable, leaving them no alternative but to return the government to the civilians they did not trust. But other officers drew the opposite conclusion: It was Ongania and not military authoritarianism that had failed. Consequently it still could work, they believed, if a more determined and better organized effort were made. Meanwhile civilian politicians learned their own lessons from the same experience, namely, that Argentina's political parties and labor unions could survive repressive military rule. Patience had served the military's civilian opponents quite well, leaving them confident that should the need arise again, they could do the same.

Military officers were given the chance they had been waiting for to try again when the Peronista government elected in 1973 fell into disarray in 1976. Perón had returned to Argentina and, at age 78, won the 1973 elections only to die one year later. His wife and successor Isabel could neither hold the government together nor deal successfully with her many opponents within the Peronista movement and among the middle and upper classes. The economy deteriorated rapidly in 1975 and inflation rose to record levels. To make matters worse, segments of the extreme right and left turned to terrorism, causing panic among the country's economic and military establishments and the middle class. Finally, in April 1976 the military stepped in and deposed the Peronistas.

It marked the triumph of the hardliners within the armed forces who had said all along that constitutional democracy would not work. They quickly banned all political parties and took over the labor movement. They also unleashed a ruthless antiterrorist campaign that did not end until the military and civilian paramilitary forces had killed from 15,000 to 20,000 people.

This time the military had bigger plans for the country. Unlike General Ongania who had been content to work for the restoration of business confidence in order to complete the nation's industrialization with foreign help, General Jorge Videla announced his intention to transform the country's economy and drastically reorient Argentine society. Henceforth Argentines would have to rely on the rules of the free market rather than political chicanery, patronage, and economic subsidies for their well-being. Without asking the public for its permission the armed forces announced its intention to reduce government to minimal activities and end the protection of Argentine industry from foreign competition; public enterprises would be sold off, budgets cut severely, tariffs reduced, and restrictions on foreign investment removed. If Argentines were going to survive, they were told, it would be through their success in the marketplace and not in political meeting halls and ministerial chambers. His reasoning was quite simple: Without patronage to distribute or subsidies to disburse, political parties as Argentines knew them would go out of business, leaving the country's governance to technocrats and the officers who backed them.

Ingenious in theory, the scheme never made much sense in practice. But that never stopped Videla and his colleagues. Their initial self-confidence was reinforced by the successful repression of terrorism and the economy's gradual improvement. By 1979 it was growing at a 7.3 percent annual rate and substantial capital was flowing back into Argentina. Then, to the dismay of the military, everything suddenly fell apart. Over the next three years the economy went into a tailspin; then Argentines fought and lost a war with Great Britain; and finally in 1983 new elections were held, allowing the Peronistas and Radicals to reassert themselves once again.

What went wrong? There is no simple answer; several things combined to bring the military down, though unlike in the Ongania case, public protest was not one of them. Instead, the actions of the military, both in its economic policies and its foreign relations, are largely responsible. First of all, public confidence in the government's economic policies declined in 1981 after a record number of bankruptcies, caused by reductions in subsidies and less tariff protection, suggested the possibility of economic disaster. Capital fled Argentina, its foreign debt rose to record levels, and the value of the peso dropped from 2,000 to the dollar at the end of 1980 to 24,000 a year later. To make matters worse, it was not clear what the government was going to do about the situation. In March 1981, as scheduled, President Videla was replaced by fellow officer and close friend General Roberto Viola. But instead of keeping Videla's economic team on board, he replaced them with one of his own, touching off speculation that he was about to abandon Videla's free market program in response to complaints by Argentine businessmen. Investor panic and government indecision followed, as did a worldwide economic recession causing economic growth to come to a halt, prices to rise by over 200 percent during the year that followed, and confidence in the government to virtually disappear.

Although errors of policy and unanticipated economic events were the most obvious causes of the collapse, the military must also accept some of the blame. Critical to the program's success was a drastic reduction in public expenditures and the sale of government enterprises. That was fine in theory but when it came to doing it the military balked, fearing that some of the cuts would come from their own budget. So rather than carrying through with the plan, the government's technocrats were forced by their uniformed employers to back off, letting the armed forces buy all of the weapons it wanted and protect their industries from being sold. As a result, Argentina's huge public sector escaped the bitter medicine that was intended for it.

When President Viola was replaced by Army Commander Leopoldo Galtieri only ten months after his inauguration, the junta announced that it was going to buckle down again and get on with the original program of economic reform. But just when it appeared that they were doing so, Galtieri went to war, seizing the Falkland Islands off Argentina's coast, occupied since 1833 by the English but always claimed by Argentina (who calls them the Islas Malvinas). The invasion on April 2, 1982, took everyone by surprise.

Argentine and British diplomats had failed repeatedly to resolve the issue of sovereignty over the islands. The Argentines demanded complete sovereignty, but the British deferred to the islands' 1,800 British residents who refused to live under the Argentine flag. The Argentines had threatened invasions in the past but had never been taken seriously by successive British governments, who feared the domestic political repercussions of turning the islands back to Argentina. The price they paid for their procrastination was a two-month war with Argentina.

General Galtieri had assumed that the British would not respond militarily given the islands' distance from London, their relative unimportance strategically, and the cost to the British of mounting an invasion force. He guessed wrong. Not only did the British invade the islands and inflict a swift and humiliating defeat on the Argentines in June, but they also punished Galtieri economically by securing a three-month European blockade of trade with Argentina. In the end Galtieri had nothing to show for his adventure but defeat and an economy in worse shape than before, and a bitter and confused Argentine people who had supported what was for them a patriotic cause. To save face a deeply divided armed forces sent Galtieri into retirement, replaced the entire junta, and announced their intention to hold free national elections within eighteen months. As in 1970, when Ongania was deposed, the moderates picked up the pieces and called on their military colleagues to take another rest.

There certainly seemed to be a pattern to Argentine behavior. Within twenty years two military authoritarian regimes had attacked serious economic problems and attained some initial success only to watch things fall apart, each forced to withdraw less than a decade after it had begun. The causes of their failures were not identical nor were they very simple. But it is obvious that neither regime sustained its economic program or altered the nature of civilian politics. The Peronistas, Radicals, and other parties all survived repression, as did a labor movement loyal to the Peronistas. Politically the Argentines could not imitate the Brazilian armed forces with their official party and rigged elections. The Argentine military does not have an electoral following like the Brazilians do, nor does it face civilians who are as reluctant as the Brazilians to take the all-or-nothing approach in their dealings with the military. Brazilian parties and interest groups recognize that the military has the upper hand and can sustain its rule using the very powerful Brazilian state, perhaps indefinitely; the Argentine parties, in contrast, have won battles with the military many times before and are always confident that they will do so again.

Does this mean that military authoritarianism survives longer in some circumstances than it does in others? Probably. The military is part of an established political process and can do only as much as the distribution of power in that process allows it to do, no matter how great its physical force. Even though it aspires to change national politics permanently, it seems especially ill equipped to do so. The Brazilians managed to invent devices that allowed them to hold off opponents, but all were ad hoc and of only temporary value. The Argentines never got that far. Political inventiveness is not a skill known to contemporary Argentine officers. Formal, bureaucratic, and simpleminded in political matters, they are more comfortable jailing or ignoring their opponents than they are playing politics with them.

Peru: The exception?

One is tempted to conclude that military authoritarian regimes all have the same purpose and serve most of the same class and sectoral interests. Not only did the Brazilians and Argentines interrupt competitive politics and repress their opponents in order to implement the conservative modernization development strategy, but so did the Chileans and Uruguayans beginning in 1973. Moreover, all professed faith in the National Security Doctrine as the guide to the reconstruction of their nations. Clearly they had much in common, enough perhaps to lead one to believe that military authoritarianism comes in a single package adaptable with slight adjustments to most South American settings. But politics, even when directed by authoritarians, is not that neat. While the militaries of the Southern Cone region were mimicking each other, the Peruvian armed forces set out to invent their own version of the military authoritarian game. How different it actually became is still a matter of some dispute.

The causes of the Peruvian coup in 1968 were more complex than those that prompted coups in Brazil and Argentina. In the past the

Table 8.8. *Postwar Peru: historical background*

1945	José Bustamante, conservative diplomat, elected president
1948	Military overthrows Bustamante government and governs through presidency of conservative General Manuel Odria for eight years
1956	Manuel Prado, president between 1939 and 1945, again elected president
1962	None of three major candidates—Haya de la Torre of APRISTA party, Fernando Belaúnde Terry of Popular Action party, or Manuel Odria of National Union party—receives required one-third of popular vote, nor can Congress agree on one of three. Military then annuls election
1963	New election won narrowly by Fernando Belaúnde Terry
1968	In October Belaúnde government overthrown by military; General Juan Velasco Alvardo is named president and in 1969 announces sweeping agrarian reform program
1975	In August General Velasco is replaced by General Francisco Morales Bermúdez, who shifts policy in more moderate direction and purges most reformist officers from government
1978	Constituent Assembly elected and constitution approved
1980	Fernando Belaúnde Terry elected president

Peruvian military had frequently intervened in politics to protect conservative interests. It had also developed a strong antipathy toward APRISTA, the country's primary reform party since the 1930s, because of APRISTA's strident antimilitarism. On the surface the 1968 coup appeared to be a calculated response to a probable election victory by the APRISTAs in 1969. In fact, it was a response by nationalistic officers to Peruvian subservience to foreign investors and to civilian failures to cope with discontent in the Peruvian countryside.

During the first half of the twentieth century Peru's conservative leaders had successfully absorbed the country's small but growing middle sectors by giving them a role in the management of the export economy and the state bureaucracy. At the same time, the leaders ignored the plight of the peasantry and dealt harshly with the labor movement and the political parties that encouraged it. But Peruvian society continued to change, promoted by the expansion of copper mining, the growth of local industry and commerce, and accelerating urbanization in the 1950s and 1960s. The Conservatives' failure to adapt their policies to these changes yielded land invasions by disgruntled peasants, student protests, illegal strikes, strident nationalism, and the formation of a small but potentially disruptive guerrilla movement in the countryside during the 1960s. The election of reformer Fernando Belaúnde Terry in 1964 marked the first serious attempt to adapt public policy to these new conditions. Belaúnde modeled his Popular Action party (AP) after the democratic reform movements already active in the hemisphere and campaigned on a platform of agrarian reform and economic modernization. But his ability to fulfill his campaign promises was hindered by the opposition of APRISTAs and Conservatives in Congress. As a result, instead of delivering sweeping reforms, Belaúnde inadvertently increased the frustrations of those who desired immediate solutions to the country's growing social problems.

The military's reaction to Belaúnde's travail was hard to predict at the time. In the past it might have welcomed his failures as evidence of the strength of the old order. But the military had changed during the 1960s, and many of its younger officers, fresh from battles with guerrillas in the countryside that had awakened them to the increasing political costs of defending traditional social institutions, saw Belaúnde's failures as heightening the possibility of radical upheaval. No longer, it appeared, could Peru afford the kind of reformist politics that became immobilized by interparty squabbles. The only solution, some officers concluded, was the suspension of democratic politics in order to permit a more direct assault on the country's development problems by a military-led state bureaucracy.

The officers who led the Peruvian coup were more audacious than either the Brazilians or the Argentines. They intended not only to control the nation's politics, but also to build a popular foundation for a reorganized Peruvian state. Though they began like the Brazilians and Argentines with the closure of political parties and the repression of potential opponents, they were not content to rely on repression alone. Instead they hastily created new *campesino* and labor organizations that they hoped to use to create a corporatist-type political regime capable of both improving the condition of the poor and denying the political left a base for political action.

The new regime was organized hierarchically and by economic sector, starting with government-sponsored local economic organizations, which were joined into sectoral organizations and finally into a national body called the National System for the Support of Social Mobilization (SINAMOS), created in June 1971. Within each economic sector production organizations were created. Under the 1969 Agrarian Reform Law, for example, the largest private holdings were reorganized into collective enterprises known as Agrarian Production Cooperatives (CAPs) and Agricultural Societies of Social Interest (SAISs). And in 1970 firms involved in manufacturing, mining, telecommunications, and fishing were forced by the new Industrial Law to admit worker participation in their ownership and management. Such measures were intended to involve the masses in the economic decisions that affect them most directly.

SINAMOS was supposed to join all social classes within the new political system and to regulate their involvement in the making and implementation of government policy. In fact, it achieved much less, never advancing beyond a means for government control over the Peruvian masses. Social classes were actually kept divided in order to facilitate the government's regulation of each separately.

At the top of the government hierarchy was the president – until mid-1975 General Juan Velasco Alvarado – and the Presidential Advisory Committee (COAP), an all-military body charged with designing legislation and coordinating its implementation. They were advised by a host of civilian technocrats, but they did not consult directly with the leaders of peasant, labor, or other mass organizations when designing their policies as promised. They were, however, occasionally forced to revise their programs when they met resistance from such groups.

Policy innovation, more than government organization, distinguished the Peruvian officers from their neighbors. Though they called their program revolutionary, it more resembled the progressive modernization strategy than the revolutionary one. It began with initiatives in three areas. First came the nationalization of some foreign and domestic enterprises. The petroleum and fish-meal industries, most banks and insurance companies, the import and export trade, and most utilities were placed under state control. These measures appeared quite radical within the context of Peru, but they actually did little more than raise the level of state ownership to one commensurate with that already achieved in the more industrialized Latin American countries. Second came agrarian reform. A modest program had already been begun by President Belaúnde before the military overthrew him in 1968. But in three years Belaúnde had expropriated only 795 estates, covering 1.5 million hectares. In a similar amount of time President Velasco expropriated 1,939 estates covering 3.2 million hectares, including the valuable foreign-owned sugar estates along Peru's Pacific coast. Only 20,000 peasant families gained land under Belaúnde compared with approximately 87,000 under Velasco. The third component of Velasco's program was industrial reform. This included a scheme for joint ownership by workers and entrepreneurs. In practice this meant the government would require the country's larger firms to implement profit- and stock-sharing plans that would gradually turn over a large share of the firm to its employees.

In the short run, the bureaucrats and military officers who manned state agencies were the principal beneficiaries of reform and the expansion of the Peruvian state. Those peasants who were fortunate enough to receive land under the agrarian reform also profited. But a majority of the rural work force, both hired laborers and subsistence farmers, were bypassed by the reforms which were restricted primarily to the transfer of the ownership of the largest *latifundios* to the *campesinos* who worked on them. The third to gain were a minority of industrial workers who participated in the profit-sharing programs required of major industries by the government.

Velasco accomplished much, but it was far less than he had sought. Like civilian reformers he repeatedly ran into obstacles, some human and others natural, and despite his power, he could not overcome most of them. Take the rural sector, for example. It might appear that the Peruvians had solved their rural development program by redistributing land to peasants and organizing the land into various types of cooperatives. But not all peasants benefited from agrarian reform. In fact, after the completion of land redistribution, 300,000 rural families remained landless because there was not enough land to go around. Only 2 percent of Peru's total area – the lowest proportion in Latin America – is under cultivation. More land could be made available, but only at a very high cost because the project would require the irrigation of desert regions or the clearing of tropical lowlands.

Nor did the military government escape the kinds of externally induced balance-of-payments deficits and foreign debt burdens that plagued previous Peruvian governments. In June 1976 it faced a crisis similar to that which it had inherited in 1968. The problem was largely one of resources. Velasco and his advisers, encouraged by foreign bankers who foresaw an oil boom for Peru in the mid-1970s, borrowed heavily abroad to finance the most ambitious development program in the country's history. In a period of four years Peru took on a host of new creditors, raising its foreign debt fivefold to $5 billion (American billion) and its annual debt servicing to 43 percent of its total export income in 1976. But little oil was discovered.

Military reformism was halted in 1975 when Velasco was deposed by more conservative officers. During the next five years they supervised the gradual restoration of constitutional government, starting with a constitutional convention in 1978 and free presidential and congressional elections in May 1980. Confident that moderates would triumph, they made no effort to rig the elections as the Brazilians would do two years later. Ironically, it was moderate Fernando Belaúnde Terry, the person overthrown by Velasco twelve years before, whom the Peruvians again elected president. As expected, Belaúnde announced his intention to respect the results of Velasco's agrarian reforms while disbanding all of his mass organizations.

Whatever his shortcomings, Velasco's actions remind us that the military is not always compelled to be conservative in its policies. But it also indicates that there is no reason to believe that the armed forces can achieve lasting structural reforms any more easily than civilians can. Their actions are often swifter, but seldom more enduring. Nor is the military especially adept at securing control over society, even when attempting popular measures. The Peruvian military did achieve some autonomy from the social classes usually thought to influence military authoritarians, but its control over the government was never enough to secure its complete hegemony. On the contrary, by the time he was deposed Velasco had managed to alienate all social classes either with his policies or with forced participation in the state's organizations.

Military authoritarianism: experiments that failed

Two decades have passed since the Brazilian armed forces launched a new authoritarianism that was enthusiastically replicated by their colleagues in neighboring countries. What do any of them have to show for their efforts today?

Nowhere have the visions of the good society proffered by the national security ideology become reality. Nor has rapid and steady economic development been achieved. Instead, some militaries gave up, others are still looking for the exit, while a few hold on stubbornly. What went wrong for this generation of ambitious crusaders?

To begin with, most were ill equipped for the task. Military education, even in advanced war colleges, offered little preparation for the reorganization of complex economic and social institutions traditionally managed by citizens reluctant to change their habits. Officers acted like children who wanted to fly to the moon. They knew where the moon was and believed that rockets might take them there but had little idea about how to build their own rocket. Undaunted, they tried anyway, only to find themselves stifled during the first stage.

But why did they try, given the obvious obstacles? We need only recall that during the 1960s and 1970s Latin American officers were not only more ambitious for themselves and their nations, but also more frustrated by repeated economic instability and the appearance of a skilled and determined political Left that threatened the military institution as much as it did the propertied classes. Fidel Castro's disposal of Batista's army in Cuba reinforced military fear of the Left. Sooner or later military officers were bound to conclude they alone could preserve themselves as well as the society of which they were a part. And each time they stepped in, they were cheered by conservatives at home and allies in the United States, as well as by frightened members of the middle class.

Officers were always more short-sighted than their official statements made them appear. Plans were announced and new societies promised, but once in office most officers worked incrementally, dealing first with the liquidation of the Left and then the promotion of economic growth. Politics was marginal, something either to be manipulated by government organizations, like SINAMOS in Peru or official parties in Brazil, or just ignored as in Argentina. This is why military rule seems to follow a similar pattern in different countries, starting boldly, achieving some order and economic stabilization and growth, and then weakening, either because of rising economic problems or uncertainty about political reconstruction, especially when faced by civilian recalcitrance long after the military thought it had the population under control.

One of the primary sources of the military's weakness as a ruler is its inability to retain some of its initial supporters. Militaries do not depend on popular legitimacy to survive, but they do need the cooperation of producers and the conformity of labor. They usually get the first with policy and the latter with repression, at least for a while. They also want the backing of the middle sectors, since they are the ones who keep society operating from day to day. Usually, middle-sector dread of economic crisis and civil unrest causes these groups to accept military rule in times of crisis. Although they claim to prefer constitutional government, they have a habit of welcoming military intervention when constitutional government no longer serves their immediate interests. They are, however, quite fickle, as most militaries have discovered. Once order is restored and economic conditions improved, they are among the first to demand that the armed forces step aside so that civilian politicians can return to their offices. Most often they consider military rule to be a temporary expedient, a necessary evil to be used and then discarded. Their support is not essential to the military's governance of the nation, but it is crucial for its political reorganization. If the middle sectors want their own parties rather than the military's when democratization begins anew, officers have little choice but to work with them.

The military authoritarians' primary achievements are economic. Without a doubt, they can do things that popularity-seeking politicians find hard to do: cut wages, raise prices, give concessions to foreign investors, and so on. But one should be careful not to rate the military's performance too highly. First, its economic programs never do all that they are supposed to do. It can control wage levels and repress the working class, but the cutting of budgets often eludes it due in large part to the military's vested interests in the public sector, both as manager of public enterprises and as purchaser of arms. How cooperative it is depends on how much it will lose from following the edicts of its economic advisers. Second, as we have seen repeatedly, though austerity policy may be compelling from time to time in a capitalist economy, it never guarantees recovery once it has served its purpose. What is required is the strengthening of the Latin American economies so that they can either withstand the vicissitudes of the world economy or compete successfully within it. The conservative modernization strategy promises to do the latter but has yet to prove that it can do so in more than a few marginal areas. Moreover, by creating greater national dependence on the world economy it risks making the nation more vulnerable than before, as occurred in the early 1980s when world recession forced heavy borrowing abroad, record foreign debts, and the acceptance of the bitter medicine dispensed by international bankers. Of course, other economic strategies did little better, but this being the case, one should be just as skeptical

Table 8.9. *The political structure of military authoritarianism*

	Brazil (1964–76)	Argentina (1966–9) (1976–83)	Peru (1968–75)
Composition of government elite	Military officers Civilian technocrats	Military officers Civilian technocrats	Military officers Civilian technocrats
Political organizations	Official party (ARENA) Opposition party (MDB) Congress, state, and local governments controlled through official parties and presidential interventions	None outside executive Provincial governments placed under military commanders	Military-led mass organization (SINAMOS) and constituency of groups of peasants and laborers
Structure of interest-group participation	Traditional dependence on state with authoritarian government acting as coordinator of private group participation	Government isolation from contesting groups modified by selective, informal contacts	Abortive corporatist system in which government controlled functional groups through bureaucracy and mass organization
Treatment of political opposition	Physical repression Expulsion from politics	Physical repression Isolation from policy-making process	Mild repression Co-optation of rank and file through mass organizations

Table 8.10. *The initial economic programs of the military authoritarians*

	Castelo Branco (1964–7)	Ongania (1966–9) Videla (1976–80)	Velasco (1968–72)
Objectives	Price stability Balance-of-payments equilibrium Acceleration of economic growth Increased private investment Alleviation of sectoral and regional economic disparities Expansion of exports	Price stability Industrial growth Attraction of foreign investment Increased efficiency of public and private sectors	Reduction of public debt burden Integration of peasantry into market economy Sharing of industrial wealth with workers Reduction of dependence on foreign investors
Instruments	Fiscal restraint Wage controls Unification and freeing of exchange market Tax incentives to encourage private domestic and foreign investments Increased efficiency of tax collection	Wage freeze Devaluations of currency Tariff reductions Removal of restrictions on foreign investors Tax increases	Credit restraint Devaluation of currency Tax increases Redistribution of rural property Nationalization of selected foreign and domestic enterprises Worker participation in ownership of private firms

of the claims of growth and development made by the advocates of conservative modernization as one is of the claims of its competitors.

It is tempting to conclude that during the past two decades the military learned its lesson and in the future it will be less eager to intervene directly in national politics. But such an inference would be naive and incorrect. No matter how much one might wish otherwise, militaries remain active players in most national political games. Whether in office or not, they are preoccupied by the nation's governance and concerned about its economic strength as well as their own well-being. Moreover, others still believe they can turn to the armed forces for assistance when it is needed. It is wrong to speak of "the" military and the lessons "it" learns. The military is led by officers who are separated by rank and age. One generation's failure does not necessarily convince a later generation that it too will fail. On the contrary, if their past behavior is any guide, one must suspect that there are young officers today who believe that when their time comes they will accomplish what their authoritarian elders failed to achieve. Civilian politicians know this and will be among the last to disregard the military as a competitor in the national game.

Further reading

General

Collier, David, ed. *The New Authoritarianism in Latin America.* Princeton, N.J.: Princeton University Press, 1979.

Comblin, Jose. *The Church and the National Security State.* Maryknoll, N.Y.: Orbis, 1979.

Huntington, Samuel. *Political Order in Changing Societies.* New Haven, Conn.: Yale University Press, 1968.

Johnson, John. *The Military and Society in Latin America.* Stanford, Calif.: Stanford University Press, 1964.

Malloy, James., ed. *Authoritarianism and Corporatism in Latin America.* Pittsburgh: University of Pittsburgh Press, 1977.

O'Donnell, Guillermo A. *Modernization and Bureaucratic-Authoritarianism: Studies in South American Politics.* Institute of International Studies. Berkeley: University of California, 1973.

Thorpe, Rosemary, and Lawrence Whitehead, eds. *Inflation and Stabilization in Latin America.* New York: Holmes and Meier, 1979.

Argentina

Mallon, R. D., and J. V. Sourrouille. *Economic Policymaking in a Conflict Society: The Argentine Case.* Cambridge, Mass.: Harvard University Press, 1975.

O'Donnell, Guillermo. *The Bureaucratic Authoritarian State*. Berkeley: University of California Press, 1983.
Potash, Robert A. *The Army and Politics in Argentina, 1945–1962: Perón to Frondizi*. Stanford, Calif.: Stanford University Press, 1979.
Snow, Peter. *Political Forces in Argentina*. Boston: Allyn & Bacon, 1971.
Wynia, Gary W. *Argentina in the Postwar Era: Politics and Economic Policy in a Divided Society*. Albuquerque: University of New Mexico Press, 1978.

Brazil

Bruneau, Thomas C., and Philippe Faucher, eds. *Authoritarian Capitalism: Brazil's Contemporary Economic and Political Development*. Boulder, Colo.: Westview Press, 1981.
Evans, Peter. *Dependent Development: The Alliance of Multinational, State, and Local Capital in Brazil*. Princeton, N.J.: Princeton University Press, 1979.
Flynn, Peter. *Brazil: A Political Analysis*. Boulder, Colo.: Westview Press, 1978.
McDonough, Peter. *Power and Ideology in Brazil*. Princeton, N.J.: Princeton University Press, 1981.
Schneider, Ronald M. *The Political System of Brazil: Emergence of a "Modernizing" Authoritarian Regime 1964–1970*. New York: Columbia University Press, 1971.
Stepan, Alfred. *The Military in Politics: Changing Patterns in Brazil*. Princeton, N.J.: Princeton University Press, 1971.
  Authoritarian Brazil: Origins, Policies and Future. New Haven, Conn.: Yale University Press, 1973.
Syvrud, Donald. *Foundations of Brazilian Economic Growth*. Stanford, Calif.: Hoover Institution, 1974.

Peru

Astiz, Carlos. *Pressure Groups and Power Elites in Peruvian Politics*. Ithaca, N.Y.: Cornell University Press, 1969.
Bourricand, Francois. *Power and Society in Contemporary Peru*. New York: Praeger, 1967.
Collier, David. *Squatters and Oligarchs: Authoritarian Rule and Policy Change in Peru*. Baltimore: Johns Hopkins University Press, 1976.
Dew, Edward. *Politics of the Altiplano: The Dynamics of Change in Rural Peru*. Austin: University of Texas Press, 1976.
Einauldi, Luigi. *The Peruvian Military: A Summary Political Analysis*. Santa Monica, Calif.: Rand, 1969.
  Revolution from Within? Military Rule in Peru Since 1968. Santa Monica, Calif.: Rand, 1971.
Fitzgerald, E. V. K. *The State and Economic Development: Peru Since 1968*. Cambridge: Cambridge University Press, 1976.
International Bank for Reconstruction and Development. *The Current Economic Position and Prospects of Peru*. Washington, D.C.: 1976.
Lowenthal, Abraham, ed. *The Peruvian Experiment*. Princeton, N.J.: Princeton University Press, 1976.

North, Lisa, and Tanya Korovokin. *The Peruvian Revolution and the Officers in Power: 1967–1976.* Center for Developing Area Studies Occasional Monograph Series, no. 15. Montreal: McGill University, 1980.
Stepan, Alfred. *The State and Society: Peru in Comparative Perspective.* Princeton, N.J.: Princeton University Press, 1978.

9. The revolutionary game: Mexico

Real revolutions

Real revolutions are quite rare in Latin America. It is not for lack of trying but rather the simple fact that most revolts have met with defeat or betrayal. This may seem a bit surprising given the abundance of conditions in the region that are conducive to revolution. Social structures tend to be rigid and repressive, the economic exploitation of the many by a few is common, and subordination to foreign economic power is a fact of life. Whether one's theory holds that revolution is caused by imperialism, class conflict, "relative deprivation," or merely the escalation of political conflict, Latin America has always seemed ripe for it. Nevertheless, revolutions there are infrequent and often abortive. Why is this so? Are the theories that predict revolution faulty or are they merely inappropriate for Latin America in particular? Perhaps a little of both, as we shall see.

Theories of revolution are drawn primarily from the study of successful revolutions like the Russian, Chinese, and Cuban ones, but there is little reason to believe that the way it happened in these countries will be replicated today in Latin America. For one thing, it is harder now than before. Since Fidel Castro's triumph in Cuba over two decades ago thousands of Latin American soldiers have been trained by the United States in counterinsurgency warfare, and though such training does not guarantee battlefield success, it does make guerrilla warfare riskier and costlier. It does not make revolutionary triumph impossible though, as Anastasio Somoza and his National Guard discovered in 1979. But to succeed, revolutionaries must defy heavy odds, constantly adapt their strategies to new realities, and exploit any advantages they have, all the while paying a high price in human lives for their conquests.

Revolutions are rare for another reason. Real revolutions involve much more than the military defeat and expulsion of autocrats (or democrats). Many who have seized power in Latin America have claimed to be revolutionary, but few have achieved anything more than marginal modifications of the status quo. A real revolution involves the transformation of a nation's politics, social structures, and economic institutions. In other words, to qualify for the title they covet, revolutionaries must achieve fundamental and pervasive change throughout society.

To succeed, the revolutionary has to do three things. First comes the defeat and destruction of the existing government, second the adoption and enforcement of new political rules, and third the design and construction of new social and economic institutions. The incumbents' defeat could require anything from a brief insurrection to a protracted and costly internal war. The path taken is dictated by the political and military advantages held by the rebels and the tactics used by their opponents. Mass insurrections, tightly controlled guerrilla warfare, and terrorism directed at selected targets have all been tried, and each has contributed to victory in some instances but not in others. The fact that more revolts have failed than succeeded testifies to the difficulty of the task.

Triumph on the battlefield is necessary but hardly sufficient for the achievement of revolutionary change. Revolutionaries, no matter how popular they are with the masses, have to work hard at establishing some control over the nation in the face of inevitable opposition both from within the country and from without. Those whom they have evicted will do all they can to make their defeat only a temporary one. Accordingly, the new government must defend itself militarily and do whatever is necessary to strip opponents of the resources they might use to undermine the revolution. It is here that revolutionaries face one of their most troublesome and potentially divisive decisions. Can they tolerate opponents who demand the freedom to compete openly with the new leadership in democratic elections if their adversaries are opposed to radical economic and social change? Or should they limit freedom, creating a revolutionary dictatorship to replace the reactionary one they deposed? Contemporary revolutionaries seem to prefer the latter, though they claim theirs is a true social democracy, something more valuable to the poor than liberal democracy.

Equally crucial to the construction of the new society is the winning and holding of the support of the masses. Here ideological education is important, for though most may have welcomed the creation of a new order, they may not agree on what form it should take. They have to be taught to believe in it and to accept its organizations as their own. A charismatic leader might facilitate the process by buying some time while the learning goes on, but by itself charismatic authority cannot hold the new society together. Here too revolutionaries face a major dilemma, namely, how much conformity with the new values is required and how far to go in enforcing conformity against the will of those who choose to resist. What to revolutionaries is necessary reeducation for the unification of their society will seem to nonconformists nothing more than unrelenting repression.

Revolutionaries are driven not just by a desire for power, but also a vision of a new society. The translation of this vision into reality is a never-ending project. Like all other advocates of change, they have to overcome well-entrenched traditions as well as resist the temptation to sacrifice revolutionary objectives to satisfy personal ambitions or the dictates of economic expediency. There are many models of the new order to draw upon, but history teaches that revolutionaries have been no more successful in creating the perfect society than have nonrevolutionaries. In the end the best they can do is select the objectives that for them are most important and pay the price required to pursue them.

Mexico, Cuba, and Nicaragua offer three contrasting examples of the revolutionary game in contemporary Latin America. Each tells us something about the possibilities for radical change and the price that is paid to achieve it. Moreover, by comparing these three cases we can also learn about the different forms that revolutionary politics and policy take and the choices and compromises that are made along the way. We will start with Mexico in this chapter and then turn to Cuba and Nicaragua in the next.

The Mexican insurrection: 1910–17

Controversy still haunts the Mexican revolution. The revolt that started in 1910 became a long and bloody struggle, filled with violent battles in which Mexicans of all social classes participated. When it was ended in 1917 the victors proclaimed an end to elitist, autocratic government, announcing that henceforth Mexico would be governed by leaders dedicated to social justice for everyone. Land that had been taken from *campesinos* over several generations would be returned to them, and all laborers would be guaranteed respectable minimum wages and an eight-hour day. Moreover, foreigners would no longer be allowed to control the nation's economy through their ownership of its utilities and extraction of its natural resources. By the standards of the time it all seemed quite revolutionary.

Sixty-five years later things look different. Many in Mexico complain that what the insurrection accomplished politically was simply the replacement of one oligarchy by another. What the revolutionaries created, their critics tell us, was not an egalitarian society but a stratified, bourgeois one. Its leaders were not from the peasantry as mythology would have it, but from a growing middle class who resented their exclusion from the Díaz dictatorship. The poor did become participants in the new government, but only at the cost of accepting their subordination to the country's new rulers. In other words, a regime that claimed to be revolutionary never really became so, for though it changed the nation's leadership it never truly rebuilt the country's social structure by transferring substantial wealth and power from the rich to the poor.

The revolution is not without its defenders, of course; most are in the Mexican government. They claim that the promises made in 1917 were kept, and they cite data on the vast amounts of land that have been given to *campesinos*, the growth of organized labor and the improved welfare of its members, and increased education and social services as their evidence. Mexico is not an egalitarian society, they admit, but to have expected the creation of one in a nation as poor as Mexico was in 1917 is naive. Before wealth could be redistributed it had to be created, and that required the Mexican state's concentration of resources in productive development projects, paving the way for industrialization. A comparison of the Mexico of 1984 with that of 1917 indicates how much, not how little, was achieved, the revolution's defenders tell us.

Differences of opinion about the revolution are not surprising. Such is the nature of politics, especially when much is expected from it. But in assessing competing interpretations of the Mexican Revolution we need to keep the standards we are using in mind. Comparisons with the Díaz regime it replaced will lead to one conclusion, comparisons of its actual achievements with its promises will lead to another, and comparisons with Marxist revolutions like Cuba's still a different conclusion. All of these comparisons are essential, but we need to be conscious of which ones we employ as we make our assessments.

We will start with the insurrection and its initial results. The revolt began in 1910 with opposition to the reelection of Porfirio Díaz, the dictatorial ruler of Mexico since 1877, and ended seven years later with the adoption of the Constitution of 1917 and the gradual organization of a new political regime. The struggle was led by men as diverse as Emiliano Zapata, a peasant leader; Francisco ("Pancho") Villa, a rural outlaw; Venustiano Carranza, a landowner politician; Alvaro Obregón, a small farmer; and Francisco Madero, a cultured gentleman from an upper-class family. It took an immense toll in Mexican lives, not just among the masses who fought it but also among its leaders as they tried to consolidate power after 1917. By 1928, Zapata, Villa, Carranza, Obregón, and Madero had all met violent deaths.

Principal among the long-term causes of the Mexican Revolution was opposition from the emerging middle sectors, labor unions, and *campesinos* to the repressive elitist rule of Porfirio Díaz. Díaz, an inheritor of the liberal regime created by reformer Benito Juárez in 1857, was dedicated to the economic development of Mexico through the exploitation of its resources by foreign investors and domestic capitalists. This exploitation was supported by a strong government that could impose its will on the peasants who resisted the transfer of their communal lands to commercial farmers and the laborers who protested harsh conditions and depressed wages in the mines and factories. Through the use of a system of loyal regional political bosses backed by their local *rurales* police forces, Díaz secured the political order and rapid economic development that strife-torn Mexico had lacked before 1880. Yet, by monopolizing the fruits of economic growth for distribution among a small elite, he added to the frustration of those in the middle sectors, peasantry, and working class whom he denied a share of his political power or the country's increasing economic bounty.

When Díaz announced in 1908 that he would not seek reelection and then backed away from his pledge, he provoked a violent reaction by his frustrated opponents. The opposition, inspired by the radical writings and agitation of intellectuals like Ricardo Flores Magón, turned to the more moderate Francisco Madero for leadership. Madero, the son of a wealthy northern Mexican family, was dedicated to the restoration of constitutional government rather than radical economic or social change. As the candidate of the Anti-Reelectionist

Table 9.1. *Mexico: historical background*

1821	Independence from Spain declared
1848	Texas ceded to United States in Treaty of Guadalupe Hidalgo
1857	La Reforma revolt led by Benito Juárez ends in creation of liberal constitution of 1857
1872	President Juárez dies in office
1877	General Porfirio Díaz becomes president and creates personal dictatorship that lasts thirty-four years
1911	Porfirio Díaz forced to resign by revolt led by democrat Francisco Madero Madero becomes president
1913	President Madero overthrown and killed by troops of General Victoriano Huerta, touching off civil war
1914	In face of violent opposition, General Huerta resigns from presidency
1916	At end of year, warring factions declare truce and convene constitutional convention
1917	New constitution announced, and Venustiano Carranza declared president
1920	Carranza forced from office by rival revolutionary generals and killed while fleeing
	General Alvara Obregón, collaborator of Carranza during revolution, declared president
1924	Plutarco Elias Calles elected president
1928	General Obregón assassinated while campaigning for reelection
	Revolutionary party (PNR) created and Calles rules indirectly until 1934 through handpicked presidents
1934	Lázaro Cárdenas elected president; agrarian reform accelerated and foreign petroleum companies nationalized
	Revolutionary party reorganized along corporate lines composed of peasant, labor, and popular sectors and renamed Party of the Mexican Revolution (PRM)
1940	Manuel Avila Camacho elected president
1946	Miguel Aleman Valdes elected president
	Party name changed to Institutional Revolutionary party (PRI)
1952	Adolfo Ruiz Cortines elected president
1958	Adolfo Lopez Mateos elected president
1964	Gustavo Diaz Ordaz elected president
1970	Luis Echeverria elected president
1976	Jose Lopez Portillo elected president
1982	Record foreign debt causes unprecedented financial crisis
	Miguel de la Madrid elected president

party, he campaigned vigorously against Díaz before the 1910 election, only to be arrested and jailed for his efforts. After his release Madero reluctantly took to arms, joining an uprising already in progress in several parts of the country. One year and several minor battles later, Madero's forces captured the border city of Juárez, embarrassed Díaz's army, and forced the seventy-eight-year-old patriarch to abandon the presidency and flee into exile in Europe, where he spent the last four years of his life. What followed, however, was not a simple transition that added a few new players to the game, but a decade of turmoil and civil war that changed many aspects of Mexican life.

The first phase (1911–13) was dominated by the figure of Francisco Madero, elected president after Díaz's departure. Madero's goal was not the economic transformation of Mexico, but the creation of a political democracy whose procedures individual Mexicans could use to improve their condition. He was a constitutional democrat concerned more with political means than socioeconomic ends. Instead of eliminating the traditional elite and Díaz's army and bureaucracy, he invited them to accept a place in the new constitutional order. And rather than responding immediately to the demands of Emiliano Zapata and other peasant leaders for the return of the village land sugar planters had taken, he asked them to wait until their claims were duly processed and evaluated by the new authorities. Nevertheless, it was not Zapata or Madero's other disappointed supporters who did him in: Instead it was Victoriano Huerta, an army general backed by antidemocrats in the elite and by archconservative American ambassador Henry Lane Wilson (who sought the restoration of a government more sympathetic to foreign investors), who deposed and killed Madero on February 22, 1913.

Huerta's coup, which represented a last-ditch attempt by the followers of Porfirio Díaz to reestablish their political control, touched off the second and most violent phase of the Mexican Revolution (1913–16). Those who had seen their reformist aspirations frustrated by the proceduralism of Madero and ignored altogether by Huerta's vengeful autocracy turned to the battlefield to accomplish what they could not secure through the political process. Northerners Carranza and Obregón wanted to create a constitutional democracy and promote Mexican nationalism; peasant leaders like Zapata wanted their land returned; labor leaders wanted their rights protected by the state; and an assortment of urban intellectuals aspired to lead Mexico down a path of liberty and social reform. Between 1913 and 1916 they waged war, first against Huerta, who was forced to resign in 1914, and then against one another for the right to create a new government. In late 1914 Villa and Zapata took control of Mexico City, and then in 1915 both were evicted by Obregón and Carranza. For nearly three years Mexico was engulfed by one of the most violent struggles in Latin American history. The revolution was, in the words of revolutionary novelist Mariano Azuela, "like a hurricane, and the man who enters it is no longer a man, but merely a miserable dry leaf beaten by the wind."

Exhaustion and the military superiority of the forces led by Carranza and Obregón finally brought peace in 1916. Soon thereafter the revolutionary generals met in Querétaro to settle their differences and write a new constitution. Conspicuously missing from the convention were the *latifundistas*, clergy, bureaucrats, and army officers who had been the mainstay of the old Díaz regime. Instead, it was the opposition middle sectors from northern Mexico, labor leaders, intellectuals, and peasant leaders who met in Querétaro. Though most of the document was inspired by the same kind of liberalism that had influenced the 1857 constitution, written a half century before under the leadership of Benito Juárez, the proponents of social reform did secure the inclusion of significant new powers that would later enable the implementation of social and economic reforms. Article 3 limited the power of the church by prohibiting religious instruction in Mexican schools. In Article 27 the traditional right of the Spanish Crown to all land and water within its domain was allocated to the Mexican state, as was the right to expropriate land and pay for it at declared tax value using twenty-year bonds that carried a five percent rate of interest. And laborers were guaranteed an eight-hour day and given the right to strike in Article 123.

Through the inclusion of these statutes the door was finally opened to social and economic reform in Mexico. Or so many hoped in 1917. Still to be settled were equally important issues of how the new Mexican political game would be organized, who would dominate it, and how dedicated revolutionary leaders would be to fulfilling the promises contained in the Constitution of 1917.

The consolidation of power

Revolutionary upheavals produce political vacuums that must be filled quickly. But the creation of new institutions is often hindered by disagreements among leaders about the exact form the new regime should take. In Mexico conflicts among members of the insurrectionary coalition developed immediately after the fighting stopped and lasted for over a decade. What later came to appear as one of the most cohesive, well-organized regimes in the region started slowly and suffered many strains before achieving the qualities for which it is known today.

The revolutionary generals who emerged victorious in 1916 were handicapped by two weaknesses when they began. First, they had no coherent plan or ideology to direct their reconstruction of the Mexican state. Second, they were a disparate group with diverse interests, who had fought almost as much with one another as they had with the Díaz regime. In 1916 Mexico was emerging from the chaos of a long and destructive war. New aspirations had been codified in the 1917 constitution, but the truce was an uneasy one. The constitution allocated formal authority to the president and the legislature, but political power remained in the hands of the many armed leaders whose forces had shared in the victory. Only by establishing practical control over such groups could anyone hope to govern the war-ravaged country.

It is helpful to view the consolidation of power in postrevolutionary Mexico as involving successive choices among very few real options. There was first the matter of whom to include in the new game. Clearly the old order would never be the same again. The revolution had destroyed the army, broken the grip of the regional bosses who had enforced the will of the Díaz regime, drastically reduced what was left of the power of the clergy, and weakened the strength of the landed elite. There was no question of restoring any of the old elite to power. Rather, it was a matter of deciding which of the victors would rule. The most obvious choice was the revolutionary generals, men like Carranza and Obregón, each the leader of an army that had fought in the revolt. All of them expected rewards, either in the form of sinecures in the new government or some of the property and other spoils of war. But they were not alone. Also demanding entry into the new regime were the *campesino* leaders who, like Zapata, demanded some assurance that their village lands would be returned to them by the new government. Some had seized *hacienda* lands during the war but needed legal recognition of their titles and state protection against their return to the rural elite. Labor leaders also wanted a place at the top, fearing that without their participation the rights given them by the new constitution would go unenforced. Last but certainly not least were the middle-sector professionals and intellectuals who saw the new government as their means to rapid advancement.

The challenge was to create a government strong enough to rebuild a nation torn apart by a decade of internal war, one that could rise above the narrow interests of any single group or sector yet retain the support of each for its reconstruction program. A handful of revolutionary generals met it by seizing the initiative after the constitutional convention and gradually incorporating carefully selected representatives from each of the popular sectors and from each region into a new regime. Though they adopted the trappings of liberal democracy with a president, bicameral legislature, and independent judiciary, what they actually created was a highly centralized political machine whose leaders exercised immense control over the nation.

The study of postrevolution politics lays to rest the fiction that the revolutionary regime emerged quickly and painlessly. Consolidation came only after intense and often bloody struggles led by Alvaro Obregón, president from 1920 to 1924, and Plutarco Calles, president from 1924 to 1928. They jailed, bought off, or shot their rivals. Zapata was ambushed in 1919, President Carranza was shot while fleeing in 1920, and Villa was assassinated in 1923. The key to consolidation was not just the calculated use of violence but also Obregón's and Calles's skill in outmaneuvering their opponents. Piece by piece they created a coalition composed of the revolutionary army, peasant leaders, labor bosses, and public employees by offering something to each without allowing any one of them to dominate. Radical peasant leaders were replaced by moderate ones willing to play by the government's rules, and the labor movement was reorganized to make it more dependent on the state for its privileges. Mexican nationalism was spread throughout the nation using an expanded education system, art, and music, and the Roman Catholic church was stripped of its property and its defenders crushed violently when they resisted the authority of the new state. In sum, after a decade of intense infighting Mexico's new leadership had laid the foundation of the regime that would govern the country for decades to come.

The Mexican state

Revolutionaries rely heavily on three things when they govern: an ideology, a mass-based political organization, and strong and loyal civil and military bureaucracies. Ideology is used to orient the government and transform the political beliefs of the masses. It instructs citizens about the new rules of the game, motivates them to work for common ends, and gives them a new political ethic for determining right and wrong. The normative values of the ideology, rather than physical force or personal charisma, should become the primary source of the government's authority if it is to endure. A mass-based political organization is needed to spread the ideology, mobilize supporters, and isolate opponents of the regime. The political party is the preferred form of organization, but unlike political parties in liberal democracies, the revolutionary party does not limit itself to campaigns, elections, and legislative politics. In fact, none of these activities is as important as the mobilization of mass support for the regime. Finally, revolutionaries must have a strong and loyal bureaucracy to implement government policy. Working closely with the official party, government agencies carry the burden of reorganizing social and economic institutions and coordinating diverse efforts to achieve revolutionary goals. Because state control over much, if not all, of the economy is essential to the revolutionary's task, state agencies find themselves with more power and responsibility than ever before. How well they use that power determines the fate of the revolution.

Ideology is important to the governing of Mexico, though more as a means for legitimizing the government than as a guide to the selection of policy. According to the official rhetoric – which has changed little since 1917 – the Mexican government is the servant of a nation that liberated itself from its oppressors by means of a heroic struggle, and it is dedicated to securing social justice, economic development, and national independence for all Mexicans. The ideology is taught in schools, expressed in popular art, repeated in political campaigns and used in nearly every presidential speech. Many Mexicans consider it a sham, cynically manipulated by authorities to retain their power over the masses; nevertheless, it remains the primary source of Mexican nationalistic thought and patriotic rhetoric.

Authorities adroitly exploit popular affection for the nation and its revolution. In so doing they have become the envy of politicians throughout the hemisphere. While others are constantly threatened by opponents who challenge their right to rule, the leaders of Mexico's ruling party can defend themselves by claiming that they alone are the legitimate heirs of the revolution. It is as if American Democrats could defend themselves against Republicans by making a popularly accepted claim to being responsible for the American Revolution and are, therefore, the only legitimate guarantors of the Constitution. Though the transparency of the tactic seems obvious, it can nevertheless be a very popular tool for legitimizing existing authorities when it is skillfully exploited as it has been in Mexico.

Ideologies, though essential, do not implement revolutions; people and organizations do. When they began the Mexican revolutionaries needed a means for enforcing the new rules in every region of their rebellious country. The obvious solution was a political party able to control national, state, and local governments. The party's creation was made possible by the triumph of Plutarco Calles over his rivals soon after Alvaro Obregón's death in 1928. One year later he launched the National Revolutionary party, an organization built from a coalition of regional revolutionary generals. That is how it stayed until president Lázaro Cárdenas reorganized the geographically structured party in order to assure the party's hold on the masses. Rather than working primarily through local party officials as Calles had done, Cárdenas wanted direct contact between the president and the leaders of mass organizations. Accordingly, in 1938 he created a corporatist-like party organization composed of three sections: the Mexican Confederation of Labor, the National Peasant Association, and a third called the "popular" sector, which included teachers, public employees, small farmers, and the military. Now labeled the Institutional Revolutionary party (PRI), its organization is much the same as it was under Cárdenas, though the military was later removed.

The original inclusion of the military in the party was a radical departure from conventional practice. It was made possible by the destruction of Díaz's army during the revolution. When Cárdenas brought it into the party he was not making a pact with well-established armed forces, such as the AD party did in Venezuela, but was only formalizing the president's control over an army that the revolutionary elite had created a decade before. The Mexicans' subordination of their armed forces is the envy of civilian leaders elsewhere. Emulating Mexico is no easy task, however, for to make the Mexican

solution work one must destroy the military before incorporating it.
In other words, subordination comes only after the armed forces have
been defeated in battle by popular forces, something few of the region's civilian politicians are willing or able to do, especially since the
military is so intolerant of mass movements that include its destruction among their primary objectives.

The rules of the Mexican game

The Mexican political game defies simple characterization. Constitutionally, it retains the trappings of liberal democracy with a president, legislature, judiciary, and regular elections. It even guarantees
opposition parties one-fourth of the seats in Congress. In practice,
however, the system is run by PRI leaders and the president, who
together control the masses much more than they are controlled by
them.

The dependence of the rank-and-file on the party elite derives
largely from the government's immense patronage powers. Rule by
the PRI is somewhat analogous to that of the political machines that
once governed some of the larger North American cities. It controls
access to thousands of public jobs, which it distributes annually to
grateful supporters. And regardless of profession or business, every
person is affected by decisions of the economically powerful Mexican
government. Favorable treatment is not claimed by right but secured
in exchange for political support, personal favors, and bribes. Moreover, all villages and towns are dependent on central authorities for
their public works; should they not support the PRI in elections, they
deny themselves access to the resources on which they must rely to
meet their minimal needs.

Equally important to the PRI's power is its ability to co-opt opponents before they are strong enough to do the party any harm. Instead
of insulating themselves from opponents, pretending that they do not
exist, as is the practice among less secure ruling elites, PRI leaders try
to absorb them into the party, offering them government posts and
policies aimed at satisfying the people they claim to represent. In this
way they have persuaded many critics to abandon their cause for an
opportunity to pursue their interests from within the government.
The critic's choice is seldom easy: To stay outside a government as
invulnerable as the Mexican one usually means a futile struggle; but

joining it may allow one to act with authority but never with the freedom to do most of the things one wants to do.

Despite the PRI's near monopoly over national politics, it cannot claim the allegiance of all Mexicans. Presidents do receive 60 and 80 percent of the popular vote, but many people, especially in the middle sectors, despise the PRI machine. They especially resent being deprived of the option of effective independent political action. Unwilling to rebel against their government, they have become more and more cynical and alienated, many of them giving up entirely on politics as a way to shape their own destinies.

If the PRI is one key to political control in Mexico, the presidency is the other. Disputes are common at every level of government in Mexico, as elsewhere, and an effective mechanism is required for their ultimate resolution. Few Latin American nations have managed to establish a reliable means for conflict resolution. The Mexicans, in contrast, did so long ago. Ultimate authority resides in the Mexican presidency. For six years one person uses that authority to direct the nation, but once his term is completed, he relinquishes all authority to his successor. Thus, by holding to a fixed term the Mexicans have prevented control by any person for more than a single term. And the longer the rotation of the office works, the more people accept it as part of the natural order of things.

The Mexican president is given substantial formal authority by the constitution, but he gets his real power from the PRI's control over society. The rules of the Mexican game require that he use his authority constantly. He is the initiator of all domestic and foreign policies and is the final arbiter of disputes among governors, cabinet members, labor and management, and peasants and commercial farmers. He is also the supervisor of a very complex economy and the person ultimately responsible for the nation's development.

To sustain his authority, the president must successfully do three things: secure the cooperation of the PRI's labor, peasant, and popular constituencies with official policy, work closely with powerful business interests that are not included in the party, and assure a smooth presidential succession. The first task is managed through patronage, co-optation, and the adoption of policies aimed at satisfying minimal constituency demands. The second is more challenging. The party, though broadly based, is not all-inclusive. Two of the country's most

powerful forces – the domestic and foreign business communities – are
deliberately excluded in order to maintain the popular character of the
party. Yet, the government relies very heavily on the private sector to
finance and manage much of the country's mixed, capitalist economy.
Consequently, private entrepreneurs are quite influential over presidential policy decisions, often securing the assistance they need to
maximize their corporate gains. The relationship is not always a congenial one since entrepreneurs resent the president's ability to use his
immense power against them on occasion, and the president is per-
petually displeased with corporate defiance of his demands for subordination to the state. Nevertheless, the fact that Mexican and foreign
businesses have prospered and Mexican presidents have survived indicates the relative success of both in achieving a very productive accommodation of their respective interests.

Finally, Mexican presidents must handle the succession problem
smoothly in order to sustain public faith in the presidential institution. Clearly they have done so, for with the exception of a brief
interlude after President-elect Obregón's assassination in 1928, each
Mexican president has relinquished the office to a successor at the end
of his term. Mexicans, unlike some Latin Americans, do not have to
fret about whether they have a president or how long he will be
allowed to govern, but need worry only about who he will be.

Party primaries and convention battles are unknown to Mexicans.
Their mode of selection is much simpler and less conflictual: The
new president is simply chosen by the departing president in consultation with a handful of party leaders. Usually a member of the
cabinet or party leadership, the one chosen is informed of his selection eighteen months before the end of the incumbent's term. Soon
thereafter his candidacy is ratified by the national PRI convention,
launching a campaign that will take him to towns and cities
throughout the country to reaffirm the symbolic link between the
president and his people. Once this ritual is concluded the election
is held and his victory confirmed by millions of his subjects at the
polls.

The presidency is the last stop for only a few of the thousands of
Mexican politicians who begin their careers aspiring to the highest
office. They do not compete openly, in public campaigns, but by
working from within the PRI or the government to get close enough

to the incumbent president to become his chosen successor. Rising that far traditionally has required a person to devote his life to moving up the hierarchy, taking what advantage he can from the personal networks that abound within party and government. Each office holder relies on networks of colleagues and subordinates devoted to his advancement and their advancement with him. A political aspirant usually starts by attaching himself to an office holder, serving him as a political operator or technical aide. If his mentor rises higher in the official hierarchy, he may be rewarded with a post in the government or the party. Once established, he then builds his own network of followers whom he uses the same way his mentors used him. If one's leader does not rise, however, the aspirant for higher office will leave him for someone whose mobility is more probable. In short, the successful Mexican politician operates like an investor who hedges his bets by investing in several firms simultaneously, only to transfer his money from the least to the most profitable enterprise as often as necessary.

On the surface Mexican politicians appear to be quite cordial, giving the impression of a large, fraternal association. But they are neither as secure nor as collegial as they pretend, for to survive in this very competitive system, duplicity and betrayal often become necessary. Ultimately only a few reach the cabinet; nevertheless, many of the rest do establish sinecures for themselves elsewhere within the party or government and do quite well financially.

To the displeasure of PRI politicians, the route to the presidency changed in the 1970s. Once a monopoly of revolutionary generals, after 1950 it became the residence of career politicians. Now the technocrats are moving in. Presidents José Lopez Portillo (1976–82) and Miguel de la Madrid (1982–8) were not traditional politicians. In fact, neither had run for public office before his selection as president. Like many who rose to cabinet positions after 1970, they were highly educated specialists who began in technical and managerial positions within the national government and worked their way up within one or two agencies to become cabinet members a few years before their nomination for president. Increased reliance on such people to direct the country evidences the governing elite's loss of confidence in the ability of the pure politician to manage a very complex economy and direct an increasingly sophisticated bureaucracy.

Unrevolutionary economics

Nowhere are the mixed motives behind the Mexican Revolution more obvious than in the nation's economics since 1917. Between 1920 and 1940 substantial land was taken from the *hacendados* and returned to the *campesinos*, and some foreign enterprises were nationalized as promised. But after 1940 attention turned to the nation's industrialization, and through the combined efforts of the rapidly growing Mexican state and native entrepreneurs, Mexico sustained one of the fastest and steadiest rates of economic growth in the hemisphere during the next twenty years. In the 1960s they were joined by multinational firms who came to see Mexico as the land of opportunity. But the more officials placed their faith in industrialization, the more the gap between the rich and poor grew, for little of the nation's new wealth trickled down to *campesinos* and unorganized laborers. What the descendants of Obregón and Cárdenas had created, it turned out, was not socialism but a very Mexican version of capitalism.

A closer look at how this occurred needs to begin in the Mexican countryside. In 1910, 97 percent of Mexico's land was owned by just 830 people or corporations, an incredible degree of concentration, even for Latin America at the turn of the century. Ending this condition became the objective of the agrarian activists who fought in the 1910 insurrection. Some seized *hacendados* in the midst of battle: *campesinos* recovered village lands taken from them during the Porfiriato and revolutionary generals secured their own *haciendas*. Yet most of the rural elite survived the war, and it was up to the new government to strip them of property and power.

The cause of agrarian reform was embraced by Obregón and subsequent Mexican presidents primarily because it was necessary for the maintenance of order in the countryside. By redistributing land they hoped to deprive the oligarchy of its primary means of control over the masses while at the same time securing the political support of *campesinos* by making them indebted to their new benefactors in Mexico City. Land expropriation by the government, which began slowly in the 1920s, was accelerated by President Cárdenas during the 1930s; in only six years he expropriated twice as much land as had been taken during the preceding seventeen years. Most of the land was redistributed in units known as *ejidos*, an indigenous mode of organization in which property is owned by the entire village and farmed either communally or individually. Today 43 percent of Mexican farmland is held by 18,000 *ejidos*, and 4,000 of them are communally farmed. The other 57 percent is privately owned, nearly half of it held by families or corporations in farms over 250 acres, some of which supply the United States with its winter fruits and vegetables.

Agrarian reform, while necessary for social justice in the country-side, is certainly not sufficient. Most *campesinos* remain poor and a majority are still landless. And now Mexicans face another problem: Once self-sufficient in grain and bean production, they are no longer, and beginning in 1980 they had to import $2 billion worth of grain from the United States. Farm production, which stagnated in the 1970s, no longer keeps up with population growth. Obstacles to in-creasing production abound. Only 17 percent of Mexico is arable, and the land that is cultivated is plagued by soil erosion and erratic rain-fall. And only 25 percent of the nation's farmers have access to credit, fertilizer, and other things essential for modernization. This is no accident, however, for a few decades ago government officials chose to devote their limited resources to assisting the development of large agribusiness operations in northwestern Mexico. Theirs was a choice between spreading resources widely but thinly among the needy *ejidi-tarios* and concentrating them among a few hundred very productive farms able to earn dollars needed to finance the nation's industrializa-tion. They chose the latter, convinced that economic objectives should prevail over social ones. In doing so they took the revolution another step away from one of its original purposes. Nevertheless, Mexican presidents still claim dedication to the elevation of the poor farmer and from time to time allocate resources to the modernization of se-lected *ejidos*. In 1980, for example, President Lopez Portillo promised to devote a substantial share of the nation's income from petroleum sales to rural development, but this promise, like many before it, was never kept.

Mexican leaders discovered long ago that the nation could not rely on agriculture and mining to promote rapid economic development. Like the Brazilians and Argentines, they chose import-substitution industri-alization after 1940, and also like them, they used public enterprise and investment to do the job in areas where private investment was slow in developing. The Mexican government has supplied an average of 30 percent of national investment, and by 1970 it had accumulated 600 of its own businesses. What distinguishes the Mexican public sector from that of other Latin American countries is the immense variety of activities in which it has become engaged. In no other country except Cuba has the state entered into so many markets. This is due, it seems, to the government's need to assure that certain goods and services reach their principal constituents and to supply jobs to thousands. The result is a powerful and paternalistic state on which most Mexicans depend directly or indirectly for their welfare.

Mexican nationalism, which led to the eviction of many foreign firms in the early days of the revolution, did not prevent their return in large numbers after 1960. Eager for modern technology and help in the financing of industrialization, the Mexican government has unofficially encouraged foreign investment. And despite restrictions on foreign ownership of enterprises in some sectors and requirements of Mexican investor participation in most, foreign investment increased 11-fold between 1950 and 1979 when it reached $6.9 billion (70 percent of which came from the United States). By the 1970s it was estimated that foreign firms were responsible for 35 percent of Mexico's industrial production and owned 45 percent of the share capital in the nation's 290 largest firms. Here too the Mexican economy has come to resemble that of unrevolutionary Brazil and Argentina more than that of revolutionary Cuba.

In sum, industrialization, and not agrarian reform, is primarily responsible for Mexican development and the current structure of its economy. After 1950 the officials who directed the country's development behaved more like conservative bankers eager to bolster investor confidence in the nation's future than adventuresome directors of a reformist society. Having begun in 1920 with something resembling the progressive modernization development strategy, they gradually incorporated many of the elements of conservative modernization, emphasizing monetary and foreign exchange consistency and capitalization over distribution.

But even the carefully managed Mexican economy proved vulnerable. The nation's economic growth slowed in the early 1970s, picked up again a few years later, and then came to a crashing halt in 1982. A world recession in 1973 reduced demand for Mexican exports, slowing growth and causing many to fear that the country had reached the end of a thirty-year era of steady economic progress. Mexico's suffering was quite brief, however, for just as its planners were beginning to reconcile themselves to slower growth, new petroleum discoveries were made along the country's eastern seaboard. The timing could not have been better, for the OPEC nations had raised international prices in 1973 and again in 1979, making Mexico's newly acquired oil surplus a potential source of immense income. Not surprisingly, the Mexican government, which owned all of the nation's petroleum, quickly recast its plans in anticipation of an unprecedented capacity to finance new development projects.

But prosperity and rapid growth did not follow, at least not for very long, for by 1982 the Mexican economy was engulfed by the highest inflation and greatest foreign debt the nation had even known. Suddenly a Mexican government that had struggled for decades to reduce the nation's dependence on its northern neighbor was forced to go hat in hand to its creditors in the United States and Europe to plead for emergency financial assistance. Why the sudden change and why had no one predicted it only a year before?

Oil discoveries in the mid-1970s elevated Mexico to the elite among the holders of petroleum in the world, placing it sixth internationally. Mexican officials welcomed their good fortune but proceeded cautiously at first, aware that if national income rose too swiftly, high inflation would follow. President Lopez Portillo announced a limitation on oil production, holding output to 2.5 million barrels a day, keeping 1 million for national use and exporting the rest to the United States and Latin America. Nevertheless, things quickly got out of control. The cause was not oil production per se, but the optimism it bred among Mexican bureaucrats and entrepreneurs and among foreign bankers.

The Mexicans rushed to take advantage of foreign confidence in their economy by grabbing all of the loans that eager foreign bankers would supply (with one-fourth going to private business and the rest to government enterprises). Within three years they had accumulated the largest foreign debt in the Third World. Nevertheless, this caused little concern at first. It was only when income from the sale of oil and other commodities suddenly fell as demand dropped during the world recession in 1981, causing prices to fall, that the Mexicans discovered that they were in trouble. In August 1982 they simply ran out of the dollars that they needed to pay their creditors in the United States and Europe, so their only choice was to call for help, since defaulting on their debts was out of the question to the trade-dependent and

financially conservative Mexican leadership. Thus, like the Venezuelans, the Mexicans discovered that oil was not enough, for even
though it gave the country a source of new wealth, like other commodities it yielded only what foreigners were willing to pay for it.

Help came quickly, first from the United States government, which
did not dare let the Mexican crisis undermine the credibility of major
American banks, and then from the International Monetary Fund,
which secured additional private bank loans for Mexico by promising to
assist it with funds of its own after the Mexicans agreed to slow their
spending and restrict expenditures abroad in order to increase their net
dollar income. It was a high price to pay, especially for Mexican consumers, for it meant both a rise in the price they paid for public services
and basic foods and accepting limits on wage increases at a time of
record inflation. Yet pay it they did as the Mexican authorities accommodated themselves to the demands of their creditors.

Where Mexico goes from here is uncertain. It still enjoys an abundance of oil and gas and will profit from the sale of both in the years
ahead, whether they are sold at current prices or higher ones after the
world recession ends. Yet, by itself petroleum cannot solve the more
fundamental problems facing Mexicans. Raising farm productivity
will be neither easy nor cheap, and even if substantial progress is
made, most *campesinos* will remain landless and without much hope of
finding employment in industry. Moreover, the nation's economic
dependence on the United States will continue even if some progress
is made in diversifying the nation's trade and reducing its borrowing
abroad. And to make matters worse, the country's rapidly growing
population is making unprecedented demands on its resources. The
actual rate of growth has declined during the past few years, from 3.5
percent to an estimated 2.9 percent annually as a result of government-sponsored family planning, middle-sector affluence, and several
hundred thousand illegal abortions every year. Yet because 40 percent
of the Mexican population is now under 15 years of age, the population will double again in only 35 years.

What will be the political impact of the failure to deal with these
problems satisfactorily? It does not take much imagination to envision
a scenario that includes another revolution of some kind. But before
we forecast another insurrection, it would be prudent to recall why
the PRI has survived this long and ask whether or not its strengths
will keep it on top in the future.

Table 9.2. *Mexican economic performance, 1979–82*

	1979	1980	1981	1982
GDP Annual Growth Rate (%)	9.2	8.3	8.1	−2.0
Annual consumer prices growth rate (%)	18.2	26.4	27.9	100.0
Foreign debt ($U.S. billions)	37.0	50.0	75.0	80.0
Public sector deficit (% of GDP)	7.0	7.5	11.0	16.5

Source: Inter-American Development Bank, *Economic and Social Progress in Latin America 1982 Report*, p. 281; *The Economist*, November 20, 1982, p. 68; *Business Week*, February 28, 1983, p. 60.

The PRI has not given Mexicans everything they desire, but it has always worked closely with handpicked leaders from each sector. Using its huge propaganda and patronage machinery, it has conditioned most Mexicans to believe that in bad times as well as good ones their only alternative is to let the president decide their fate. Discontent is common and will grow in the days ahead, but the government is still well equipped to cope with it. Should co-optation, bargaining, and propaganda fail, the government will not hesitate to use physical repression, selectively at first, and then more generally if necessary. One should not forget that few governments in the region are as well equipped to police their populations as the Mexican one. Its military is relatively small, though growing in response to the security requirements of the country's oil industry, but its police forces have always been large and active.

Repression alone will not guarantee the survival of the PRI in Mexico. Should it become necessary on a large scale, it might sow the seeds of the regime's eventual destruction. But meanwhile there is much that the PRI can and no doubt will do to avert a political disaster. There will be more wealth to distribute when petroleum revenues rise once again and Mexican industrialization will continue. And no one wants the PRI to survive more than its neighbors to the north, who require a politically stable and economically growing Mexico for their own security and commercial well-being. The American government was the first and the fastest to respond to Mexico's financial crisis in August 1982 and, out of self-interest, will do so again if the need arises. Though Mexicans would prefer to deny the reality of their heavy dependence on the United States, that reality is and will continue to be one of the primary obstacles to radical change in Mexico in the years ahead.

How unique is Mexican politics?

Mexicans pride themselves on having avoided the kind of conflictual politics found in the rest of the hemisphere. For over sixty years their government has been strong, their presidential transitions orderly, and their military subservient to civil authority. No other nation in Latin America can make that claim. But is Mexico all that different from the rest? Certainly it is in some respects, but how far should we go in granting it the status of being truly unique?

We need only compare Mexico with a few of the other Latin American nations to discover that it does indeed share much with them despite its peculiar political history. For example, the PRI may be the most successful party in Latin America, but it is not the only one to gain its strength from the creation of a coalition of middle-sector politicians, labor unions, and peasant organizations. Venezuela's Democratic Action party, it will be recalled, did much the same thing with substantial success electorally. Where the two parties differ is in the AD's inability to construct the kind of political monopoly that the PRI secured in Mexico through its use of the revolutionary mythology to legitimate its rule.

Though it boasts of having kept its military out of politics, the Mexican government nevertheless also shares some things with the military authoritarian governments we studied in Chapter 8. Its democratic pretensions notwithstanding, Mexico is governed by a strong central government that uses the power of the state to rule over sectoral interests just as the military has in Brazil for over two decades. Where they differ is in the manner in which they have legitimated this kind of heavy-handed, corporatist government: The Mexicans claim that their people want it that way, whereas the Brazilians could do little more than argue that it was the most practical way of governing their rapidly industrializing nation. Mexican leaders have a political machine, well oiled by patronage, that guarantees their triumph in national elections; the Brazilian military, in contrast, can do little better than rig elections and representation to remain in office.

It is its unusual blend of populist, authoritarian, and democratic rules and practices that makes Mexican politics similar to and yet distinct from the politics found elsewhere in the region. It is also what makes it so hard to label as either democratic or authoritarian. But that is exactly the way Mexican authorities like it. Ambiguity makes it difficult for their critics to judge them according to any single set of principles and it gives them the latitude they need to do contradictory things without being held accountable for them.

If its politics is still distinguishable from that of the other nations in the hemisphere, Mexico's economic condition is becoming less so every day. But this should not be surprising. Despite its revolutionary pretensions, Mexico, like Brazil and Argentina, followed the path of import-substitution industrialization, combining the resources of what became a very large public sector with an aggressive though sheltered private sector. Later both were joined by hundreds of multinational corporations. Yet, though it was quite productive in aggregate terms, industrialization did not increase Mexico's economic autonomy significantly, and today economic independence is as much a myth as ever. To be sure, the discovery of petroleum is cause for optimism, but petroleum will not overcome rural stagnation, rapid population growth, and government corruption, at least not for some time to come.

Further reading

General

Berger, Peter. *Pyramids of Sacrifice*. New York: Basic Books, 1974.
Gurr, Ted Robert. *Why Men Rebel*. Princeton, N.J.: Princeton University Press, 1971.
Hagopian, Mark. *The Phenomenon of Revolution*. New York: Dodd, Mead, 1974.
Huntington, Samuel. *Political Order in Changing Societies*. New Haven, Conn.: Yale University Press, 1968.
Johnson, Chalmers. *Revolutionary Change*. Boston: Little, Brown, 1966.
Rejai, Mustafa. *The Comparative Study of Revolutionary Strategy*. New York: McKay, 1977.
Skocpol, Theda. *States and Social Revolutions*. Cambridge: Cambridge University Press, 1979.
Tilly, Charles. *From Mobilization to Revolution*. Reading, Mass.: Addison-Wesley, 1978.

Mexico

Brandenburg, Frank. *The Making of Modern Mexico*. Englewood Cliffs, N.J.: Prentice-Hall, 1963.

Cumberland, Charles. *Mexico: The Struggle for Modernity.* New York: Oxford University Press, 1968.

Glade, William P., and Charles W. Anderson. *The Political Economy of Mexico.* Madison: University of Wisconsin Press, 1963.

Hamilton, Nora. *The Limits of State Autonomy: Post-Revolutionary Mexico.* Princeton, N.J.: Princeton University Press, 1982.

Hansen, Roger. *The Politics of Mexican Development.* Baltimore: Johns Hopkins University Press, 1971.

Hellman, Judith Adler. *Mexico in Crisis.* New York: Holmes and Meier, 1978.

Hewlett, Sylvia, and Richard S. Weinert, eds. *Brazil and Mexico: Patterns in Late Development.* Philadelphia: Institute for the Study of Human Issues, 1983.

Johnson, Kenneth F. *Mexican Democracy: A Critical View.* New York: Praeger, 1978.

Johnson, William W. *Heroic Mexico.* Garden City, N.Y.: Doubleday, 1968.

Padgett, Vincent. *The Mexican Political System,* 2d ed. Boston: Houghton Mifflin, 1976.

Reyna, Jose Luis, and Richard Weinert, eds. *Authoritarianism in Mexico.* Philadelphia: Institute for the Study of Human Issues, 1977.

Reynolds, Clark W. *The Mexican Economy: Twentieth Century Structure and Growth.* New Haven, Conn.: Yale University Press, 1970.

Tannenbaum, Frank. *Mexico: The Struggle for Peace and Bread.* New York: Knopf, 1956.

Peace by Revolution. New York: Knopf, 1933.

Vernon, Raymond. *The Dilemma of Mexico's Development.* Cambridge, Mass.: Harvard University Press, 1965.

Wilkie, James. *The Mexican Revolution: Federal Expenditure and Social Change Since 1910.* Berkeley: University of California Press, 1967.

Womack, John. *Zapata and the Mexican Revolution.* New York: Knopf, 1969.

10. The revolutionary game: Cuba and Nicaragua

Cuba

One half century after the Mexicans staged their revolution the Cubans had one of their own, but when it came it was quite unlike the Mexican one. First of all, the Cuban insurrection was much briefer and did not involve most of the Cuban people in the fighting. Second, what the rebels created was not a multiclass coalition government that supervised a mixed capitalist economy, as happened in Mexico, but a communist regime that directed one of the most socialized and highly planned economies in the world. And third, the Cubans defied the United States, preferring to take their chances within the Soviet camp rather than risk further domination by the *yanquis*. How do we explain such striking differences? The answer can be found only by going back to the beginning, to the 1950s, when 7 million Cubans were ruled by dictator Fulgencio Batista and controlled economically by the United States and a small band of guerrillas set up camp in the Sierra Maestra mountains to prepare to do battle with Batista and his army.

The 26th of July movement

When it comes to explaining Batista's overthrow in December 1958, memories differ, as do the casting of blame and the distribution of credit. The history of the period is rewritten frequently to bolster the causes of victors and vanquished alike. Some claim that the struggle was largely one of peasants against their oppressors. Others say that most of the resistance to Batista was in the cities and not in the countryside, and that were it not for the urban resistance, the guerrillas who were credited with Batista's defeat never would have won. Still others, such as French Marxist Regis Debray in his provocative book, *Revolution in the Revolution*, argue that Castro won because he adapted guerrilla tactics to Cuban conditions, placing emphasis on the

272

military *foco* rather than the mass insurrection. The issue would be of interest only to historians were it not that so many Latin American strategists have tried to extract from the Cuban experience lessons that would aid them in their own guerrilla campaigns.

In many ways Cuba did not appear to be the prime candidate for Marxist revolution in the late 1950s. It was neither the poorest nor the most industrialized of the Latin American countries. In per capita income it ranked third, behind Argentina and Venezuela. It ranked fifth in industrialization, and 57 percent of its population was urban. At the same time, however, Cubans suffered from many frustrations. Their fate was tied to sugar, and as in any monoculture economy, economic growth fluctuated with the performance of the primary export crop. The Cuban class structure was also conditioned by the sugar economy, most notably in the creation of a rural proletariat of seasonal laborers who divided their time between six months in the sugar harvest and six months of unemployment. And sugar also tied the Cuban economy and polity to the United States, its principal trading partner. American businessmen dominated the Cuban economy, American tourists occupied the capital, and the American underworld managed the country's flourishing gambling and prostitution industries. The political control of Cuba by Americans after its independence in 1898 and their economic domination thereafter bred an intense nationalism that was used as an effective instrument of the Cuban revolutionaries.

If there was a catalyst in the Cuban revolution, it was the increasingly brutal dictatorship of Fulgencio Batista. Batista had long been active in Cuban politics, beginning with his leadership of a "sergeants' revolt" in 1934 and then his legitimate election in 1940 under a democratic constitution he helped create. More opportunistic than ideological, Batista sought to please both the United States and the Cuban nationalists. He retained close ties with the American economy, while at the same time defusing his nationalist critics by securing the abrogation of the Platt amendment, which since 1901 had permitted American intervention in internal Cuban affairs. He also promoted the country's economic growth through the Sugar Act and Reciprocal Trade Agreements of 1934, which guaranteed Cuban access to American markets. And Batista even stepped aside when a successor from the opposition was elected president in 1944. After two well-meaning but corrupt, patronage-ridden, reformist administrations proved themselves incapable of providing Cuba with a progressive, well-managed government, Batista intervened once again in 1952. Backed by foreign investors, the United States government, and the sugar industry, he rejected political democracy, this time in favor of a corrupt and harsh dictatorship. In doing so he left his opponents only one option: To stop him they would have to bring down his government, and the only way to accomplish that was through a violent struggle.

The war against Batista was waged on several fronts after 1952, the two most prominent being the urban resistance and the guerrilla campaign of the 26th of July movement. Both were led by the idealistic generation of 1953 who, as university students and young professionals, had opposed Batista's return to power and his perpetuation of a corrupt, elite-dominated regime subservient to the Americans. Because it was more diffuse and produced no leaders to match the charisma of Fidel Castro, the urban resistance has received less credit than it deserves for the overthrow of Batista. While Castro was trying to consolidate his position in the Sierra Maestra in 1957 in preparation for his attack on the Cuban army, many Cubans were already at work in the cities, bombing government installations, assassinating government leaders, and undermining public confidence in the Batista regime. Several thousand of them were killed and many jailed and tortured by government police forces between 1953 and 1959.

The other front belonged to Fidel Castro and his guerrilla army. His campaign began with an ill-fated attack on the Moncada military barracks in Oriente province on July 26, 1953, which led to his capture and imprisonment. Before his conviction, however, he delivered his famous "History Will Absolve Me" speech announcing his commitment to the overthrow of Batista and the creation of a nationalistic, reform-oriented social democracy to replace the dictatorial regime. A general amnesty in mid-1955 allowed Castro to flee to exile in Mexico, where he met Argentine Marxist Ernesto ("Che") Guevara and prepared for his return to Cuba and the guerrilla struggle that followed. After a near disastrous landing on the Cuban shore on December 2, 1956, from which only twelve of Castro's eighty-two-man force escaped capture and fled to the Sierra Maestra, the guerrilla struggle was launched.

Most remarkable about the 26th of July movement was the speed of its military success. It did not begin its attacks on government outposts in earnest until early 1958. Yet, less than a year later Batista had fled the country and Castro was welcomed as a national hero in Havana. Several factors accounted for Castro's unexpectedly brief campaign, including an American embargo on arms sales to Batista, a decision that hurt the government's morale more than its military strength; the persistent agitation of the urban resistance; and middle-sector disaffection with the repressive Batista regime. The most critical factors, however, were the incompetence and corruption of Batista's army and the ability of the 26th of July movement to exploit this weakness through the use of guerrilla tactics that harassed and demoralized poorly led government troops.

The beginning of the government's collapse came in May 1958, when it overextended itself in an all-out offensive against the guerrillas, who were still lodged in the Sierra Maestra. Fidel Castro and his army absorbed the offensive with only moderate losses and counterattacked with great skill, gradually transforming the offensive into an embarrassing retreat that led to the rapid demoralization of Batista's troops. Despite its larger size and heavier armament, the army was no match for the dedicated guerrilla fighters within the confines of the Sierra Maestra, where the latter enjoyed superior intelligence, better knowledge of the terrain, and greater mobility. In August two columns led by Che Guevara and Camilo Cienfuegos moved from the mountains into Las Villas province to cut communications in the middle of the island. Then in December the guerrillas launched their own offensive, which hastened the collapse of Batista's defenses. On December 31, much sooner than Castro and Guevara had anticipated, Batista gave up the fight and fled to the Dominican Republic, leaving his army to surrender to the guerrillas the next day. The final victory came so swiftly, in fact, that several days were required for Fidel Castro to organize his triumphal march across the island to Havana to join Guevara and the victorious troops.

What then was the Cuban insurrection? We can begin by establishing what it was not. It was not a mass-based revolutionary war like the struggle of the Chinese Communists against Chiang Kai-shek and his Nationalists. Although several thousand people were involved in the fight against Batista, the striking force was more concentrated and much smaller than that of the Chinese. Nor was it a peasant uprising like those led by Zapata in Mexico or Ho Chi Minh in Vietnam. To be sure, Castro could count several peasants among his guerrilla army, and some peasants did assist the guerrillas with food and communications. However, it was not the Cuban peasantry that Castro led, but a small group of students, professionals, and workers drawn from the lower middle sectors. Had the struggle lasted longer a peasant army might have been created, but victory came swiftly, making it unnecessary. And finally, the Cuban insurrection was not an urban proletarian revolution. Organized labor, which was largely controlled by the Communist party, opposed the guerrilla struggle until near its conclusion, when labor leaders belatedly lent their support to Castro. When we strip away the rhetoric and revolutionary mythology, we are left with a focused, armed insurrection by a small band of dedicated revolutionaries supported by elements of the urban middle sectors and rural poor who sought the defeat of a corrupt tyrant. That the revolution would turn into something more ambitious than many who sought Batista's removal had expected did not become clear until after Castro had consolidated his power and begun his program of radical reconstruction.

The new order

In Cuba the postrevolutionary consolidation of power came more rapidly than in Mexico, but it too involved a series of strategic decisions by the leaders of the insurrection. The almost complete domination of Fidel Castro and his colleagues over Cuba since the early 1960s should not obscure the severity of the political problems Castro faced when he entered Havana in January 1959. The swiftness of his victory and the involvement of so few Cubans in it had left much of the old political power structure intact. Only Batista and a few thousand army officers, police, and bureaucrats fled the island. Most of the landowning elite, foreign and domestic businessmen, middle-sector professionals, clergy, and other powerful groups remained behind, hopeful that they could survive under a new regime by influencing the course it followed. Castro had to contend with the expectations and power of such players, while at the same time fulfilling his pledge to supporters to create a more just political order and a more equitable economic system.

After the celebration had ended, Cuba's revolutionary leaders turned their attention to the consolidation of their control over the Cuban state and the initiation of a program of radical social and economic reform. Neither could be accomplished without a confronta-

Table 10.1. *Cuba: historical background*

1898	Cuba achieves independence from Spain at end of Spanish-American War
	Cuba occupied by American troops until 1902
1901	Platt amendment to new Cuban Constitution gives United States right to intervene in Cuba to "maintain government adequate for the protection of life, property and individual liberty"
1906	American governor appointed to replace Cuban president
1909	Jose Miguel Gomez elected president
1913	Mario Garcia Menocal elected president; United States continues to intervene frequently with troops and advisers
1921	Alfredo Zayas elected president and advised by American General Enoch Crowder
1925	Gerardo Machado becomes president and rules in dictatorial manner
1933	Machado overthrown by popular revolt
1934	American President Franklin Roosevelt abrogates Platt amendment
	Provisional government overthrown by "sergeants' revolt" led by Fulgencio Batista
1940	Batista elected president under new constitution
1944	Opposition candidate, Grau San Martin, elected president
1948	Carlos Prio Socarras elected president
1952	Fulgencio Batista seizes power through coup
1953	Rebel attack on Moncada barracks fails, and revolt leader, Fidel Castro, is jailed
1955	Fidel Castro flees to Mexico after general amnesty
1956	In July Castro-led rebels sail to Cuba and twelve survivors of government attacks on landing party flee to Sierra Maestra to organize guerrilla campaign
1958	In December urban and guerrilla insurrections force Batista to flee island
1959	Fidel Castro creates coalition government in January
	In June moderates in cabinet resign, leaving control to Castro and 26th of July movement
1961	In January United States breaks relations with Cuba and imposes trade embargo
	Bay of Pigs invasion of island by Cuban exiles supported by United States government fails
1962	Cuban missile crisis in October in which President John F. Kennedy forces Russians to withdraw offensive missiles from Cuba in exchange for American promise not to intervene militarily in Cuba in future
1965	Cuban Communist party created
1975	In December first Communist party congress held
1976	New system of local, provincial, and national assemblies created and representatives to each elected
1979	Cubans celebrate the Revolution's twentieth anniversary

tion with the many players opposed to Castro's revolutionary objectives. Castro needed a strategy for winning that confrontation as quickly as possible. His plan of action emerged gradually through a process of trial and error during the first half of 1959 and involved the isolation of his potential opponents one by one, followed by their forced withdrawal from the new regime. At first glance, Castro's strategy appears to have been inspired by political genius, but in retrospect it is obvious that good fortune and the ineptness of his opponents had as much to do with his success as the brilliance and ruthlessness of his tactics.

Castro's political choices came down essentially to three options: First, he could use his triumph over Batista to propel himself to the head of a broad coalition of anti-Batista groups, and then begin the slow process of creating a new democratic regime that he would likely head as president; second, he could ignore all other players and create a government drawn entirely from the 26th of July loyalists; third, he could take a position somewhere between these two extremes, creating a smaller coalition of those groups who shared his vision of radical reform and using them to consolidate enough control to isolate and defeat his opponents.

He began with the first option, adopted some reform policies, and then, after his enemies had identified themselves through their outspoken opposition to such measures, moved to the third strategy, dropping other players one by one from his coalition until only the 26th of July loyalists and the remnants of the Communist Party (PSP) were left in the government. By then, however, he had consolidated his support among the rural and urban masses through a host of popular reform measures and had organized a revolutionary army large enough to defend him from most enemies, both domestic and foreign. What made the strategy so successful was Castro's ability to avoid a confrontation with all opponents at the same time. By dealing with each separately, he prevented their organization into a united opposition that might have stopped the march of his small band toward the execution of a Marxist revolution.

Castro relied on four fundamental policy decisions to flush out his opponents. First came the use of revolutionary tribunals in early 1959 to judge and then execute approximately 500 members of Batista's police and security agencies. The tribunals not only fulfilled a need for revenge, but also forced many of those who had been associated with the dictatorial regime to seek refuge abroad. At the same time, they prompted moderates who were opposed to the crude process of revolutionary justice to disassociate themselves from the regime. Second came the long-awaited announcement of an agrarian reform program in June 1959. Moderates in the cabinet, such as acting president Miguel Urrutia, resigned in protest, taking much of the leadership of the old democratic parties and landed elite into exile with them. And as the moderates began leaving the cabinet their places were taken by 26th of July loyalists, giving Castro increasing control over the bureaucracy. Third was Castro's open alliance with the PSP in late 1959. Castro did not completely trust the PSP and refused to be dominated by it, but he recognized it as a source of political operators who could staff his talent-starved agencies. He also knew that his open association with the Communists would drive the remaining democratic reformers from his regime.

Finally, Castro decided to seek Russian allies, a decision that helped drive the United States from the island. From mid-1959 until the United States broke relations with Cuba in January 1961, Castro skillfully baited the American government and then used its often clumsy reprisals to justify even more drastic anti-American measures. For example, after he signed agreements to import cheap Soviet oil, President Eisenhower ordered American refineries in Cuba not to process it. Castro retaliated by nationalizing the refineries. Then when Eisenhower terminated Cuba's sugar quota in July 1960, Castro nationalized sugar refineries and most other foreign-owned enterprises. When the cutting of American diplomatic relations with Cuba failed to force any change in Cuban policies, the Americans resorted to the ill-conceived Bay of Pigs invasion a few months later. But in surviving the invasion, Castro increased his following among Cuban nationalists and rid himself of direct American involvement in the country's internal affairs.

The swift consolidation of power was also aided by the small size and relative homogeneity of Cuba, in contrast to the larger and more diverse Mexico. It is one thing to gain control over a relatively small island nation and another to dominate a large country plagued by regionalism. Cultural diversity caused by the presence of large indigenous populations and a strong tradition of local political control had long troubled Mexico. As a result, the consolidation of control by the revolutionary generals required the repression of local elites and the neutralization of several hundred rivals to leaders like Obregón and Calles. Cuba, in contrast, despite some racial divisions, was a relatively homogeneous nation. Moreover, Castro did not have to contend with a host of revolutionary generals, but could count on the loyalty of most of the 26th of July movement and the new revolutionary army it created. For him, consolidation was a matter not of uniting the nation but of defeating potential opponents in the Cuban elite and middle sectors, a task that, though beset by obvious hazards, required less political engineering than did the unification of a country as large and diverse as Mexico.

By a process of elimination Castro drove his most likely enemies from the government and quickly consolidated his personal control over Cuba: first Batista and his army, then foreign firms and the rural elite, and then moderates who questioned his ultimate goals. As the ranks of his opponents dwindled, it became easier to identify counter-revolutionaries and jail or exile them. The new regime Castro created was built by those who survived: the 26th of July loyalists, the leadership of the PSP, the new revolutionary army, and the laboring masses whose support Castro cultivated with his charismatic appeal and his economic reforms.

The communist way

Ideology has played a more central role in the formation of the new Cuban state than it did in Mexico. We will never know if Fidel Castro was a committed Marxist before he began his insurrection, but we do know that he has built the new Cuban regime on the foundations of a well-developed and well-worn ideology. Castro's adoption of Marxism-Leninism not only gained Cuba a powerful ally in the Soviet Union. It has also given the country a model to use in the creation of new political and economic institutions. Marxist-Leninist ideology offered a vision of a new society that was the antithesis of what Cubans knew before 1959. Equality was to replace rigid class distinctions, public ownership of the means of production was to end the evils of private ownership, and community needs were to prevail over individual self-interest.

Fidel Castro does not have to rely entirely on Marxist-Leninist ideology to sustain his political authority, however. He has also enjoyed a reservoir of popular support gained from his leadership of the insurrection and his unparalleled ability to communicate with the Cuban masses. In fact, it is tempting to begin and end a study of the Cuban Revolution with the person of Fidel Castro. That he has dominated the revolutionary regime through the strength of his character and political genius is obvious. Nowhere in the region does authority seem to rest so heavily on the "charismatic" appeal of one person. Castro earned his popularity not only by leading a revolt, but also by being so different from his predecessors. Unlike the pompous, aloof leaders of old, he spoke in a simple language to workers and intellectuals alike, appearing to be just a young amateur who was one of them. To a people exhausted by terror and violence, bitter about government corruption, and ashamed of their domination by the American underworld, Castro represented a fresh beginning. Even without knowing where he would lead them, most Cubans found it easy to believe that his rule would be a vast improvement over Batista's.

What has kept Castro in power for over two decades has not been his rhetoric, however, but his skill as a politician. Few leaders in the hemisphere have matched his dexterity in dominating his supporters and exposing and disposing of his opponents. A revolution needs politicians if it is to survive the euphoria of military triumph, for though idealism will inspire change, leadership and administration are required to achieve it. New loyalties and chains of command have to be created, rules enforced, and economies rebuilt. And therein rests one of Castro's greatest strengths. He knew that to sustain his authority he had to act continuously, repeatedly showing initiative, even if he knew that some failure was inevitable. Wherever one looked during the early years he was announcing something new on television, and at rallies, factories, schools, and farms all over the island.

Castro's personality contrasted sharply with that of Che Guevara, the revolution's inspirational leader and principal ideologue. Guevara, the Argentine expatriate who had fought with Castro in the Sierra Maestra, was a disastrous administrator, never at home running government agencies after the revolution. A very private and ascetic individual, Che was once described as a person who combined the idealism of Mahatma Gandhi with the aggression and zeal of Leon Trotsky. His cause was liberation, not governance, and it was in fighting for his cause that he was killed by U.S.-trained counterinsurgency forces in Bolivia in 1967. All revolutions have their Che Guevaras and their Fidel Castros, leaders with opposite personalities whose individual strengths initially complement each other. Yet, it is the Castros, the ambitious *politicos* who want to rule over others who triumph in the end, and the idealistic Guevaras who become the saints enshrined by the politicians they leave behind.

As important as leadership is in Cuba, it would be a mistake to ignore the political institutions that are employed to govern Cuban society. Like Mao Tse-tung in China and Ho Chi Minh in Vietnam, Castro has used his personal authority not just to effect social change, but also to construct a communist state intended to outlive its founding fathers.

No organization was more critical to the governing of Cuba in the early years than the revolutionary armed forces that Fidel and his brother, Raúl Castro, created from the remnants of the 26th of July movement. Armed and trained by Soviet advisers, the 300,000-member Cuban military has been as involved in the execution of domestic policy as it has in the nation's defense. Its officers have staffed government agencies and have played a direct role in the mobilization of the Cuban work force. No organization has been more loyal to Castro or was more useful in the establishment of his effective control over Cuban society in the early 1960s. But Castro's is not simply another military regime; the military is only one part of an elaborate set of organizations that has been developed to govern Cuban society and execute revolutionary policy.

The first mass organization created by Cuban leaders was the Committees for the Defense of the Revolution (CDRs). Originally designed in 1960 for security purposes, the CDRs acted as the eyes and ears of revolutionary leaders in each neighborhood, reporting on the activities of counterrevolutionaries and enforcing government policy at the local level. At their peak they numbered 3 million members, but as the counterrevolutionary threat declined in the mid-1960s, the CDRs were gradually transformed into smaller organizations responsible for neighborhood ideological education and social organization, communicating government decisions to the masses, and reporting unrevolutionary behavior to authorities.

Neither the military nor the CDRs provided the kind of strong civilian organization needed to transform Cuban society. That task was given to the Cuban Communist party (PCC), created in 1965. The party's origins can be traced to July 1961 when Castro formalized his alliance with the existing, prerevolution Communist party (PSP) through the creation of the Integrated Revolutionary Organization (ORI). The ORI was, however, only a transitional organ, which temporarily assisted in the implementation of the initial socialist phase of the revolution. In February 1963 the ORI, which had grown to a membership of 16,000 in two years, was reorganized as the United Party of the Socialist Revolution (PURS). The most important achievement of PURS appears to have been its recognition by the Soviet Union, Cuba's principal foreign ally and financier, as a legitimate Communist party. The final stage of party development began in October 1965 with the launching of the Cuban Communist party, an organization modeled after the Soviet Communist party.

What was the significance of a Soviet-style party? Initially, very little. Castro did not even call the first party congress until late in 1975, ruling until then much as he had before, using well-tested chains of command. But after 1975 the party's responsibilities did grow, and by 1980 party members occupied nearly all of the important positions within the government ministries, the armed forces, and the educational system. It was, however, like other Communist parties an elite organization whose membership included no more than 5 percent of the population.

The Cuban government, like most, has never functioned as smoothly or as efficiently as its creators had intended. During the early years costly planning and administrative mistakes were made, some owing to the zeal of the country's new leaders, others to Castro's capricious meddling with policy, and still more to the difficulty of organizing a centrally controlled economy. One of the most sobering of the early policy failures occurred in 1970 when the Cubans failed to achieve a 10-million-ton sugar harvest after an all-out mobilization of the country's resources. The failure, for which Castro personally accepted blame, was later attributed to the unresponsiveness of Cuba's centralized bureaucracy to economic and social conditions at the local level. Consequently, throughout the early 1970s Cuban officials reassessed their rigid planning and bureaucratic processes in search of ways to make them more effective in implementing revolutionary policy objectives. Their efforts yielded an unprecedented plan of political reform that Castro announced at the first party congress in December 1975.

Castro proposed the creation of a new system of popular representation designed to make the bureaucracy more responsive to local conditions. It involved the selection of delegates to municipal, provincial, and national assemblies to supervise government agencies active within their jurisdiction.

As had been promised, elections were held during late 1976 and delegates to all the assemblies were chosen. The process began at the local level with the selection of 10,743 delegates to 169 municipal assemblies. They, in turn, chose delegates to 14 provincial assemblies (1 for every 10,000 citizens), and to a national assembly (1 for every 20,000 citizens). Each assembly appointed its own executive committee to supervise the day-to-day implementation of government policy. Municipal executive committees, for example, were assigned supervision of schools, hospitals, retail stores, hotels, public utilities, and sports; provincial committees assumed responsibility for intercity transportation and trade.

These reforms have made the Cuban bureaucracy a little more responsive to local needs and more efficient in the delivery of goods and services. But they have not changed the distribution of power and authority within the nation. Of the 481 delegates elected to the National Assembly 441 were members of the Cuban Communist party. Moreover, the Council of State, which serves as the executive arm of the National Assembly, is chaired by Fidel Castro, who is assisted by Raúl Castro as first vice-president and five other vice-presidents, three of whom are veterans of the 26th of July movement.

Socialist economics

Fidel Castro had revealed little of his economic philosophy before 1959. He promised social justice to the Cuban *campesino* and worker, stressing his belief in agrarian reform and the eviction of foreign exploiters. But whether he would become a moderate reformer or a socialist dedicated to the economy's reconstruction from top to bottom could not be determined until he had begun to rule the nation in 1959. In the end he chose the latter and in only a few years transformed a very capitalist economy into one of the world's most socialized ones.

Central to Castro's plan was putting an end to American domination over the Cuban economy. Americans owned substantial property and industry in Cuba and controlled much of its foreign trade, making the Cuban economy more dependent on decisions made in New York and Miami than almost any other country in Latin America. If economic reform was to succeed, most concluded, the Americans would have to be moved out of the way.

As we learned, foreign investors were among the first to be forced out of Cuba. When the Cubans began importing crude oil from the Soviet Union in late 1959, American and English oil companies refused to refine it at their facilities in Cuba, causing Castro to expropriate them in retaliation. And when the United States reduced the volume of sugar imported from Cuba, the Cubans expropriated all U.S. assets in the country. It was a costly move, for the United States imposed a trade embargo on Cuba that hindered the country's development for several years; yet it was a price that the Cuban revolutionaries believed they had to pay in order to end American domination over them.

The Cubans had hoped to replace U.S. capital with funds supplied by the Soviet Union and the Eastern European nations, but their assistance, though substantial, was far less than the Cubans needed to finance their ambitious development programs. Moreover, industrialization, their initial objective, proved to be much more expensive than they had expected. Instead of becoming an industrialized nation, Cuba remained dependent on traditional exports and was forced to ration many essential goods in order to assure a fair distribution of its insufficient supplies. Moreover, sugar, which was intended to become less important to the nation's economy, accounted for 85 percent of the nation's exports in 1965, compared with 74 percent in 1959. Thus, it was not rapid economic development that the Cubans achieved during the first decade of their revolution, but the eviction of American capital and the improvement of life for the poorest third of the population at the expense of the rest.

The socialization of the Cuban economy was not hard to accomplish; once the government's authority was established, the expropriation of property came rapidly. What was hard was the management of the centrally directed economy and the determination of how the nation's scarce resources were to be used to foster its development. It involved the determination of such things as the relative importance of investments in agriculture and industry, in capital investment and consumption, and in defense and nondefense activities. The Cubans never found a perfect formula to guide them; instead, they have experimented with many different mixes, occasionally shifting course in order to deal with obstacles imposed by nature, foreigners, and their own mistakes.

Distributive objectives were stressed in an effort to gain mass support during the first phase of the revolution (1959–60). Driven more by revolutionary ardor than a clear plan of attack, Fidel Castro and his colleagues from the 26th of July movement concentrated their energies on agrarian reform, health care, education, and public housing. As a result of their zeal and inexperience, technical errors, bureaucratic waste, and disorganization accompanied the implementation of most policies. The second phase (1961–2) began with an increase in central control through the emulation of the Soviet model of economic development with its emphasis on economic planning, bureaucratic regulation, capital accumulation, and industrialization. A third phase (1963–7) resulted from a reassessment of the high costs of industrialization and a decision to return to an emphasis on agricultural rather than industrial growth. Again, Soviet planning methods were applied, but now their goals were agricultural production and diversification. The fourth phase (1968–70) saw a shift to more radical methods, such as the use of revolutionary ideology and moral incentives, to inspire the Cuban masses to greater effort in the implementation of the government's economic and social programs. This "revolutionary offensive" culminated in an unsuccessful attempt to produce a record 10-million-ton sugar crop in 1970 and a reassessment of the development effort. Since 1970 greater emphasis has been placed on material incentives, more realistic objectives, and the improvement of economic administration through greater public control over the bureaucracy.

The Cubans' occasional frustrations and constant search for improved modes of economic management have not reduced their determination to make socialism work in their country. As in Eastern Europe and the Soviet Union, disputes among leaders have concerned primarily issues of short-term economic strategy and administration rather than fundamental questions about ultimate purpose. The disputes reflect the frustrations of ambitious revolutionary leaders who must direct an island economy condemned by nature to depend on the production of a few crops and plagued by traditions that have not been easily eradicated during the transition to socialism.

The Cubans' most notable achievements have been in the area of social welfare. Universal education, basic health care, housing, nutrition, and the economic status of women have all been improved markedly since 1959. Unlike all other Latin American countries, Cuba now meets the basic physical needs of its citizens. The costs of this effort have not been meager. The feat required the redistribution of resources by the state to programs aimed at improving the condition of the masses. Several hundred thousand middle- and upper-class Cubans have been forced into exile, depriving the country of skilled personnel for some time. There has also been a persistent shortage of consumer goods, and rationing continues in the 1980s, over two decades after Batista's demise. By the standards of the urban middle sectors of other countries, most Cubans are not well off. Yet, in comparison with the majority of Latin Americans, they are doing quite well.

The long-term development of the Cuban economy is more problematic. Statistics are scarce and incomplete, but the unevenness of Cuban development since 1959 is apparent. After an abortive attempt to industrialize quickly between 1961 and 1963, Cuban leaders were forced to rely on agriculture once again. Industrialization was not abandoned, but it was pursued at a reduced pace thereafter. During the 1960s the Cubans built for the future by holding down consumption in order to finance infrastructure, agricultural, and industrial investments. As a result, total output, though impressive in such areas as nickel mining, milk and paper production, and electricity generation, has been low in most other sectors.

The many successes of the socialist development strategy in China, the Soviet Union, and Eastern Europe must be weighed against the chronic problems that repeatedly limit its effectiveness. One such problem is its apparent need to impose a very depressed standard of living on the population for an extended period. To be sure, many of those who suffered the most under the old economic system do enjoy an improved living standard, even under socialist austerity. Nevertheless, because a relatively small proportion of the national income is allowed for current consumption during the initial capital formation phase of socialist development, citizens often do without a wide range of goods. A second problem is the inefficient use of labor. Socialists are dedicated to full employment and have the power to compel people to work wherever the economic planners believe they are needed. Seldom, however, can they resist the temptation to overallocate labor in order to assure the achievement of high-priority objectives. Waste and temporary labor shortages in other areas often result. Third is the problem of the uneconomical allocation of materials in the production process. The lack of prices that accurately reflect shortages or the real demand for materials, along with the zeal of planners to achieve certain objectives, leads to the overallocation of materials, which proves costly when resources are already scarce.

These problems, which appear to be endemic to centrally planned socialist economies, have also plagued Cuba. During the first phase of the revolution, for example, materials and labor needed in industry were lavishly allocated to the construction of housing for the rural poor, a noble objective but one that proved costly to the pursuit of the government's other development objectives. Similar misallocations occurred in the industrial sector during the 1961–2 phase, as revolutionary leaders tried to apply the same enthusiasm to industrialization that they had used so successfully in the guerrilla struggle. And, as already noted, the rationing of consumer goods has persisted since the early days of the revolution. During the 1960s rationing could be justified as necessary for capital accumulation or as an unavoidable effect of the economic blockade of Cuba by Western Hemisphere nations, but as the Cuban Revolution passed its twentieth anniversary it became increasingly difficult to justify austerity. Undoubtedly, the government will be forced in the years ahead to give greater attention to consumer demand; hopefully, two decades of investments in productive enterprises will allow it to meet much more of the demand.

What stands out from the Cuban experience, however, are not such problems as inefficiency and austerity, for they were predictable, but the willingness of public officials to acknowledge their economic errors and change direction. Much more rapidly than the leaders of most socialist countries, the Cubans have responded to their failures with policy reassessments and minor shifts in course. Few leaders, in fact, have been more adept than Fidel Castro at absorbing the political costs of policy failure and, in some instances, even turning failure to his advantage and rallying the public behind each new campaign to overcome the shortcomings of the last one. This capacity for reassessment and absorption of failure does not, of course, prevent waste and inefficiency from occurring, but they are less costly if the government can adapt its program quickly enough to avoid their accumulation.

After more than two decades of socialist development, agriculture remains the driving force in the Cuban economy. The original agrarian reform of 1959, which authorized the expropriation of all properties over 995 acres, created a dual system of tenure composed of private farms owned by ex-tenant farmers who had been given their land by the state and a cooperative sector composed of expropriated sugar plantations and cattle ranches. In 1963 the second agrarian reform converted most cooperatives into state farms and authorized the expropriation of the remaining large private farms. It left an estimated 200,000 farms of less than 168 acres each – or 30 percent of the country's arable land – in private hands. These private owners, whose prices and marketing are controlled by the state, have been encouraged to join the socialized sector, but few have done so. The anomaly of 200,000 private farms in an otherwise socialized economy continues, it appears, because the government recognizes the private sector's ability to supply badly needed fruits and vegetables to urban consumers and because it is reluctant to seize the land of peasant farmers who acquired their property as a result of the 1959 agrarian reform.

Nothing illustrates the problems faced by planners and administrators better than the ill-fated campaign to produce a 10-million-ton sugar crop in 1970. Cuba had averaged 5 to 6 million tons of sugar in its annual harvest prior to the revolution. After a decline to only 3.8 million at the end of the intense industrialization campaign in 1963, production rose again to 6.2 million in 1967. To raise it above that level required the reallocation of resources from other activities, a risky endeavor that threatened the production of other goods and offered no guarantee of a 10-million-ton harvest. Nevertheless, Cuban leaders decided to take the risk, and beginning in 1965, they implemented an investment plan designed to modernize the sugar industry in preparation for the 1970 harvest. In addition, they initiated a "revolutionary offensive" in 1968 to mobilize the Cuban people to an all-out assault on the sugar-production problem. Through unprecedented human effort, the heavy involvement of the army in the production process, and the expenditure of record amounts of public funds, the scheme was implemented. Nevertheless, the Cubans produced only 8.5 million tons of sugar in 1970. Administrative problems, technical difficulties, and inflated expectations all contributed to the disappointing results. The experience was a sobering one. Reassessments of the campaign led to the abandonment of several other grandiose plans and the initiation of a more balanced and pragmatic approach to the agricultural development.

During the 1970s Cuba's economic fortunes rose and fell with the international price of sugar, much as they had before the revolution.

Two-thirds of the crop was committed through trade agreements to the Soviet Union and Eastern Europe at a price of 32 cents a pound, with the remainder being sold on the open market. The sudden rise of the world price to 65 cents a pound in November 1974 gave the Cuban economy its biggest boost since the revolution began. Immediately, the Cubans increased the share placed on the world market to 50 percent of their crop and soon thereafter revised public investment plans upward with the expectation that the added income would accelerate the pace of the country's development. But, alas, prices fell in 1976, descending to only 8 cents a pound, making Cuba once again the victim of its reliance on sugar. As a result, the goals of the ambitious 1976–80 development plan were slashed and proposals for immediately improving the general standard of living postponed.

Cuban leaders did not have to be reminded by collapsing prices of their excessive dependence on sugar exports. Although they have been forced by short-term financial exigencies to return to sugar repeatedly since 1959, they have not given up their campaign for agricultural diversification and self-sufficiency in food production. Since 1970 they have been trying to lay the foundation for a major breakthrough in agricultural production. Thousands of technicians and managers have been trained at home and abroad, experiments in plant and animal genetics have reached advanced stages, and new production processes have been tested successfully. Livestock, dairy, and poultry production have been emphasized under the program. New feeds created from domestically produced molasses and fish meal have been developed to reduce dependence on imported grains, and new breeds of livestock more compatible with the tropics were created. The long-term objective of the program was the doubling of livestock, dairy, and poultry production by 1980, an ambitious objective, but one that was not attained. Instead, the rationing of many basic foods continued into the 1980s.

The Cubans do not regard their economic reliance on the Soviet Union as being as onerous as dependence on the United States was. Nevertheless, most wish it were not necessary. The Russians pumped nearly $4 billion into the Cuban economy in 1982 (or $11 million a day, which is equal to more than one dollar per head for Cuba's 9.8 million people). Total Russian assistance equals one-fourth of the Cuban GDP. It takes many forms: soft loans, artificially cheap oil supplies ($12.80 per barrel in 1982), and generous prices for one-half of

Cuban sugar exports. Moreover in 1979 Russia bought 72 percent of Cuba's exports and provided three-fifths of its imports. Cuba is trying to increase its trade with the West, which reached 23 percent of its total trade in 1982, to earn hard currency for purchasing needed technologies. To do the latter it has also begun to borrow from banks and governments in Europe and Japan, accumulating a debt of $3.3 billion by 1983. Due to the fall of world prices for sugar, nickel, and tobacco, Cuba, like nonsocialist Venezuela and Mexico, was forced to reschedule its debts in 1983. The Cuban government has also announced new laws designed to lure multinational firms into joint ventures with government enterprises; in return for their investments, foreigners have been assured freedom to repatriate their after-tax profits and dividends. Once again, it seems, the Cubans are adjusting to a world over which they still have little control. It does not mean, however, that they are preparing to abandon socialism. As they see it, tightly regulated foreign investment is merely another means to socialist ends.

The achievements of Cuban socialism are no longer in doubt. It has not generated affluence, but it has eradicated poverty, provided minimal economic security, and given most Cubans a new sense of dignity. At the same time, its costs have been high. The gains of the Cuban masses have come at the expense of those who owned and managed the economy before 1959. Individual diversity and private competition for economic gain have been replaced by political orthodoxy and conformity to the dictates of a bureaucratic elite. Moreover, Cuba has not overcome some of the economic problems that have plagued the island since Independence. Its leaders still rely heavily on the Soviet Union for the financing of economic projects, its economy is still dependent on a single crop, and consumer goods remain in short supply. The Cuban experience does not offer other Latin Americans a formula for solving all development problems, but it does suggest one way of redistributing the burdens of underdevelopment so that the common people retain some faith in their society.

Nicaragua

Almost twenty years after Fidel Castro and the Cuban guerrillas sent Batista to Miami the Nicaraguan people rose up and did the same to Anastasio Somoza. Suddenly one of the hemisphere's poorest and most repressed peoples had won a chance to build a very different Nicaragua.

When access to authority is callously denied a people, as it was in Nicaragua by the Somoza family for decades, they can acquiesce to dictatorial rule, resist it nonviolently, or take up arms against it. Acquiescence was a way of life in Nicaragua until the mid-1970s, when large groups of people turned to strikes and boycotts and, under the leadership of well-armed guerrillas, physical violence to end the Somoza tyranny. In 1979 they succeeded, but only after nearly 50,000 people had died during the three-year struggle.

The rebellion

The Somoza dynasty started in 1938, when Anastasio Somoza Garcia, head of the Nicaraguan National Guard, was made president. Somoza ruled the nation like an unpopular monarch until his assassination in 1956 when his eldest son Luis, the regime's crown prince, succeeded him. Only a decade later Luis died of a heart attack, leaving the reins of government to his younger brother, Anastasio Jr., who, some years before, had assumed the leadership of the National Guard after completing his education at West Point in the United States. He ruled until the revolution in 1979.

From the beginning the Somozas governed because the United States government wanted them to. The Americans considered building a canal across Nicaragua at the turn of the century, and though they never did, interest in the country and its political and economic condition remained high. American banks lent money to the Nicaraguan government during these years and frequently called upon officials in Washington to help them collect what was owed them when the poor and bickering Nicaraguans were slow in meeting their obligations. American presidents responded by sending in the Marines, who occupied the country during most of the 1909–33 period. When it was finally decided that the Marines should leave, an American-trained National Guard replaced them, and Anastasio Somoza was made its commander.

The guard's first test actually came during its formative years when in 1927 guerrilla forces led by an anti-American populist, August Cesar Sandino, began harassing it. The guerrillas' struggle lasted until the Americans agreed to go home in 1933; but one year later Somoza had Sandino murdered, making Sandino a hero to future generations of Somoza haters. It was natural that the rebels of the 1970s should take Sandino's name as their own when they mobilized the Nicaraguan people against the dictator.

Somoza was very ambitious. Not wealthy when he began, he used his authority once in the presidency to build an economic empire that controlled about 40 percent of the nation's wealth by the 1960s. It was secured not just with plunder but also through the development of the country's agricultural economy, first by increasing the land devoted to cotton and sugar production, and later through the construction of cotton gins, sugar refineries, banks, insurance companies, a steel mill, a national airline, and many complementary enterprises, all owned by the Somoza family. It was this veneer of national development that made it easy for many Nicaraguans and foreigners to rationalize the Somozas' rule as highly beneficial to the nation's modernization. But as their enterprises multiplied, so did the family's control over the country; eventually nearly all Nicaraguans found themselves dependent on decisions made either by the Somozas' government or their family enterprises. Moreover, when elections were held, the results were always the same: two-thirds of the legislative seats went to the Somozas' National Liberal party and the rest to an impotent Conservative opposition.

Why then, if the Somoza regime was so strong, was it finally defeated in 1979? Two things figure most prominently in its demise. The first was the political ineptitude displayed by the youngest Somoza son after he succeeded his brother Luis in 1967. Anastasio Somoza Debayle proved to be even greedier than his father and brother and much less willing to share the spoils of development either with other members of the elite or with the growing middle sectors. Nothing evidenced this greed more than the way Somoza handled relief efforts after an earthquake destroyed much of Managua, the nation's capital, in 1972. Rather than distributing reconstruction projects among the nation's entrepreneurs, he kept nearly all of them for himself and pilfered most of the emergency aid sent from abroad before it reached those in need. When the public protested, Somoza's National Guard smashed them. As repression increased, moderate Nicaraguans, originally unsympathetic with the tactics of anti-Somoza guerrillas, moved closer to them, gradually giving up any hope of nonviolent solutions to the Somoza problem. Like Porfirio Díaz in Mexico over a half century before and Fulgencio Batista in Cuba, Somoza became increasingly isolated from his own society, and in the end could rely only on the National Guard to protect him against the entire nation.

The other thing that caused Somoza's demise was the way the rebels took advantage of the opportunities he gave them in 1978 and 1979. The guerrilla opposition was led by the Sandinista National Liberation Front (FSLN), an organization created in 1961 by university students and Nicaraguan Socialists, who took their inspiration from Castro's triumph in Cuba two years before. Frequently defeated in skirmishes with the National Guard, they initially were forced to retreat into the countryside from where they quietly built support networks in the capital and in some remote areas. Only 1,000 in number, they limited their efforts to bank robberies, kidnappings, and encouraging student and union protests against the government until the late 1970s, when the opportunity for bolder initiative finally arose.

It started with the assassination of popular opposition newspaper editor Pedro Joaquin Chamorro in January 1978, an act for which everyone blamed the intemperate Somoza. Instantly Nicaraguans took to the streets in protest, and before it was over the country's business community had joined in a boycott that halted 80 percent of the nation's commerce for two weeks. Soon thereafter opposition political parties, professionals, and businessmen created the Broad Opposition Front (FAO) in the hope of leading their own campaign for Somoza's ouster. While they busied themselves with matters of strategy, the FSLN struck again, this time sending twenty-five disguised guerrillas into the National Palace where they held the nation's legislature and most of Somoza's cabinet hostage until they were paid a $500,000 ransom, imprisoned guerrillas were freed, and the culprits were allowed to drive triumphantly amid the cheers of hundreds to the airport and then safely leave the country.

Finally in early 1979, the FAO agreed to join with the FSLN to form a broadly based National Patriotic Front that united nearly every sector and organization in Nicaraguan society against the Somoza regime. Their final offensive came in June; it was intense and bloody as guerrillas seized cities and the National Guard shelled them with artillery and bombed them from the air, killing thousands of innocent civilians. An estimated 15,000 people died during the last six weeks of combat, but the FSLN overcame the guard's superiority in numbers, mobility, and air power, driving them back bit by bit from city to city until finally isolating and defeating them in Managua. On July 17, Somoza fled to Miami and three days later the FSLN's ragged columns marched into the rubble of Managua that Somoza had left behind. A year later Somoza was assassinated outside Asunción, Paraguay.

Sandinista political economy

Victorious rebels cannot afford to spend much time in celebration. By destroying a dictatorship that had run Nicaragua for decades, the revolution created a political vacuum that had to be filled quickly, if order was to be maintained. The unity built on the battlefield is always short-lived, and knowing this, the victors must get on with the less spectacular work of establishing a new political chain of command, filling bureaucratic posts, and assuring that the people's immediate economic needs are met.

Initial decisions are made even more important by the fact that once the new rules are set, they are not easily reversed. Vested interests quickly develop around them, and those who challenge the new rules are often excluded from the new order to protect it. This is why the people who seize the initiative and define the rules usually govern for a long time. In Cuba Fidel Castro adroitly took advantage of his popularity and his disciplined organization to establish his control over the new government, eventually excluding all of his potential rivals. In Mexico it took much longer, nearly a decade, but the revolutionary generals organized a coherent power structure that has ruled Mexico ever since. Nicaragua falls somewhere in between Cuba and Mexico in this regard, for there was no charismatic leader like Castro to exploit his personal popularity, but there was the FSLN, a stronger and more disciplined organization than anything the Mexicans had to start with.

The FSLN's control over the new government was not automatic. Nearly the entire society had joined the war against Somoza and each group had its own vision of how the country would be governed in the post-Somoza era. Traditional political parties wanted elections, businessmen wanted a moderate government that would allow them larger shares of the market than Somoza had permitted, organized labor wanted immediate economic benefits and political influence, and *campesinos* wanted land. But the leaders of the FSLN had plans of their own. They were determined to establish a strong government, one able to implement major economic reforms swiftly and to defend the nation against counterrevolutionaries from within and outside the country. The FSLN alone, they were convinced, should lead such an effort.

Like most revolutionaries, FSLN leaders were reluctant to clearly define the organization of the new government until they knew how the others would respond to their agenda for the nation's reconstruction. They did not want to concede to their opponents enough participation to foil their plans. Though they claimed to believe in democratic government, they refused to hold free elections, fearing that political parties, less devoted to social reform than they were, might upset their program before it had a chance to prove itself. Naturally, the parties cried foul, claiming that the FSLN was denying them the rights they had fought for, but the FSLN held firm.

Gradually a new government was created, composed of the Governing Junta of National Reconstruction, the Cabinent, and the Council of State. Initially the junta was broadly representative, one member coming from the FSLN and the other four from business, opposition parties, and other sectors. The Cabinent was composed of technocrats and Sandinistas who were placed in charge of government ministries, including a couple of sympathetic Catholic priests. It was their job to implement the junta's policies. The Council of State, which was created in May 1980, was given a kind of legislative role, though a very weak one. Its forty-seven members were to be consulted by the junta regarding its legislation, though the council's approval was not always required. Representation was corporatist in nature, with delegates from the FSLN, other parties, labor, peasants, and the private sector.

What made the government work, however, was the FSLN. Most initiatives did not originate in the junta but in the FSLN Joint National Directorate, the movement's collegiate leadership, who designed nearly all policy, controlled the armed forces, and dominated the administration of justice. What gave them their strength was not their physical force but their following at the grass roots. The Sandinistas' populist, antiimperialist ideology took hold among most Nicaraguans, since they believed they were threatened more by American-financed counterrevolutionaries than by the occasional heavy-handedness of the FSLN.

The government also secured the support of most labor, peasant, women's, and student associations. Equally important were the Sandinista Defense Committees (CDSs) modeled on the Cuban Committees for the Defense of the Revolution, which were created in neighhborhoods to implement health and educational programs, mobilize support for the FSLN, and maintain order.

The FSLN's control was far from complete, however. Most businessmen and private landowners, the opposition parties, conservative clergymen, and some dissident unions were highly critical of its methods and its refusal to hold elections. They were a minority but a powerful one that hoped the nation's severe economic troubles and the FSLN's failure to deal with them would drive people away from it. But as long as the FSLN was able to meet the basic needs of the poor and exploit their fear of the Somocistas' return from exile, their grass roots support would remain intact. The Sandinista game is not a very neat one with clearly defined rules and lines of authority. It has avoided reliance on a single leader, and the FSLN is not as tightly disciplined as Castro's Communist party. Moreover, some opposition and criticism are tolerated, at least as long as they lack enough force to block major government initiatives.

As the revolution entered its fifth year in mid-1983 it was troubled by three things: criticism from Nicaraguan church leaders, the attacks of well-armed counterrevolutionaries, and economic hardship.

The Nicaraguan clergy had enthusiastically endorsed the war against Somoza and many have worked for the Sandinista government, both at cabinet and grass roots levels. But after five years of participation and support church leaders became quite critical of the regime, attacking its propagation of Marxist ideology in schools and its restriction of personal freedom. In doing so it deeply divided its own clergy, weakening its authority over it and making enforceable church positions on most issues unattainable. Were the Nicaraguans not one of the most devoted Roman Catholic peoples in the hemisphere, the issue might be only a minor one. But for the time being, the Sandinistas will have to deal with the almost irresolvable problem of overcoming the incompatibility of their ideology with the teachings of an unsympathetic church leadership.

The threat posed by counterrevolutionaries was quite real and very serious. Ex-National Guardsmen and disillusioned one-time Sandinistas living in exile declared their intention in 1982 to militarily harass and defeat the Nicaraguan government. Guerrilla groups established bases along the Honduran-Nicaraguan border and, with the assistance of the United States, Argentina, and other governments, trained and equipped a few thousand troops who entered Nicaragua in early 1983 to set up positions from which to wage a long guerrilla war. For their part the Sandinistas built up their defenses, creating a 22,000-member force equipped and trained with help from the Cubans, Russians, and any other nation who would sell the country the material it needed. No one in the Sandinista leadership feared military defeat by the guerrillas as long as the United States did not intervene with its own troops. Moreover, they were confident that only a minority of the Nicaraguan people were willing to trade the Sandinista government for one created by mercenaries from Somoza's exiled National Guard. Nevertheless, the cost of dealing with the guerrillas was high and unwelcomed by a regime already plagued by enough distractions.

The most serious problem facing the Sandinistas is the one that haunts all Central American governments regardless of the forms their politics take, namely, economic survival. From the beginning the Sandinistas took a more cautious approach to revolutionary development than the Cubans had. Where the latter turned immediately to socialism and state planning, the Nicaraguans chose to mix capitalist economics with the socialization of certain parts of the economy much as the Mexicans had done under Cardenas in the 1930s. Their decisions were dictated as much by economic necessity as by philosophy. Sandinistas want a more equitable economic system for Nicaragua; some among them prefer Marxist economics while others are less dogmatic about the form socialism should take, recognizing that need, not utopian visions, must guide policy.

Whatever their economic faith, the Sandinistas' job is not an enviable one. Nicaragua is one of Latin America's poorest nations ($660 per capita income in 1980) and was damaged badly by an earthquake in 1972 and the war in 1979. To make matters worse, when Somoza fled, he took most of the Nicaraguan treasury with him, leaving his successors nothing but huge foreign debts. Moreover, unlike the Cubans who marched into cities virtually untouched by combat, the Nicaraguan victors inherited a lot of rubble and thousands of homeless, unemployed people to care for.

In poor countries socialists always face a cruel choice between either moving immediately to the redistribution of the nation's property and wealth to those most in need or concentrating resources and promoting capital development, asking their people to sacrifice in order to improve conditions for future generations. In the euphoria of victory one is always tempted to divide the spoils instantly, but reason and experience teach how disastrous that can be. The FSLN designed its own mix of welfare and capital development. Substantial effort was made to improve public health, sanitation, and basic education, relying on volunteers from Nicaragua and abroad. At the same time, resources were devoted to restoring the nation's production. What made the Nicaraguan effort unique was that the new government inherited nearly 40 percent of the economy when Somoza fled, leaving his many enterprises behind. From the outset then the state became the country's largest entrepreneur. To assure its control over the nation's development the government also nationalized all business involved in mining, lumber, and fishing, and major services like banking and insurance. The private sector was allowed to retain ownership of two-thirds of the nation's internal commerce, half of all agriculture, and three-fourths of industry. Thus, about 60 percent of the nation's product stayed in private hands. Thereafter the state and private entrepreneurs were locked into a relationship that both disliked but neither was in a position to change: The government could not manage the entire economy on its own and the private sector could not reduce the will or power of the government to direct the nation's development according to its own plan. Not surprisingly, businessmen repeatedly accused the government of sabotaging their enterprises with regulations and controls, and officials charged entrepreneurs with trying to use their economic power to undermine the reform effort.

The new government also contended with the international economy. Rather than defaulting on their debts and cutting themselves off from the capitalist nations, they renegotiated or paid them. Agricultural production declined sharply during the insurrection, but by the time it had risen again in the 1980s, world prices for coffee, cotton, and sugar had dropped precipitously, forcing the Nicaraguans to borrow even more heavily abroad, just as their neighbors had done. And when the Reagan administration cut off foreign assistance, ostensibly to punish them for encouraging revolutions in neighboring countries, the Nicaraguans borrowed wherever they could, both in Western and Eastern Europe and from the Soviet Union.

There is no easy way out for the Nicaraguans, even if the country is left unharassed by counterrevolutionaries. Nicaragua is favored to some extent by its low population/land ratio, rich soils, good metal mining potential, and a decent transportation network, but it relies heavily on the import of petroleum for the production of electricity and its primary exports are, like those of most Latin American countries, subject to wide fluctuations in price, making the country's economic growth very insecure. For the time being the new leadership is trying to make the burdens of underdevelopment more bearable by improving the welfare of the poorest. Simultaneously they are slowly restoring the nation's productive capacity. But whatever they try, the road ahead will be a very rough one.

The revolutionary game: lessons learned

Revolutions have many causes and take several forms, making any single theory inadequate. Each one requires separate study if it is to be understood.

Yet though their differences were many, the Mexicans, Cubans, and Nicaraguans did have a few things in common when their revolutions began. One was the general discontent with the maldistribution of wealth and the cruelty of the ruling classes who monopolized it. Another was the elite's smug denial of political participation to potential rivals who refused to accept complete subordination to those in power. In each case armed rebellion became an effective means for gaining admission to the game, not just for peasants and workers but also for the middle-sector intellectuals, students, and politicians who led them.

What makes armed revolt against dictatorships so likely is the apparent impossibility of accommodation between the dictator and his opponents. The autocrat always fears that compromise will lead to his own demise rather than to his opponents' subservience. Since the dictator has nothing to rely on for his authority except the power of intimidation, he believes that concessions will be taken as evidence of weakness, provoking more and more challenges to his rule. So the dictator holds his ground, but in doing so only forces his opponents to an all-or-nothing violent struggle. Dictatorial government can survive for many years this way, but eventually the autocrat, be he a Díaz, Batista, or Somoza, will meet a violent end.

Today few of the old dictators remain. Instead the revolutionaries' paths are obstructed primarily by military authoritarians whose governments were designed expressly to eradicate armed nonconformists, and by elected civilian governments that are forced to rely on the military for their protection. Does this mean that the era of armed rebellion is over? Not at all. Many revolutionary movements, like the Tupamaros in Uruguay in the early 1970s and the Montoneros in Argentina a few years later, have been crushed. Nevertheless, the revolutionary's cause is far from hopeless. The risks are greater and the probability of success anywhere but in Central America is lower than before, but there is nothing to prevent revolutionaries from adapting their tactics to changing conditions, thereby improving their chances of victory, just as they did in the past.

The performance of revolutionary governments is another matter. Nothing as controversial as the revolutionary regime ever receives the same marks from those who comment on it. Personal beliefs shape our assessments of revolutions even more than they do other kinds of politics because of the intensity of feelings about both the means and ends of radical change. Nevertheless, judge them we must, just as we did the other types of governments in Latin America.

Two features of revolutionary governments have preoccupied the people who study them. One is their demand for strict conformity with a single set of values and the ways they achieve this conformity; the other is the manner in which they promote social welfare and economic development.

Revolutionaries are not the only ones who demand political conformity, but they expect much more of their people than do the leaders of nonrevolutionary regimes. They demand that people change their ways, often substantially, in order to become part of a society held together by a new, community-based ethic. And, because their vision of the new order is quite precise, they expect conformity in the details of social life. Moreover, like those they deposed, they face antagonists eager to expel them from power. Revolutions always create enemies, both foreign and national, who resent being deprived of their property and privileges. Unlike constitutional democrats who take their chances with the rules of competitive politics, revolutionaries want to control their own fate totally, if possible. Consequently, internal and external security absorbs much of their attention and, when threatened, they may decide to turn their society into a fortress dedicated to the revolution's defense.

Each revolutionary regime develops its own ways of building conformity with its values. They were quite different in Mexico in the 1920s than they were in Marxist Cuba, and Nicaragua differs from both. The Mexicans were less certain than the others about what they wanted their new society to become, and they were more bound by the breadth of interests within their multiclass coalition. For the PRI conformity meant doing nothing to halt the maintenance of its political monopoly, but little else. How Mexicans made their money and how they used power informally was their own business. Such laxity was never tolerated in Cuba. Once its leaders had chosen the Marxist-Leninist model to guide their construction of the Cuban state, very specific rules were written and enforced in economic as well as political affairs. Strict discipline in all things became common in Cuba, in contrast to Mexico, where doctrine and discipline were never taken very seriously.

In Nicaragua the Sandinistas have been neither as lax as the Mexicans nor as strict as the Cubans. It is their ambivalence on the issues of state control that has caused such a divergence of opinion about the exact character of their revolution. Thus far they have been content to direct a mixed economy (something akin to Mexico) while mobilizing followers into a disciplined defense of the country against counterrevolutionaries (similar to Cuba in its early years). The Sandinistas' opponents clamor for elections but their demands are ignored by a revolutionary leadership that wants to establish its control over the state before going to the polls.

The other distinguishing feature of revolutionary government is the way it provides social services and promotes economic development. Leaders quickly learn that the redistribution of wealth, no matter how equitably it is done, will not by itself meet the needs of their people. Like everyone else revolutionaries must also increase their nation's product in order to provide adequately for all. How to do that without abandoning the revolution's social welfare objectives poses one of the toughest problems faced by revolutionary governments throughout the Third World. And few of them have dealt with it in the same way. The Mexicans, for example, began with land reforms and the nationalization of foreign properties and later added minimal social services for the organized working class and food subsidies for the poor generally, but for the most part Mexicans were left responsible for their own welfare.

Many Mexicans have risen from poverty as the nation's economy has grown, but most have not. Nothing about Mexican economics is very revolutionary today. Moreover, what preoccupies its leadership a half century after they came to power is not how to redistribute wealth but how to create enough of it using capitalistic means to prevent a frustrated Mexican people from turning against them.

In contrast, the Cubans concentrated on improving the average Cuban's welfare; as a result, in no Latin American country are education, medical care, and sanitation available to a larger proportion of the people than in Cuba. It is such achievements that the Cubans point to when defending themselves against critics from the more capitalistic Latin American countries whose economies have grown much faster than Cuba's. Revolutionary economics, as the Cubans readily admit, has not brought affluence to their society, but it has mobilized the nation's resources for national development and rationed goods that are still in short supply. Cuba remains a modest, tropical island heavily dependent on the export of sugar, a few minerals, and other agricultural crops for its economic survival, and it must rely on its Soviet allies for capital and technology. But the old oligarchs are gone, the United States government and the multinational firms enter the country only on the terms dictated by the Cubans, and the Cuban leadership feels free to send its troops anywhere in the world where ideology and geopolitics suggest a need for them. Middle-class Mexicans would not enjoy life in Cuba, but one wonders how uncomfortable Mexican *campesinos* would find it.

The plight of Nicaragua is grimmer than that of either Mexico or Cuba. One need only recall that it is one of the poorest countries in the hemisphere and one of the most dependent on the export of a few crops for its survival. There is nothing that the Sandinistas can do to increase the country's wealth significantly in the short run. They have raised literacy and have given some relief to a people whose economic productivity remains low. But to expect them to achieve even as much as Castro did during his first decade is to ignore what little they have to work with. The principal task facing them after four years is the same as it was when they began, namely, producing enough to employ and feed all Nicaraguans, using private, state, and borrowed capital.

What are we to conclude about the revolutionary game? Clearly its appeal is strong to anyone who resents how conservative modernization increases foreign penetration of an economy without improving the condition of the poor significantly, or who is displeased with the way reformers make concessions to the defenders of the old order while failing to deliver on their promises of a better life for the masses. Until it is tried, revolutionary change will always seem better than the status quo to the disenfranchised. But, as the Mexicans, Cubans, and Nicaraguans have discovered, revolutionary politics is neither cheap nor easy. Costly mistakes are often made, disappointments are common, and substantial personal freedom may be sacrificed. To dismiss the latter as an expendable bourgeois luxury only ignores the fact that most people, regardless of their social class, covet the opportunity to do some things as they wish. Of course, they also want liberation from oppression, and as long as they do, revolutionary politics of the socialist variety will retain its appeal.

Books usually end with conclusions, but this one does not, for there is little that we are ready to conclude about Latin America, even after spending several hours getting acquainted with the region. To be sure, patterns are apparent and tentative generalizations can be made about the way authority is exercised, militaries behave, classes are formed, dependency works, and different games are played. But we should tread carefully lest we prematurely conclude that we really understand Latin America. Nothing will serve us less well than the false sense of wisdom that comes from reading a book about a world rich in people, places, and problems.

What happens next is up to you. Much more is to be learned and more informed judgments must be made. Libraries are full of books and documents about Latin America and periodicals offering the latest news from below the border. But the story of Latin America cannot be told entirely on the printed page or in the statistical table. Equally important are the stories told by the millions of people who are Latin American. And it is to them that we need to turn for instruction if we are to comprehend who they are, who we are, and where we both are going in the days ahead.

Further reading

Cuba

Bonachea, Ramon L., and Marta San Martin. *The Cuban Insurrection: 1952–1959*. New Brunswick, N.J.: Transaction Books, 1974.

Bonachea, Rolando, and Nelson Valdes, eds. *Cuba in Revolution.* Garden
City, N.Y.: Doubleday (Anchor Books), 1972.
Debray, Regis. *Revolution in the Revolution.* New York: Grove Press, 1967.
Dominquez, Jorge. *Cuba: Order and Revolution.* Cambridge, Mass.: Harvard
University Press, 1978.
Dumont, Rene. *Cuba: Socialism and Development.* New York: Grove Press,
1970.
Is Cuba Socialist? New York: Viking Press, 1974.
Fagen, Richard R. *The Transformation of Political Culture in Cuba.* Stanford,
Cal.: Stanford University Press, 1970.
Goldenburg, Boris. *The Cuban Revolution and Latin America.* New York:
Praeger, 1965.
Gonzalez, Edward. *Cuba Under Castro: The Limits of Charisma.* Boston:
Houghton Mifflin, 1974.
Guevara, Ernesto "Che." *Reminiscences of the Cuban Revolutionary War.* New
York: Grove Press, 1968.
Halperin, Maurice. *The Rise and Decline of Fidel Castro.* Berkeley: University
of California Press, 1972.
Horowitz, Irving Luis, ed. *Cuban Communism,* 4th ed. New Brunswick,
N.J.: Transaction Books, 1981.
Huberman, Leo, and Paul Sweezy. *Socialism in Cuba.* New York: Monthly
Review Press, 1970.
Karol, K. S. *Guerrillas in Power.* New York: Hill & Wang, 1970.
Mesa Lago, Carmelo. *Cuba in the 1970s: Pragmatism and Institutionalization.*
Albuquerque; University of New Mexico Press, 1974.
Revolutionary Change in Cuba. Pittsburgh: University of Pittsburgh Press,
1974.
The Economy of Socialist Cuba. Albuquerque: University of New Mexico
Press, 1981.
Ruiz, Ramon Eduardo. *Cuba: The Making of a Revolution.* Amherst: Univer-
sity of Massachusetts Press, 1968.
Seers, Dudley, ed. *Cuba: The Economic and Social Revolution.* Chapel Hill:
University of North Carolina Press, 1964.
Suarez, Andres. *Cuba: Castroism and Communism, 1959–.* Cambridge, Mass.:
MIT Press, 1967.
Thomas, Hugh. *Cuba.* New York: Harper & Row, 1971.

Nicaragua

Black, George. *Triumph of the People: The Sandinista Revolution in Nicaragua.*
London: Zed Press, 1981.
Booth, John. *The End of the Beginning: The Nicaraguan Revolution.* Boulder,
Colo.: Westview Press, 1982.
Borge, Tomas. *Sandinistas Speak.* New York: Pathfinder, 1982.
Gettleman, Marvin. *Central America in the New Cold War.* New York: Grove
Press, 1981.
Macaulay, Neil. *The Sandino Affair.* Chicago: Quadrangle Books, 1967.
Millet, Richard. *Guardians of the Dynasty: A History of the U.S.-Created Guardia
Nacional de Nicaragua and the Somoza Family.* Maryknoll, N.Y.: Orbis,
1977.

Randal, Margaret. *Sandino's Daughters: Testimony of Nicaraguan Women in Struggle.* London: New Star Books, 1981.

Somoza, Anastasio Debayle, and Jack Cox. *Nicaragua Betrayed.* Belmont, Mass.: Western Islands, 1980.

Walker, Thomas W. *Nicaragua: The Land of Sandino.* Boulder, Colo.: Westview Press, 1981.

   ed. *Nicaragua in Revolution.* New York: Praeger, 1982.

Appendix: Tables

Table A.1. *Latin American demographics*

	Area (sq. miles)	Population, 1981 (millions)	Average annual population growth, 1970–81 (%)
Argentina	1,072,000	28.1	1.5
Bolivia	424,000	5.8	2.7
Brazil	3,286,000	121.5	2.5
Chile	292,000	11.1	1.6
Colombia	440,000	26.7	2.1
Costa Rica	20,000	2.3	2.8
Cuba	44,000	11.0	1.8
Dominican Republic	19,000	5.6	2.4
Ecuador	109,000	8.2	3.0
El Salvador	8,000	5.0	3.0
Guatemala	42,000	7.2	2.9
Haiti	11,000	5.1	1.7
Honduras	43,000	3.8	3.2
Mexico	762,000	72.3	3.4
Nicaragua	50,000	2.5	2.2
Panama	29,000	1.9	2.4
Paraguay	157,000	3.3	2.5
Peru	496,000	17.0	2.1
Uruguay	72,000	3.0	0.5
Venezuela	352,000	14.0	2.7

Source: Inter-American Development Bank, *Economic and Social Progress in Latin America 1982 Report.* Washington, D.C., 1982, p. 346.

Table A.2. *Latin American economic and social conditions*

	Per capita gross domestic product, 1981 (1980 dollars)	% Population with safe water, 1979	% Literacy rate	% Population urban
Argentina	1,796	57	93	86.3
Bolivia	550	38	63	33.0
Brazil	1,555	47	75	69.0
Chile	1,675	87	92	80.6
Colombia	925	62	86	78.1
Costa Rica	1,446	80	93	47.0
Cuba	–	98	95	–
Dominican Republic	1,044	61	68	55.5
Ecuador	1,053	46	79	44.0
El Salvador	605	44	63	40.5
Guatemala	1,183	42	50	32.2
Haiti	271	10	26	26.0
Honduras	616	59	60	36.8
Mexico	1,954	55	81	65.9
Nicaragua	889	41	62	59.2
Panama	1,983	82	82	54.7
Paraguay	1,205	17	82	36.5
Peru	1,294	53	76	72.6
Uraguay	2,156	83	94	81.6
Venezuela	2,615	91	82	79.0

Note: Dashes indicate figures not available.
Source: Ruth Leger Sivard, *World Military and Social Expenditures, 1982*. Leesburgh, Va.: World Priorities, 1982; Inter-American Development Bank, *Economic and Social Progress in Latin America 1982 Report*.

Table A.3. *Latin American military and educational expenditures, 1979 (U.S. dollars)*

	Military		Education
	Public expenditures per capita	Public expenditures per soldier	Public expenditures per capita
Argentina	55	11,256	75
Bolivia	18	4,174	20
Brazil	14	6,004	64
Chile	88	11,247	52
Colombia	9	3,118	20
Costa Rica	–	–	92
Cuba	79	4,116	122
Dominican Republic	18	5,263	24
Ecuador	24	5,606	43
El Salvador	10	6,857	24
Guatemala	12	4,722	19
Haiti	3	2,285	4
Honduras	15	4,546	20
Mexico	10	6,330	80
Nicaragua	23	6,750	19
Panama	8	1,364	74
Paraguay	13	2,800	14
Peru	25	4,728	20
Uruguay	59	6,179	48
Venezuela	42	16,595	135

Note: Dash indicates figures not available.
Source: Ruth Leger Sivard, *World Military and Social Expenditures, 1982*. Leesburgh, Va.: World Priorities, 1982.

Table A.4. *Relative importance of the external sector to national economies*

	1970	1980
Panama	89	196
Venezuela	45	108
Honduras	59	96
Costa Rica	63	90
Chile	39	80
Ecuador	33	78
El Salvador	42	74
Nicaragua	52	74
Bolivia	43	72
Dominican Republic	43	60
Uruguay	27	59
Haiti	27	59
Argentina	21	51
Colombia	34	47
Guatemala	29	47
Peru	30	46
Paraguay	25	44
Mexico	20	44
Brazil	16	30

Note: Measured as the ratio between the combined value of exports and imports of goods and services and the gross domestic product (percentages).
Source: Inter-American Development Bank, *Economic and Social Progress in Latin America 1982 Report*. Washington, D.C., 1982, p. 24.

Index

Acción Democrática party (Venezuela), 68, 78, 168, 190–3, 194–6, 196–200, 201, 203, 204, 269
agrarian reform, 18, 20–1, 48, 57, 63–5, 68, 79, 113–17, 205–6; in Argentina, 155; in Chile, 178, 183; in Cuba, 284, 288–9; in Mexico, 263–5; in Peru, 237–8; in Venezuela, 191, 196, 199
Alemán Valdés, Miguel, 252
Alessandri, Arturo, 171
Alessandri, Jorge, 171, 175, 176, 177
Alfonsín, Raúl, 158
Allende, Salvador, 25, 80, 171–2, 173–6, 179–90, 206
American New Deal, 112
anarchism, 151
Anglo-American democracies, 34, 74, 75
anti-reelectionist party (Mexico), 251–3
APRISTA party (Peru), 78, 235, 236
Argentina: agrarian reform, 155; agro-exporter elite, 162; anarchists, 149; conservatives, 148, 152; corporatism, 100, 153; depression of 1929, 148; economic conditions, 97, 148–50, 153–7, 228–9, 232–4; economic policy, 148–57, 228–34; elections, 157, 230–3; entrepreneurs, 156, 232; Falkland Islands War, 233; foreign investors, 95, 146, 148, 154–5, 231; General Confederation of Labor, 151; inflation, 228, 229; industrialists, 154; industrialization, 146, 149, 154–6, 226, 229; IAPI, 155; ITT, 154; labor movement, 149–51, 229, 233; middle sectors, 58, 148, 149, 152; military, 39, 86, 148–53, 158, 227–34; military

coups, 150–1, 158, 228, 230, 232; Peronistas, 39, 154–8, 229, 230, 233; presidency, 39–40, 151; Roca-Runciman pact, 148; Roman Catholic Church, 148; rural sector, 155; socialists, 149
authoritarianism, 100
Avila Camacho, Manuel, 252, 254
Ayatollah Khomeini, 33
Azuela, Mariano, 254

bankers, 97, 125, 265, 266, 292
Barrios, Gonzalo, 194
Batista, Fulgencio, 240, 272–8
Belaunde Terry, Fernando, 38, 235–9
Betancourt, Romulo, 192–4, 196–9, 203, 204
Bolivia, 67, 281
Brazil: agriculture, 221; bureaucrats, 159, 161, 214, 218, 222; commercial farmers, 213; corporatism, 100, 213; economic conditions, 220, 241; economic growth, 143–7, 159, 214, 215, 217; economic policy, 143, 145–6, 218; elections, 142, 224–6; entrepreneurs, 139, 144, 218; Estado Novo, 138, 141–2, 144, 153–4; fascists, 81, 138, 142; foreign debt, 97, 127; foreign investors, 143, 145–6, 214, 219, 241; foreign investment, 95, 130, 219, 221, 222–3; impact of 1929 depression, 139–40; income distribution, 222; industrialists, 142–6, 214; industrialization, 143, 145–6, 214; inflation, 145–6, 215, 219; Institutional Acts, 218; labor movement, 217; middle sectors, 58, 143, 221; multinational firms, 218, 221; military, 43, 82, 83, 86, 130, 138–9, 143, 146, 214, 216, 218, 241, 269; military coup of